Friends Disappear

CHICAGO VISIONS AND REVISIONS
Edited by Carlo Rotella, Bill Savage, Carl Smith, and Robert B. Stepto

Friends Disappear

The Battle for Racial
Equality in Evanston

MARY BARR

The University of Chicago Press   Chicago and London

MARY BARR is a lecturer at Clemson University.

The University of Chicago Press, Chicago 60637
The University of Chicago Press, Ltd., London
© 2014 by The University of Chicago
All rights reserved. Published 2014.
Printed in the United States of America

23 22 21 20 19 18 17 16 15 14   1 2 3 4 5

ISBN-13: 978-0-226-15632-3 (cloth)
ISBN-13: 978-0-226-15646-0 (paper)
ISBN-13: 978-0-226-15663-7 (e-book)
DOI: 10.7208/chicago/9780226156637.001.0001

Library of Congress Cataloging-in-Publication Data

Barr, Mary, 1960– author.
    Friends disappear : the battle for racial equality in Evanston /
Mary Barr.
        pages ; cm.— (Chicago visions and revisions)
    Includes bibliographical references and index.
    ISBN 978-0-226-15632-3 (cloth : alk. paper) — ISBN 978-0-226-
15646-0 (pbk. : alk. paper) — ISBN 978-0-226-15663-7 (e-book)
1. Evanston (Ill.)—Race relations.   2. Segregation—Illinois—
Evanston.   3. Social integration—Illinois—Evanston.   I. Title.
II. Series: Chicago visions + revisions.
    F549.E8B295 2014
    305.8009773′1—dc23

                                                    2013049705

♾ This paper meets the requirements of ANSI/NISO Z39.48–1992
(Permanence of Paper).

To the spirit of
the sixties activists

And in memory of
Kerry "Perkey" Foster
Arthur "Earl" Hutchinson
Antoine "Ray" Tounsel

Contents

Acknowledgments

Spend enough time in the archives and you'll get the feeling that the documents are trying to tell you something. While I was doing research at Northwestern University, I came across a letter addressed to Evanston's controversial school superintendent Gregory C. Coffin and written by William Guy, the chaplain at Morehouse College in Atlanta. Regarding Evanston's incredible story, Guy wrote: "It is frightening; it is ludicrous. It is typical; it is freakish. It is Americana suited for a tremendous sociological study." Mr. Guy was right, and I felt his nudge.

I am grateful to Jennifer and her family, Sydney, Ron, Ronny, and Suzy. I thank each of them for the love and support they've given me over many, many years. I am deeply indebted to the people whom I interviewed for this book: Carla Burnett, Regina Cartright, Fred Chatterton, Jennifer Crawford, Ronny Crawford, Jesse Floyd, Bernie Foster, Barbara Morrison, Candice Nancel, Chip Sexton, and Prince Williams. A very special thank you to Bennett Johnson.

This book is the culmination of many years of academic development. Thank you to the African American Studies and Sociology Departments at Yale University. I am especially grateful to Paul Gilroy, Jonathan Holloway, and Matt Jacobson, who guided this project at its earliest stages. This book brings together pieces of what I learned from each of them: Paul Gilroy's insistence to be political, biased, and bold; Jonathan Holloway's determined and unflinching African American history; Matthew Jacobson's scrutiny of whiteness and privilege. At various stages

Ron Eyerman and Julia Adams provided valuable insight. Laura Wexler and Jim Sleeper supported and encouraged the project. Before Yale, at the University of California, Los Angeles, Victor Wolfenstein, Brenda Stevens, Melissa Meyer, Bob Emerson, Melvin Pollner, and Kerry Ferris inspired me to know and do more.

A warm thank-you to Robert Stepto for providing opportunities and perfect bookends. He was the one to call with the good news about Yale, and then, on graduation day, he expressed interest in publishing my manuscript. For seeing promise in that first very rough draft, I must also thank Carlo Rotella, Bill Savage, and Carl Smith. At the University of Chicago Press I am forever grateful to my editor, Robert Devens, who shepherded this project through the review process. Timothy Mennel and Russell Damian deserve special thanks for the seamless transition when Devens moved on. Thank you also to Ruth Goring. This project was strengthened by the reviewers. An anonymous reader provided crucial feedback early on. Amanda Seligman provided detailed and incisive feedback twice; the book is much better than it would have been without her. John Hartigan's comments made a marked difference in the final round.

For generous support for the research and writing of this book I am grateful to the John F. Enders Fellowship, George Camp grants, a Dean's Fellowship and Summer Research Grant, and Calhoun College's Richter Fellowship, all at Yale. The writing for this book was supported, in large part, by an American Council of Learned Societies Fellowship. A Black Metropolis Research Consortium Fellowship at the University of Chicago provided crucial travel and research support. Thank you to Tamar Evangelestia-Dougherty for her generosity and support that summer. Finally, I acknowledge support from the National Endowment for the Humanities and the W. E. B. DuBois Summer Institute at Harvard University. Thank you to the institute's codirectors, Patricia Sullivan and Waldo Martin.

Much gratitude to the many archivists and librarians who assisted me over the years at the University Archives at Northwestern University; Northeastern University in Boston; Special Collections at the University of Illinois, Chicago; Evanston History Center; Evanston Public Library; Art Institute of Chicago; Center for Black Music Research; and Chicago History Museum. Thanks to Dino Robinson, director of Shorefront Legacy Center in Evanston, Illinois, who very generously shared information and made his vast collection available to me. I must also thank the Bowers House Writers Retreat and Literary Center in Canon, Georgia, where I spent two weeks poring over more than 750 primary source documents. My research assistant Chloe Judell-Halfpenny deserves special mention.

Opportunities to present my research and hash out my ideas helped this project grow and develop. Thank you to participants of the Black Liberation Authors' writing group, Photo Memory Workshop; Graduate Affiliates of the Ethnicity, Race and Migration Program; and the Center for Comparative Research, all at Yale. Thank you also my colleagues at the Black Metropolis Research Consortium, especially Doria Johnson.

The manuscript has benefited greatly from the insight, advice, and encouragement of many people. Robin Hayes has been a loyal friend since the day I first left a note in her mailbox at 493 College Street. Lynn Rapaport's enthusiasm for the project helped propel it forward. She has also been a wonderful mentor. Thank you to friends and colleagues at Armstrong Atlantic State University, especially Daniel Skidmore-Hess, and the Claremont Colleges, especially Lily Geismer. I very much appreciate my new colleagues at Clemson University for welcoming me to the institution. I'm a better writer and try not to use the same word twice on the same page because of Jonathan Holloway, Robert Stepto, Robert Devens, Ryan Poynter, and Aaron Wong. For years of listening to me talk about the photo and more, thank you to Anthony Spires, Richard Karty, Patrick Rauber, Laurie Woodard, Josh Guild, Erin Chapman, Leigh Raiford, Carrie Gray, Gabriel Acevedo, and Fred Koerner. For helping me to secure images for the book, thank you to Sydney Crawford, Suzy Crawford, Lucinda Covert-Vail, Hecky Powell, and Simon Ingall. Many thanks to Billy Kapp for allowing me to draw from his incredible collection of photographs. Thank you also to Ron Crawford for drawing maps and helping me visualize the story.

Finally, I acknowledge the important contributions of friends and family. For hosting me during research trips, thanks to Rick and Sheila Montgomery-Bower, Beverly Sexton and Katherine Sibert, and Eric and Carla Agard-Strickland. For sharing materials and vital information, thank you to Allison Burnett and Lisa Mann. My sister Melanie shared the photo and story of her beloved Ma. Finally, thank you to my parents for making the right decision to raise us in Evanston.

Who's Who on the Porch

1. Ray   2. Jennifer   3. Jesse   4. Prince   5. Mary   6. Chip   7. Perkey   8. Carla
9. Regina   10. Barbara   11. Candy   12. Anonymous   13. Bernie

Not pictured:
Ronny is Jennifer's brother and friend to the boys; he probably took the photo.
Earl is Prince's and Jesse's cousin. He met Regina when he followed her home
on his bike one day.

Introduction

Growing up black in Evanston is a totally different experience than growing up white. PRINCE

Funerals

In March 2000 Jennifer forwarded an e-mail to me from Regina containing details about our friend Earl's funeral at Springfield Baptist Church in Evanston, Illinois. She added this message: "Pretty soon there won't be any black guys left from our childhood. I hope you're still planning on writing that book." Regina had been watching television when she heard that police who mistook an eating utensil for a weapon shot a homeless man carrying a spoon in the chest. Recalling that day years later, she told me that she was devastated by the loss of her first love. Angry, Earl's cousins Prince and Jesse were suspicious of media reports. Earl wasn't homeless. "He had family and could have stayed with any of us," Prince told me. Jesse thought Earl looked too good to be living on the streets: "He had just came from the barbershop, so you could see that when they buried him it looked like he had just got real groomed." Prince and Jesse were right: the police report was filled with inaccuracies. Like too many other black males, Earl had been a victim of police harassment and brutality. It's no wonder that years earlier, when they had tried to stop Perkey, he too had taken off.

It was the summer of 1998, and I was living in Los Angeles. Jennifer's brother Ronny was visiting from San Francisco. An old snapshot of some friends and me taken in our hometown, Evanston, was hanging on my refrigerator door. There's something fascinating to most people about the fates of their childhood friends. Our curiosity piqued, Ronny and I stood together staring at it. A near even mix of black and white, this group would have benefited from the city's commitment to integrated public education and open housing during the 1960s. Growing up in an affluent suburb known best for its beautiful homes, good public schools, and liberal politics must have laid the foundation for a successful life for us all. There would have been plenty of jobs due to a flush post–World War II economy. But according to what Ronny was telling me, a racial divide limited the life chances of blacks while providing opportunities for whites. This book follows the lives of the people in the picture. They grew up in the same city at the same time but met with very different ends.

Jennifer still wears the ring that Perkey gave her. Although they hadn't seen each other in a long time, his family contacted her some years ago, and she reentered his life as it ended. Perkey was riding his nephew's motorcycle when the police signaled for him to pull over. We'll never know why he sped away. The nephew was incarcerated, so we can surmise that the bike was not registered. The resulting high-speed chase ended with an accident that left Perkey in a coma for almost a year before he died.

Ronny didn't think twice before flying back to Evanston to serve as a pallbearer in his best friend's funeral. After the service, he helped carry the casket out of the church. The driver stopped the procession: "You pay me now or this hearse ain't going nowhere." No one moved, so the driver repeated himself: "This is how it works, you pay me right now, cash, and we continue to the cemetery."

All these years later, it's still hard for Bernie to talk about his older brother Perkey except to describe him as a "free spirit." The words "I Can Fly" are carved into his gravestone. His mother chose the simple phrase because she had believed that her son could go anywhere and do anything. Perkey was buried with the hopes and dreams of 1960s civil rights activists. He never had the opportunities that I did.[1]

When I visited Yale as a prospective student in 1999, Jennifer came with me. Both of us were struck by the similarities between New Haven and our hometown. The age, architecture, and city grid felt familiar. So did the prominence of a world-class university. A bus tour around the city gave us a glimpse of its racial diversity. It wasn't until much later that I began to fully understand that New Haven and Evanston shared something much more destructive. In both cities racism serves as an organizing principle for residential areas, educational opportunities, and occupational stratification. Yale's sprawling campus impresses visitors like me. It is surrounded by a number of one-way streets, and the buildings are designed and placed so that they face inward. Blighted neighborhoods are virtually inaccessible, and it's easy to miss the poverty so cleverly hidden from sight. The university's tax-exempt status impoverishes its surroundings. In both cities a privileged white neighborhood is located alongside a poor black community, and the territorial margins of these locales are typified by interaction between middle-class whites and black service workers.

Addiction to drugs and alcohol took their toll on Ray, and he also died far too young. After his death his family scrambled to find money to bury him. Ray's brother owned some stock. Prince remembers, "They were trying to raise money for his funeral, and his older brother worked for Sears at the time, and he came into the office and was telling me that they were trying to get money together for his funeral. He wanted to sell the stock, but they were telling him it would take a few days, and he needed the money pretty quickly, and I end up buying the stock from him." Ray's brother's investment didn't help him put a down payment on a house or ease retirement; instead he liquidated it for cash to bury his brother.

My white friends and I never thought about burying siblings or paying for funerals. As Jennifer's e-mail suggests, we shared our disbelief each time we heard more bad news. With nearly half of the black boys from our small group dead, I matriculated at Yale.

The Alchemy of the Photograph

If no one recalls posing for the picture, certainly no one remembers who took it. Still, there are some clues to its origins. A sleek white Instamatic that used 126 film, my camera produced pictures with even white borders and stenciled processing dates. November 1974 was stamped on this particular photo, but the green bushes and other shots on the roll of film, more of the group on the porch and some outside Nichols Middle School immediately following our eighth-grade commencement, suggest that the snapshot was taken the summer before most of us started high school. Everyone felt welcome at Jennifer's and Ronny's house, and it's not unusual that so many of us were there. It is, however, strange that Ronny's not in the picture, and so we assume that he took it.

"We never locked the doors," Jennifer mused while reflecting on the photograph. As for the others sitting on the porch steps, we were like her "brothers and sisters," she told me, an extension of her family. Her "siblings" included her "brothers," Perkey, Ray, Jesse, Bernie, Chip, and Prince, and her "sisters," Carla, Barbara, Regina, Candy, and me. For Jennifer the image evoked bittersweet memories, and she didn't mind sharing the bad along with the good, telling me that when she was young she often felt like she had "no privacy." On another occasion, her real brother, Ronny, echoed this very sentiment. "Our kitchen was the center of it all," he told me. He knew that we, his "brothers and sisters," thought it was the "coolest fucking house in the world," but looking back he believes that his parents were far too permissive, and it felt "kinda chaotic." Closer when we were young, we drifted apart the older we got.

The photo eventually inspired me to try to find the others. Tracking them down wasn't always easy, and I felt relief each time I did. On the phone I'd mention Jennifer's and Ronny's names as quickly as possible. Next I tried to describe the photograph by explaining who was in it. The picture invariably enabled me to gain access to my old friends. Curious to see it, everyone agreed to meet with me. We met in coffee shops, bars, and restaurants across the country and around the world. Thirty years after it was taken, the snapshot was proof of our shared past, and I didn't waste much time producing it.[2] Before parting, everyone asked for a copy and agreed to meet again for an interview.

These interviews took place between 2004 and 2008. At her home in Evanston, Regina talked about Earl's untimely death. Prince knew all too well what I had yet to understand. "Growing up black in Evanston is a totally different experience than growing up white," he explained, sitting in a rented room at a Best Western hotel. On a couch in her apartment on Chicago's northwest side, Carla insisted, "I'm half black inside. I swear it's just the way I see things; it's a very real thing." In a suburb farther north I interviewed another member of the group who decided she didn't want to be in the book. At his two-flat on Evanston's southwest side, Bernie, the youngest of nine, explained the pressures that he felt to succeed. Interviews in the Chicago area complete, I made plans to travel to other cities further away.

With funding from my graduate program, I left for Chantilly, France. Candy was living with her husband and two children in a nineteenth-century chateau outside of Paris. She asked about everyone, most especially Jesse. The following summer I went to Boca Raton, Florida, to interview Barbara. She picked me up at the hotel and drove me to her house in a Jewish subdivision. "It's like the world opened up a little bit for me," she said, referring to the time in her life when the photo was taken. "I remember feeling alive."

Now a majority of the interviews were complete, but finding Jesse and Chip would prove to be a more formidable task.

When I called the number Jesse's mother, Carolyn, gave me, a man on the other end told me that Jesse didn't live there but that he did stop by once in a while to pick up messages and get something to eat. The next time, the man promised me, he would tell Jesse that I called. It would be five years before I would finally speak with Jesse. A few weeks after that phone conversation, when we met at a Starbucks in Tacoma, Washington, he didn't recognize me. No less eager to tell his story, Jesse arrived at my hotel the next day for our interview with a stack of framed photographs of his children.

Locating Chip was even harder. There were rumors that he, too, was dead. When I finally got hold of him, I made arrangements to leave immediately, flew to Chicago, and took a bus from O'Hare Airport to Beloit, Wisconsin. Chip was at the bus stop to pick me up, and we drove to his aunt's house for dinner.

Hoping to gain a deeper understanding of my friends' perspectives and experiences, I used photo-elicitation as a form of inquiry. This research method draws on the simple practice of inserting a photograph into an interview session. I asked everyone to tell me what came to mind when they looked at it. A historical document in its own right, my picture brought back fond memories of 1970s popular culture. Racial rhetoric in film, fashion, and music of the period supported prevailing ideologies of black pride and social progress.[3] Remembering the good and not the bad, participants unwittingly supported the fallacy of Evanston's "social imagination," or what historian Sarah C. Maza calls "the complicated links between representations, emotional experience, and belief that go into the making of both subjectivity and community." Early observations revealed the extent to which we embodied public narratives of racial equality and ignored institutional mechanisms of discrimination.[4]

Is Jesse's fist a reference to Black Power? He doesn't think so: "I don't even know what Black Power means. It was just something that I remember, probably from the Olympics, when those three guys got up on the podium."[5] During our interview he assures me that he was only imitating the gesture. But that televised image made a lasting impression. According to his wife, it's a sign that he still makes.[6] Chip's and Perkey's chins rest on their fists, a clear reference, Bernie informed me, to the "gangster lean," a posture he attributes to the 1972 hit movie *Superfly* and adopted from the actions of the main character and hero, a street hustler named Priest. The pose was formalized through an unrelated song released in the spring of 1974, itself more likely to be remembered for its chorus ("diamond in the back, sun roof top, / digging in the scene with a gangsta lean") than for its title: "Be Thankful for What You Got." The movie and the song are understandably associated, considering the soundtrack for the film was written and composed by Curtis Mayfield, who clearly influenced the sound and content of "Be Thankful." While the movie's script encouraged audience members to revere material goods, Mayfield's socially aware lyrics and "Be Thankful" repudiated that very idea. Teenagers at the time, Chip and Perkey may not have understood the distinction. It is more likely that they were unwittingly participating in a cultural shift that began in the early seventies with a move away from the self-sacrificing "we generation" of the civil rights movement toward the "me generation" of consumerism. According to film critic Ed Guerrero, the "militant" was displaced into a "sartorial display."[7]

Body language and fashion in the photo illustrate the extent to which we were both products and consumers of our time. Ray is wearing a headband over his afro, a style popularized by Jimi Hendrix and Sly Stone. His purple bell-bottoms are quintessential seventies fashion. Prince's tube socks, made stylish by Wilt Chamberlain, are trimmed with colorful stripes, the adornment intended to coordinate team uniforms, head, and wristbands. Bernie noticed the socks immediately: "They'd laugh at you wearin' low socks, nobody wore low socks. I don't think they existed then, you had to have the high socks." Most of the group wore canvas Converse All-Stars with rubber soles. Bernie embellished his with little chains that were strung through the two ventilation holes on the sides of the shoe, and thick, colorful shoestrings. Jennifer's pink high-tops co-opted what Nelson George calls "Black athletic aesthetic," a style of play in basketball that was resoundingly intimidating and "in your face" and was accompanied by a "b-ball look."[8] Our friend's "Jewfro" was also indicative of the decade; the term has its etymological roots in sports too, appearing for the first time in print in 1970 to describe the hairdo of a Jewish college football star. I put a blond streak in my hair using Jolen Cream Bleach. School officials frowned upon youth who looked "too black." Chip's middle school teacher did not approve of his fashion sense—plaid and flared slacks, platform shoes, a half-shirt, and 'fro parted down the middle—and on more than one occasion sent him home to change. Her disapproval didn't seem to matter much. Impressed by his own good looks, Chip would stand in front of the mirror singing "If You Want Me to Stay" by Sly and the Family Stone. Embodied cultural trends and garb were not the only markers of time. Music also defined the period. Often associated with social justice and freedom movements, rhythm and blues, funk, and soul defined our childhood experiences.

The past mediated through gesture, fashion, and song influenced the ways in which we remembered the gendered and racialized dynamics of the group. Carla pointed out the physical intimacy between some of the group members, perhaps symbolic of the hippie counterculture that flouted societal prohibitions against interracial dating and that remained salient during the era. Jennifer's arms are "locked around" Ray, and Bernie is sitting on another friend's lap. The girls loved the Jackson Five, especially Michael. Jennifer summed up the group's importance, stating, "I didn't believe in the Osmonds," an all-white boy band that rivaled the J5. She half-joked that she tried to "live the Jackson Five experience" through our black friends. For Candy, Perkey was the "closest thing to Michael Jackson you could get." Reflecting on the photo, she was reminded of a song from *Hair* titled "Black Boys." She started singing the lyrics for me during our interview and got them wrong. Later at home, I listened myself ("Black boys are delicious, / Chocolate flavored love, / Licorice lips like candy") and was struck by the song's commodification of an edible black body.[9] Bernie spoke about our interracial friendships more matter-of-factly. "It was all just curiosity," he said. "Black boys didn't know anything about white girls, and the same with white girls about black boys."

Together these memories generated a longing for the past. Appearing to be an objective representation of our youth, the photograph validates an idealized version of it. Both the absence of authorship and the directness of the shot of our group, posed in the middle of the frame, suggest that there is no point of view or distinctive style. The photo therefore conveys an unmediated depiction of reality. Recalling better times, it emphasizes humanity rather than racial division. It also understates daily activities in favor of leisure and is therefore expressive of a trouble-free stage in life. The photo is a means not only to communicate the past but to create it, the way we would have liked it to be, would like it to be remembered.[10]

Black and white youth sitting together conjures our nostalgia. We were teenagers when the picture was taken, the most innocent and least regulated members of society. Segregation did not have a firm grasp on the institutions that we frequented or customary practices that we par-

ticipated in. We were not aware of the boundaries between neighborhoods or differences in school experiences, and because we were young
we were not yet fully ensconced in a racially stratified labor market.
It is true that as adults we experienced more limited degrees of freedom and our lives became increasingly separate. As children mature,
interracial friendships often end and friends disappear. The historical
roots of this process can be found in the antebellum South. Slave narratives are replete with stories about black and white friendships that
are cut short with increasing age. Of course we didn't realize that our
relationships were coming to an end, and it is only in retrospect that
we remembered never seeing one another again. Older now, we rarely
interact with members of other racial groups.

Dissatisfaction with present conditions also can make the past look
far better than it was. The older we got, the more time we spent reflecting and reviewing life. With this renewed interest in the past,
almost everyone in the picture jumped at the opportunity to revisit
it. Preoccupied with adult problems, with disillusionment and regret,
each ruminated over the consequences of choices they made, some
being more serious than others—a sense of squandered opportunities, misplaced dreams, and educational deficiencies. Some, struggling
to survive in the present, were convinced that the hard times of their
youth were not so bad after all.[11] On the whole, black lives seemed to
deviate from youthful dreams disproportionately to those of whites.
Utopian memories of Evanston were incongruous with what I knew to
be a harsh reality.

The truth is that to some extent integration did exist. Relationships
that formed between members of the group were meaningful for those
involved and cannot be dismissed as mere teenage crushes. Captured
on film, the integrated moment was fleeting, but the effects of growing up together lasted a lifetime and affected our lives in untold ways.
Taken at face value, the photo conveys an idealized image of racial harmony. For my participants who were eager, if not determined, to remember romantic versions of their childhood and hometown, it was
validation. But these exaggerated memories left us uncritical of social
structures that either denied or supported our futures. Ultimately the
photograph consists of two competing narratives.

Today I know more than I did sitting on those steps. Haunted by the
future and by events that unfolded after the shutter clicked, I found
that the photo served as a cautionary tale. It taught me to look beyond
early observations and was a warning that we must never substitute the
superficial glance for the needed long look. The more I dug, the more

depressing the news became. Poverty, early death, and unwarranted privilege are the lived experiences behind the facade and shed light on the underlying complexities of the photograph. Life experiences determined in large part by race and class challenge a discourse that exaggerates racial integration in Evanston. Interviews offered a sobering account of our hometown. The fantasy of integration represented in the photograph played a part in perpetuating institutional racism, or power and privileges based on race.[12] It allowed us to ignore it.

The security of the class system was puzzling given the resources of good schools, social services, and exposure to middle-class values available to residents living in an affluent suburb. Outwardly at least, it seemed that everyone would benefit, but Evanston's wealth didn't seem to make a difference for poor and working-class blacks. Of the black youth in my photo, only Prince was fully able to transcend his original class position and move up the social strata. Moreover, affluent members could not fall from their place of privilege, no matter how many mistakes they made. Environment had nothing and everything to do with life chances.[13] The paucity of social mobility as well as the fixed placement of the elite reaffirmed racial hierarchies. This book explores the connections between the life course of the individuals pictured in my photograph and the social environment of our hometown. My subjects' stories were instructional as I began to look beneath the surface of the place where I grew up.

Strong Objectivity

Feminist philosopher Sandra Harding's concept of "strong objectivity" calls for science to strengthen its objective stance by acknowledging all aspects of the social world, including researcher bias and varied findings.[14] Objectivity is a value that informs how social science is practiced. It's the idea that researchers attempting to uncover truths must aspire to eliminate personal bias and emotional involvement. It's an ideal that's impossible to reach, because all research is socially situated and there is no verifiable truth in the social world. When you share the same perspective, it's difficult to recognize political and cultural biases as such. When you don't, it's much easier to see.[15] The people best positioned to critique society, then, are those who are traditionally left out. They can reveal power relations in traditional knowledge production processes hidden to the rest of us.[16] This book wouldn't be possible if I wasn't in the photograph. I'm not an outsider looking in but rather an integral part of the group I examine. To exclude myself would make my book less objective and take us further from the truth. My friends and I grew up under different circumstances, some privileged and some disadvantaged. To understand one we have to understand the other. Each of our sets of experiences and perceptions is unique. None of them are any more valid than the others. Harding's unconventional approach gives us a balanced and robust understanding of everyday life.

When I moved to California in my twenties, I had no intention of coming back to the Midwest. Still, I felt a deep connection to both the place and the people who had shaped me profoundly. It was strange returning to Evanston, but I was determined to find out what had gone wrong. In public spaces I found myself anxiously looking around for familiar faces, but I rarely recognized anyone. Structurally the city remained much the same. Some buildings had been repurposed. My favorite department store, Marshall Field, had been converted into fancy condominiums. Others had new occupants. My childhood home looked as I remembered it, but a new family was living inside. The schools where I had been a student were still standing, but other children were attending. Some places seemed frozen in time. Digging into my own past and familial history was an unsettling prospect. While my photo inspired me to take a closer look at the city where I grew-up, a picture of our housekeeper demanded that I interrogate my family's place in the history I was writing.

A hand-tinted black-and-white photograph hangs on the wall of my sister's TriBeCa loft, a tribute to the woman who gave her the emotional support that any good parent would—that particular combination of "affection, discipline, and unconditional love." She credits this woman for many of the successes she has enjoyed throughout her life. My sister doesn't remember how or from whom she received the photo. She does know that when it was framed, the penciled inscription was covered over, and she remembers only part of what was written on the verso: the woman's name, Zelma Dunlap; a date; and the place where the photo was taken, Georgia.

My sister, who called the woman "Ma," has one other treasured possession: a snapshot of Zelma dressed in her white uniform. While the two photos, the hidden caption, and the memories are all that remain, my sister insists that the maid's attire and the fact that the woman was a family employee are incongruous with the image she has of their time together. The fact is that in 1971, the year of my sister's birth, Zelma was hired not only to take care of her but also to cook and clean for our family. I was eleven years old at the time.

FIGURE 0.1   Zelma Dunlap. Photographer unknown.

My relationship with Mrs. Dunlap was far more formal. I remember that she worked Mondays through Fridays during the day and then retired to her room on the third floor of our house at night. The room was furnished with a twin bed, a small desk, and a black-and-white television. We rarely saw her after dark but knew that she was upstairs dressed in her nightgown, with her wig off, a lit Benson and Hedges to accompany her customary gin. According to my sister, she didn't drink to get drunk but rather in order "to live." My sister remembers being scared when she would see Ma after hours, dressed down and without her wig. None of us knew very much about Mrs. Dunlap beyond the services that she performed for us.

My sister and Mrs. Dunlap would spend long days together cooking, cleaning, and listening to the radio. Dinner was served every evening at 5:30. Mrs. Dunlap's specialties included fried chicken, oxtail stew, macaroni and cheese, and greens. My sister helped her by shaking the chicken in a brown paper bag to coat it with flour before frying. She learned to tie her shoelaces by practicing with a string wrapped around her beloved Ma's wrist. When Fridays would come and Zelma Dunlap would leave for her own home on Chicago's South Side, my sister would always plead with her to stay. On several occasions my sister went with her. That's where she met Ma's sister Ruby, who used to tell her, "You know, she thinks of you like you're her own." My sister maintains that she never saw "race"; she never thought of herself as white or of Ma as black.

Despite the colorblind narrative my sister tells herself, race, class, and gender do structure work arrangements and are themselves articulated through them. Mrs. Dunlap was representative of thousands of poor black women who made their way north after World War II in search of jobs as domestics in white households. Reverse commutes delivered these black workers from Evanston's west side to white neighborhoods lining the shores of Lake Michigan or, as was the case with Mrs. Dunlap, into the suburbs during the work week and then back to their own homes in Chicago on Friday evenings. My family's relationship with Mrs. Dunlap was typical of those between white employers and black domestic workers, a paradox of intimacy and distance naturalized under the guise of equality and racial indifference.[17] We can't know the hardships Mrs. Dunlap must have faced, despite the few memories that corroborate her unhappiness. My sister recalls that on more than one occasion Mrs. Dunlap would quit, pack her bags, and tell my sister that she couldn't take it anymore. Each time my sister would beg her not to go, and each time she would convince Ma to stay.

My sister was seven years old when Mrs. Dunlap died. Most likely induced by the gin she drank "to live," cirrhosis was ultimately the cause of her death. Years later, driver's permit in hand, my sister drove to the South Side of Chicago to look for the cemetery where Mrs. Dunlap was buried. She found it rundown and encroached upon by fast food restaurants. Once inside, she had a hard time finding Ma's grave. A simple plaque marked her final resting place; a headstone would have cost too much.

Barely making it in life but too poor to die: Zelma Dunlap's story was beginning to sound familiar. If my primary goal was to understand Evanston's racial structure, to identify practices and mechanisms that produce and reproduce social inequality, there was no way to pretend that I didn't benefit. My opportunities were directly related to the ones Mrs. Dunlap didn't have. This book is about the social processes that reproduce racial privilege and disadvantage in America. Interviews alone would not suffice; I began researching the city's cultural and political history.

Many Evanstons

Perpetuating an idealized past, a prevailing discourse of integration permeated the official story of Evanston. To uncover the simultaneous processes of nominal integration and continuing segregation, and to better understand the relationship between power and oppression, I drew from as many sources as possible. Like individual narratives, historical materials are composed of varying degrees of myth and reality, and I wondered if there was a connection. No single version told the entire story. There was no discernible "truth" about Evanston. The strengths and weaknesses of each source alone served as justification to include multiple versions and perspectives. Dramatization—even exaggeration, distortion, and suppression—was evident in all source materials.

The mythopoeic role of official documents cannot be denied. They can be located within systems of power, marginalization, and inequality and are mechanisms for maintaining historical narratives that privilege the stories of great white men. They assist in manufacturing an ideology that supports economic, political, and social development.[18] The stories they tell not only reflect society's norms but also continually revitalize these norms and are essential to understanding how public ideas are absorbed. Considered to be the most verifiable sources for information, official documents are filters for propaganda and can be a lens into the hidden agendas behind every representation. The consequences are enormous. In Evanston mainstream sources reinforce beliefs about racial equality, thereby weakening prospects for change. Local media illustrate this process.

The dominant news source for the community, the *Evanston Review* (henceforth cited as the *Review*), published its first paper in June 1925. I focused on issues printed between 1960 and 1970, the decade when Evanston's public schools desegregated and a fair housing ordinance was passed. In April 1968 the *Review* increased circulation from one to two issues a week—Mondays and Thursdays. The format included news columns, which detailed school board and city council meetings and, to some extent, civil rights activities. The paper took a conservative stand on social issues in its editorials and reprinted readers' letters in the "Public Forum." Published letters may not be representative, as the paper made editorial decisions about which ones to print.

The black press more thoroughly reported on protest, conflict, and the essential role of grassroots community organizations. The *North Shore Examiner* (henceforth cited as the *Examiner*) took a more radical stand on racial issues. A testament to the growing political power of the black community, the *Examiner* published its first issue in December 1968 with the promise to establish a "climate for meaningful dialogue," serving cities along the north shore from Evanston to Zion. The paper took a strong integrationist stance but was firmly rooted in the black community, especially when it came to political and economic issues. Editors hoped to reach both black and white readers. "A progressive newspaper serving a progressive community," the paper covered issues relevant to all north shore residents, but the focus was clearly on Evanston. The newspaper's office was located in Evanston. Randolph R. Tomlinson, the editor and publisher, and members of the small multiracial staff were residents. While both newspapers reflected and molded opinions, the *Examiner* contributed a critical voice to a conversation about race once dominated by the *Review*.

Invested in presenting Evanston in a positive light, libraries and museums collected materials that tended to compose what we would regard as a hegemonic account of history. These sources were, in turn, legitimated by the institutions that held them and made them available to readers. The public library, with its Prairie School–inspired design, resembles the architecture of Evanston's past. The structure has a strong civic presence and suggests the social virtues of democracy and morality—books are available to everyone and reading is good. Copies of the *Evanston Review* were readily available, but when folders containing hard copies of the *Examiner* went missing, microfilm backups were not to be had. Claiming to hold materials related to every aspect of Northwestern University's history, University Archives only recently started collecting documents pertaining to the 1968 black student uprising. Prior to this effort there was little information available about protest activities. The Evanston History Center, a turreted Victorian mansion that overlooks Lake Michigan, was once the home of Charles Dawes. A Chicago banker, Dawes achieved eminence in the 1920s as vice president to Calvin Coolidge. Today his landmark home is a museum and research center where visitors can view the documentary film *Register Me from Evanston*. The movie praises the city by touting Evanston's diversity, a reputation that the institution is all too happy to endorse.[19] A montage of still photos shows people engaged in various activities, including one of me sitting in a park eating an ice-cream cone, a near perfect display of elite leisure. Together these institutions exude civic responsibility and local patriotism, which act to legitimize the dissemination of ideas stored inside, even if they are only partly true. It is easy to be seduced by these collections and to believe that they combine to form a complete picture. For the most part, they tell us what we want to hear: Evanston does not have a racist past; racial integration and equal opportunity have largely been achieved.

Documents stored at Shorefront Legacy Center fill the void left by older research institutions. Aiming to educate the public about black history on Chicago's north shore, materials at Shorefront offer a counternarrative to the city's version of inclusivity and the mostly white and racially romanticized history available from other sources. Records demonstrate that blacks were not just victims or needy recipients but survivors with remarkable courage. They were not only domestic workers and servants but also successful businessmen and professionals who played an important role in shaping the city. Significantly, Shorefront was located on the west side of town, in the old Foster School building, an all-black institution before desegregation and a reminder to some of a time when the black community thrived and stood together undivided by social class. Correcting misrepresentations at predominantly white institutions, Shorefront collects materials donated by black families living in Evanston, all of whom must be grateful that their stories are finally being told. Overlooked in other archives, black suburbanites have also largely gone missing in academic scholarship.

New Suburban History

Through the use of racial covenants and zoning policies, suburbs sealed themselves off from groups they didn't want as neighbors during the mid-twentieth century. Many communities that line Chicago's north shore still exemplify this trend. Academics portray American suburbs as homogenous communities consisting of well-to-do whites. Sociologists tend to focus on larger cities, if only because in them social problems have been acute and visible. Chicago provides an interesting research site for scholars studying race. William Julius Wilson writes about the outmigration of middle-class blacks to suburban areas, but his work focuses almost exclusively on the inner cities they left behind. Mary Patillo-McCoy researches upwardly mobile blacks who remain in close proximity to poor communities within city limits.[20] Doug Massey and Nancy Denton have concentrated on a band of deteriorating inner-ring suburbs, almost indistinguishable from the city, where a black presence led to rapid racial turnover.[21] By concluding that suburbanization was a process in which blacks and working-class peoples played little part before the 1970s, urban historians have done a "better job excluding African Americans from the suburbs than even white suburbanites."[22] Historic narratives center on white residents living "far from their work place, in homes that they own, and in the center of yards that by urban standards elsewhere are enormous."[23] Suburban landscapes express values deeply embedded in bourgeois culture, including the idealization of family life, leisure, feminine domesticity, and a union with nature.[24] This sharply dichotomized representation of suburbanization fails to account for black life in wealthy suburbia. Richard Harris suggests that the "city-suburban dichotomy" may not be as significant as previously determined.[25] Evanston, Illinois, offers a paradigmatic corrective to this oversight.

While there is a tendency for racialized minorities to concentrate near work in cities, there were plenty of jobs located beyond the city limits, including manufacturing and service work for the wealthy.[26] Historian Andrew Wiese demonstrates that suburbs have provided a home to black residents for more than one hundred years. Hoping to improve the quality of their lives by increasing economic opportunities for themselves and educational choices for their children, southern blacks relocated to metropolitan areas in the North during the first half of the twentieth century. Of this group, one in six sought the tranquillity and resources of suburbia rather than the overcrowded ghettos of urban centers. By 1940, more than a million blacks lived in suburban areas.[27] When civil-rights-inspired suburbanization accelerated after 1960, there were more than 2.5 million African Americans in the suburbs.[28] Suburbia largely replicated well-established patterns of racial segregation. Blacks resided in run-down areas that scarcely resembled the postwar suburban ideal: "places like Maywood, a decaying blue-collar town, or Ford [Heights], one of the poorest suburbs in the country. Only a handful of upper-middle-class, white-dominated suburbs, which prided themselves on their liberality—notably Evanston and Oak Park—integrated."[29]

Neither the comparison nor the designation is fully warranted. It is true that Evanston and Oak Park are remarkably similar. Both communities employ a unique blend of welcome and rejection. They offered opportunities for blacks that did not exist in the South. Whites were not openly hostile but would not have considered blacks social equals either. Both places experienced rapid growth after the Chicago Fire and the extension of the railroad. Temperance communities, they placed importance on the family, church, and education. These values are visibly preserved in the built form by houses designed by the Prairie School, an architectural style that created large spaces for family unity. Frank Lloyd Wright lived in Oak Park and was a founder. In 1946 Paul Robeson was invited to perform at high schools in both Evanston and Oak Park. During the 1960s both places experienced an influx of progressive-minded young white families. This is where the similarities end.

Oak Park's black community was small but growing until the 1920s, when developers decided to expand the commercial district and a series of mysterious fires almost destroyed an emerging black neighborhood. African American residents and black-owned businesses were all but swept away.[30] In 1960 there were only 57 black residents in Oak Park. By 1976 that number had increased to 3,000, and neighborhoods were undergoing rapid racial transition as Chicago's massive black ghetto expanded westward.[31] In an effort to "stabilize," Oak Park employed what sociologist Harvey L. Molotch has called "managed integration," or methods for persuading whites to stay.[32] The city undertook extralegal measures such as quota systems to ensure racial balance in neighborhoods and embarked on a public relations campaign to advertise and promote integration. By contrast, in 1940 Evanston's black population was the largest of any suburban community in Illinois, totaling 6,026 of 64,000. Over the next two decades it grew to constitute 12 percent of the population, and it continued to grow. Numbering 12,861, blacks made up 16 percent of the population by 1970.[33] Evanston contained its black community less violently and more subtly—no rash of fires here.

Segregation Northern-Style

The first and largest of the lakeshore suburbs north of Chicago Evanston covers 8.3 square miles. The landscape is idyllic: there are breathtaking views of Lake Michigan from the city's scenic shore; farther to the north and west, prime real estate has been developed into exclusive suburbs for the wealthy; and to the south, Evanston's proximity to Chicago's metropolis all but secures its economic resources and development. Housing values are the highest along the lake and to the north and northwest, where large Victorian-style homes and shady elm trees line the shore. Commuters and visitors marvel at the scenery as they travel on main roads that run alongside the lake, a geographic feature with which everything else is easily aligned. These routes, however, do not take them near the west side of town, where a sizable black population is hemmed in between a sanitary canal and railroad tracks. Both areas can be distinguished not only by the identities of their inhabitants but also by the structure and texture of their social and physical environments. On the west side, housing costs are lower, streets narrower, and trees fewer and farther between. The landscape marks everyone's place in a racial order.

In this city, established as a campus town for Northwestern University, educational values are at the core. Moreover, the public school system is considered to be one of the best in the country. Well-educated adults constitute the social body. The university provides work for many of the city's residents. Additionally, Evanston's proximity to a large metropolitan area demands workers at all levels. In 1960, one-third of the workforce commuted to Chicago, while the majority lived and worked in town. Most residents held white-collar jobs. There was, however, a considerable pocket of poverty. At the lowest end of the socioeconomic scale were families and individuals receiving public assistance. A significant portion of the city's residents were wealthy and paid taxes to support organizations and institutions that provided opportunities for disadvantaged families. An abundance of financial resources, however, allowed many of the city's social problems to go undetected.[34] It would be a mistake to assume that "white flight" generated Evanston's population.

During the 1960s whites arrived from points across the United States. While some cited "neighborhood schools" when it came to segregated education, and "freedom of choice" when it came to housing, disguising their disdain for blacks with these anodyne terms, others sought out Evanston precisely because of its liberalism and racial diversity. Evanston's racial demographics were unique, and this did not go unnoticed by whites who embraced the ideal of diversity, rejecting suburbia's bland conformity. These adults internalized the message of postwar integrationists: they did not want to deprive their children of the invaluable experience of day-to-day contact with blacks. Blacks, too, made Evanston a destination, arriving from the South in search of jobs, good schools for their children, and nice neighborhoods to live in. Together these in-migrants helped shape the suburb into one that was both regionally and economically diverse. Idealism quickly turned to reality, though, when new arrivals settled in racially designated neighborhoods. Blacks were steered west by discriminatory housing practices.

Evanstonians worked hard to integrate during the civil rights era, when school board mandates and local ordinances called for the desegregation of both educational institutions and residential neighborhoods. While this process ended systematic racial segregation, it did so in the legal realm only. True integration, or creating equal opportunities regardless of race, was largely a social matter. It was at this juncture that Evanston fell short; the city never followed through on all of its promises. Nonetheless, the town's reputation was not tarnished. It had been in the making since Evanston was founded in 1857 and was deeply enmeshed in the city's social structure. On a basic level residents believed that the civil rights era had come to fruition. Both blacks and whites based their assumptions on the *presence* of the other group and prided themselves on the degree of racial integration and progressive politics embodied in the city's demographics.

Evanston is also a useful site with which to expand our understanding of the civil rights movement outside the South. Sociologists Aldon D. Morris and Doug McAdam have explained the rise and development of the "southern movement." Morris credits indigenous institutions that provided an organizational base and leadership.[35] McAdam's work has focused on opportunities presented by the political context of the 1960s.[36] This book contributes to a complementary—and at times challenging—focus on the North, which dovetails with that of historians who have increasingly turned northward to chart the "Long Civil Rights Movement." By expanding the regional and temporal framework, we challenge an artificial binary of northern innocence and southern exceptionalism. Pushing the chronology simultaneously backward and forward, we question the movement's impact. The struggle to desegregate schools and neighborhoods may be less triumphant, but the narrative becomes more explicable, replicable, and believable when we place it in a national context. Recent scholarship has called into question the self-congratulations about progressive racial politics of northern cities such as Evanston.

Historian Matthew D. Lassiter writes about the underlying and divergent structures that support a myth of southern exceptionalism. In the South, Jim Crow or de jure segregation was obvious. It was enforced by state and local law, by organized and violent retaliation. Visible signage directed movement, behavior, and usage of public space, creating little ambiguity. *Plessy v. Ferguson*, a Supreme Court ruling mandating separate but equal facilities, legitimated these practices on a federal level. The 1954 Supreme Court decision in *Brown v. Board of Education* began the gradual dismantling of this tradition. By contrast, in the North the practice and discourse of de facto segregation was mostly invisible. There were no laws or signs. Prior to the Great Migration 90 percent of the black population lived in the South, and so there was no need to legislate racial separation. With the injustice difficult to define and therefore to address, civil rights leaders devised the de facto framework as part of a strategy to extend the *Brown* mandate beyond the South. Successful in identifying segregation, the movement found it more challenging to prove malice.[37]

Coded language disguises underlying racist practices. De facto segregation suggested that inequalities were both accidental and unavoidable and therefore outside the reach of the Fourteenth Amendment. As a legal doctrine, the term actually means "innocent segregation."[38] School districts were organized using a "neighborhood model," an innocuous term connoting community and tradition rather than racial exclusion. As a result, student bodies were either all white or all black, but local politicians employed a less pejorative term, "racial imbalance," when referring to enrollment figures. Opponents of integration hoped to stir fears about individual rights quashed by dictatorial government when they used the expression "forced busing." Residential segregation was explained away as a product of "individual preference" and "free market forces," not as being caused by a discriminatory real-estate industry and racial prejudices of white homeowners. Overall, northern racism was depicted as an individual problem, not a social one. Terminology influenced public perception of these false claims.

Northern-style segregation was an early iteration of "colorblind racism," a term used by sociologists when describing present-day race relations. The colorblind perspective insists that institutional racism and discrimination have been replaced by equal opportunity and that people are now judged by their qualifications alone. Nearly identical, the term *de facto* naturalized or normalized race related matters. Like colorblindness, it explained segregated schools and neighborhoods or limited contact between whites and blacks in terms of economics or individual preference. Additionally, it completely ignored past or contemporaneous injustices, blaming individuals rather than society.[39] Like any social construct, race adapts and changes with time. In its current incarnation we don't see it. Racism is also harder to detect. This development is the product of a long process that finds de facto seg-regation as its precursor. In both cases invisibility made possible the public denial of government policies shaping segregated schools and housing.[40] During the 1960s racial inequalities in the North remained difficult to address. This book offers important insight into how racism operates in sophisticated, covert, and apparently nonracial ways.

Although the two terms are commonly conflated, desegregation did not in practice mean integration, especially when it came to housing. To be sure, many whites acquiesced to integration mandates, but that did not mean that they wanted blacks as neighbors. Violent resistance to the expansion of the black community in Chicago caused the US Civil Rights Commission to describe it as "one of the most segregated cities in the world."[41] In 1959 the commission hosted hearings in Chi-cago to determine the causes of housing discrimination. Community organizer Saul Alinsky was asked to testify. His statement defined ra-cially integrated communities in chronological terms; integration was timed, he argued, from the entrance of the first black family to the exit of the last white family, "while the blacks are moving in and the whites are moving out it's integrated."[42] Alinsky's assessment was accurate; in-tegration tends to be a fluid and fleeting process.

From binary to continuum: Evanston, Illinois, is an ideal midpoint. Even more, it is a sociological fulcrum. Like those of other US cities, Ev-anston's schools and residential areas were segregated, and its employ-ment practices were discriminatory. In Evanston it is certainly true that racial integration was ongoing and incomplete. To be sure, *true* integra-tion, or its implication that "no area of physical space be marked by racial hierarchy," was never achieved. Even a more relaxed definition of assimilation or more precisely financial and educational success as de-fined by mainstream mores and values was not reached. There contin-ues to be a contradiction between what's being said and what actually occurs in Evanston. The city is more accurately described by sociolo-gist Ruth Frankenberg's term *quasi-integrated*.[43] Popular stories of suc-cessful desegregation campaigns actually enforced social, political, and economic logics that preserved de facto segregation. *Friends Disappear* examines the ways in which actual segregation was enforced through nonracial dynamics.

Social scientists tend to think about processes of reproduction or resistance as an either-or situation, but both are usually taking place at the same time. Evanstonians participated in the creation of their perceived reality. Integration was created, was institutionalized, and became part of the city's tradition in a process that was ongoing and dynamic. Equality and justice were foregone conclusions. Evanston's reputation was invented and produced through consensus and eventual acquiescence. Compliance to structural forces is not the only defining factor of agency. This book is more than a straightforward history of the reproduction of class and racial inequality; it is also about how people fought back. Individuals resisted and transformed social arrangements. Blacks demonstrated resilience when they stayed their ground in spite of the fact that they felt unwelcome and rejected. In search of jobs, autonomy, and a middle-class lifestyle, blacks and whites moved to Evanston to improve the quality of their lives. They joined forces and to some extent overcame segregated public schools and residential neighborhoods.

The sixties was an era of intense political activity. The decade represented a move away from the conservative fifties and was a precursor to the self-absorbed seventies. Civil rights and Black Power movements took different approaches but had similar goals. Blacks demanded decent housing, decent education, and decent jobs. A bid for racial equality came to fruition in terms of new legislation including the 1964 Civil Rights Act, the 1965 Voting Rights Act, and the 1968 Fair Housing Act. Evanston's civil rights story overlaps with these national determinations. The city desegregated its public schools in 1967 and passed a strong fair housing ordinance in 1968. But racial progress threatened the privileged lifestyles that epitomized Evanston and other North Shore suburbs. A citizenry with full and equal rights would have jeopardized a standard of living that wealthy suburbanites desired and the black underclass provided. Therefore integration was quietly, if not hotly, contested and never fully realized.

Book Overview

In the mid-nineteenth century a group of Methodist ministers founded Northwestern University, infusing Evanston's economic, political, and cultural life with a religious morality. Chapter 1 presents an overview of the town's early history. Wealthy whites moved north from Chicago seeking respite from the growing metropolis, building mansions with spectacular lakefront views. Evanston's west side was already home to a well-established black community when the Great Migration began. Blacks were agents in the process, moving to escape southern racism, rejoin family, purchase homes, enroll their children in better schools, and find work. In this case the destination was a suburban city, not a colossal metropolis. They built a community noted for stability and homeownership opportunities. By the 1960s Evanston's black population was proportionally greater than the national percentage. Whites were arriving from northern cities across the country. They sought out Evanston precisely because of its liberality, racial diversity, and good schools. My own parents were among these new migrants.

Northern schools were no less segregated than their southern counterparts. Rooted in segregated residential patterns, attendance areas were organized using a neighborhood concept that sought to permit small children to walk to school and back home. As a result schools manifested considerable "racial imbalance." Chapter 2 examines Evanston's school desegregation plan. In December 1964 the board of education voted to gradually end de facto segregation and hired Gregory C. Coffin to implement its plan. Like those in other cities in the North, Evanston's strategy called for the redistribution of students from its all-black elementary school to institutions in white neighborhoods. The resulting student bodies were more representative, but black children continued to be alienated. Because they were whisked away by bus when the school day ended, interracial friendships were difficult to maintain. Without cafeterias, gymnasiums and basements served as dining areas but isolated black students while their white classmates went home for hot meals. Opposition to an all-inclusive lunch plan resulted in a series of excuses that questioned the government's role in private matters and emphasized women's responsibilities as mothers. True integration would require more than racially representative student bodies. Coffin hired black teachers and administrators. He also overhauled the curriculum to include black history and culture.

Soon the school board expressed its commitment to integration but unhappiness with Coffin. According to some members he had an abrasive personality and was moving "too far, too fast." Chapter 3 describes the battle to save Superintendent Coffin's job when his contract was not renewed. Committed to true integration, Coffin was determined to develop an inclusive lunch program, hire and promote black staff, and revise the curriculum, all of which were changing the balance of power in Evanston. Coffin was the first white superintendent in the country to have the backing of the black community. A multiracial effort, Citizens for 65, formed to elect new board members and save the superintendent's job. Coffin's policies to give black and white children an equal education threatened conservatives, who launched their own Community Education Committee to campaign against the beleaguered superintendent.

During Coffin's term Evanston made tremendous strides. Chapter 4 examines the experiences at Nichols Middle School of the young people in my photograph. This is where most of us met for the first time. Drawing from larger segments of the community than the elementary schools did, junior highs had relatively integrated student bodies. Interracial friendships formed more easily. We walked to school because we were older and the district wasn't required to provide transportation. Middle schools were built with cafeterias, and everyone ate together. They continued to be organized around a homeroom model that gave children at different academic levels a chance to get to know one another. District-sponsored after-school programming encouraged us to stay in the neighborhood when the school day ended. During interviews my friends drew maps giving insight on how neighborhoods were arranged and remembered. Not fully cognizant of boundaries separating black and white neighborhoods, we disregarded them. The older we got, however, the more impossible this became. Ultimately it was residential segregation that restricted black and white friendships.

Restrictive covenants and deeds specifying that only whites could own or occupy a residence proved to be an effective and superficially peaceful way of shaping the social geography. Zoning laws prohibited the construction of apartment buildings and kept renters out. The real estate industry, supported by widespread acts of prejudice and discrimination, sold lakefront property to whites and steered blacks west to an area marked by train tracks and a sanitary canal. Chapter 5 examines residential segregation and the fair housing movement to end it. In 1965 the North Shore Summer Project recruited student volunteers to register white homeowners willing to sell in an open market and to assist blacks looking to purchase or rent. Meanwhile the city council was given the nearly impossible job of crafting a fair housing ordinance that would be acceptable to blacks, liberal whites, conservative property owners, and real estate agents, all of whom claimed that their individual rights and freedoms were being compromised. A pervasive lack of affordable housing perpetuated a racialized east-west divide.

In chapter 6 I show how Evanston Township, a well-respected high school, created difference and promoted segregation. During the 1960s black students organized, demanding courses and faculty that reflected their experiences. They were largely successful. Semi-independent schools managed a large student population but divided friendships made in lower grades. Academic tracking or "second-generation" segregation perpetuated a tradition of separate and unequal education. Poor and working-class students were disproportionately steered toward vocational and remedial coursework. Less likely to have formally educated parents, they were the least likely to bring to school notions of how to do well there. Parent involvement made a difference in some cases but not others. White students had options even if their academic record didn't merit them. For those who were failing, special programs or private schools ensured graduation. Black and white participation in extracurricular activities was uneven, further dividing students. Friendships made in the lower grades ended as students retreated to their own racial groups. Educational experiences were varied. Not everyone in the picture graduated.

Like schools and neighborhoods, work is a key component in the articulation of race, gender, and class. Chapter 7 surveys Evanston's dual economy. During the 1960s, civil rights and Black Power movements demanded jobs and fair wages. Instead Evanston took a paternalistic approach, doling out aid and charity. Black parents and their children held jobs that were only nominally different from those obtained by early migrants—undesirable, temporary, and poorly paid. This pattern was the same for whites, many of whom had stable, well-paying professional careers. Black friends found it harder to surmount educational deficiencies. With our parents' wealth as safety net, whites were able to overcome poor educational performance and early academic disengagement. If and when we decided to attend college, we did so with ease, not having been fully prepared for it beforehand. We have successful careers despite, in some cases, lacking postsecondary training. There was some variety within these arguably racialized patterns. For the most part our group moved through an economic structure that placed whites at top levels and blacks near the bottom, regardless of credentials.

While it is tempting to ask what socializing institution had the most impact on our lives, I conclude by reiterating their interconnectedness. School, neighborhood, and work shaped individual life courses. One sphere either opened-up or limited the next. During the civil rights era, blacks and whites acted together to integrate. Despite inroads, reforms barely affected educational opportunities, residential segregation, or employment discrimination.[44] Whatever gains were made seemed to disappear quickly as the economy worsened during the seventies. It was a period of stagflation, a combination of rising prices and joblessness, due to deindustrialization and the loss of manufacturing jobs to overseas outlets. In all areas of social life blacks and whites have remained mostly separate and disturbingly unequal. White youth in the photograph had advantages that black youth did not: a public school system with varying expectations for children almost exclusively determined by race, class, and gender; the stability and financial safety nets that come with owning a home as opposed to renting; and a dual economic system that relies heavily on educational credentials, cultural capital, and social networks. Combined, these structural forces set us on separate and unequal courses. Themes of institutional failure, entrenched inequality, and moral ambiguity may take different forms, but they run throughout Evanston's two-hundred-year history.

ONE
———

Heavenston

It is of a quiet city that still prefers to call itself a village; kissed on one cheek by Michigan's waves, fanned from behind by prairie breezes, jeweled with happy homesteads set in waving green, and wreathed about with prairie wild flowers, a town as comely as a bride, even to strangers' eyes. FRANCES WILLARD[1]

The official story of Evanston begins when its "uninhabited" natural beauty is contrasted to Chicago's decay. A group of moral and religious men "discover" Evanston and build Northwestern, a world-class university. Notable entrepreneurs (railroad barons and meatpackers) and political leaders (associates of Abe Lincoln) add to the new community's spirit and greatness. University buildings, public schools, and streets carry their names and cement their accomplishments into the town's landscape. Nicknames like Heavenston illustrate the city's character. Urban legends celebrate local patriotism. Over time, collective representations create a governing identity (abolitionist, temperance worker, Democrat) thought to embody a broader social character (moral, progressive, racially integrated). These stories are told and retold by city boosters who promote an unequivocally positive image and the local media that always find the past in the present.[2] The causal importance of these visible and tangible cultural manifestations "lies less in their capacity to express mass sentiments than in their ability to elicit them."[3] Over long periods of time they become fixed to the point where it's hard to believe that things could have happened differently. This chapter reinterprets Evanston's political, economic, and cultural history.

Evanston was a destination for white elites who worked in Chicago but sought refuge from the manufacturing hub for peace on the northern shoreline and for black migrants who were mostly confined to low-paying jobs in personal service and outdoor labor. Servants living in close proximity were a convenience that whites enjoyed, so they encouraged black settlement on the west side, away from the lakefront. Vibrant and self-contained, Evanston's black community grew. Black institutions provided educational, health, and recreational services. A substantial black presence contributed to a prevailing discourse of racial and economic diversity and persuaded my own parents to raise their children in Evanston during the 1960s. For white graduates of colleges and professional schools in the North and blacks leaving the South to start new lives in the "Promised Land," moving to Evanston was the first in a series of events that would lead to the formation of our friendship group.

Fleeing the City

Economic greed was an early driver of the formation of the Chicago area. European fur traders were drawn to the region because its proximity to the Mississippi River and Great Lakes watershed facilitated the exchange of goods. The location was ideal for shipping and receiving goods, and for trading with Indians until President Andrew Jackson's Removal Program became law and the land's original inhabitants were effectively relocated west.[4] Native Americans signed away their last claims to the area as early as 1833.[5] Less than two decades later, railroads were carrying freight into and out of Chicago, and trade had moved well beyond fur to include grain, lumber, and cattle. As a gateway between eastern cities and western frontiers, the city was becoming a focal point for commerce.

According to the fable of its beginnings, Evanston was nothing but swamps in 1840. If one overlooks the Potawatomi Indians who traveled on the long trail from Milwaukee to Chicago, the area was largely uninhabited. In what was then known as Ridgeville, Major Edward Mulford built the first log cabin in 1840. Hoping to establish a place for "sanctified" learning and living, a group of Methodists headed by John Evans founded Northwestern University in 1851.[6] They purchased several hundred acres north of Chicago along Lake Michigan to establish the campus. Several years later, in 1854, the university business manager drew up the original street plans for the town that Northwestern would adjoin. The university and its property were declared "forever free from taxation for any and all purposes."[7] This arrangement structured white advantage in the economy from the beginning, creating a dual labor market where elites filled positions in the top tiers of the university and members of the working class serviced their needs, taking care of grounds and campus buildings. Without tax revenue from the city's largest institution, its ability to subsidize low wages through social services would be limited.

Exact figures are not available, but it is estimated that in 1854 Ridgeville's population was between five and six hundred. Early settlers applied to the Illinois State Legislature, and three years later, on February 15, 1857, the village was officially recognized and its name changed from Ridgeville to Evanston. Through the gradual stages of its growth, Evanston became coterminous with the township (the smallest subdivision of government at the time) of the same name. The 1860 census records two black residents, women who worked as domestics, out of a total of 831. Among Evanston's early black settlers were at least three former slaves, Nathan Branch, James Lindsay, and Richard Day. The demise of slavery also meant the end of the fugitive slave law. By 1870 Evanston's black population reached 43 out of 3,062. Ten years later it had increased to 125. The 1880 census lists five Canadian-born blacks and two northern-born blacks, all of whom had parents born in the South. The ages of these seven residents suggest that they may have been the children of slaves who fled the South via the Underground Railroad.[8] When the Civil War ended, blacks left Canada no longer fearing capture or reenslavement, and emancipated southerners moved north.

Autonomy from Chicago depended on pure water and grew out of annexation of the separate villages of North Evanston in 1873 and South Evanston in 1892. In 1896 the newly structured town absorbed a small black community reaching to its western side—the population's early growth established patterns promoting the eventual formation of a substantial black neighborhood. The process continued into the 1930s, when the last fragments of unincorporated township land were annexed and physically the city of Evanston was complete.

By the middle of the nineteenth century Chicago's elevators, lumberyards, and stockyards were the most basic symbols of the city's wealth and power.[9] Schooners carried timber from Michigan and Wisconsin to the world's largest lumber market. Environmental destruction was not far behind. Western landscapes quickly gave way to farms growing popular crops such as corn and wheat. Settling the western prairies meant cutting the northern forests; "without [this timber], houses, barns, and corncribs–not to mention churches and schools—were almost impossible to construct."[10] Moreover, "it heated homes, cooked meals, and supplied the energy that ran steam engines. No raft, boat, or railroad could be built without it."[11] Forests were quickly exhausted. By virtue of its central location and outstanding transportation system, Chicago was also a meatpacking powerhouse. The Civil War cut Texas ranchers off from their ordinary markets in the Caribbean and slave states. By 1867 hundreds of thousands of animals were making the journey north to graze before being sold as beef and pork in the bustling metropolis. As the economy grew, increasing numbers of working-class peoples (mostly foreign-born immigrants and blacks) were needed to sustain it.

Until the nineteenth century, work and residence had naturally combined, and the best location for transacting business had determined the location of one's home. Neighborhoods functioned as integrated worlds of work and family life containing a multiplicity of classes.[12] As the nation's economic and political system took shape, however, wealthy white men secured their privilege. The separation of business districts and residential areas was inevitable as the country moved from an agrarian to an industrial economy. By the mid-nineteenth century, cities were divided into distinct districts of work and home, "matched by the growing segregation of residence communities by class, ethnicity, and race."[13] Trade unions and political parties emerged as separate institutions. At work, employees were class conscious, but with a difference, for the "awareness narrowed down to labor concerns and to unions that established few ties to political parties"; away from work, "ethnic and territorial identifications became dominant." [14] Challenges to the larger social order were suppressed as the politics of class was restricted to the workplace, where workers opposed their bosses, not the capitalist system. Tension between the owners of capital and their employees drove wealthy city dwellers to Chicago's North Shore as early as 1870. Located on the periphery of major cities, suburbs were the most radical rethinking of the relation between work, power, and residence.[15]

Chicago's North Shore had been a popular spot for wealthy families to build second residences. After Chicago's Great Fire, these homes became primary as well as permanent.[16] On the night of October 8, 1871, nearly 100,000 city residents lost their homes to the burning inferno.[17] In the aftermath, while the underclass fell prey to "cheap housing that was poorly built and very dense," the wealthy, assisted by their servants, relocated north to escape apocalyptic ruin and crime.[18]

A construction boom and a move away from the city's center followed. "The higher the downtown became, the greater the horizontal spread of the residential neighborhoods that housed its daytime inhabitants: skyscraper and suburb created each other."[19] Evanston's population increased precipitously.

Elites associated the hustle and bustle of city life with the "dregs of humanity." Centrally located business districts were becoming too expensive for residential use, forcing workers into flimsy cottages located in the industrial and warehouse districts where they labored. Those who owned the factories also moved from the city centers where they conducted business. Additionally they sought to separate themselves from the working classes. An immigrant tide purportedly lacking values drove their exodus from the city to less crowded and more appealing areas in order to escape the "hordes of rats [that] lived under the wooden sidewalks of the sprawling frontier town filled with rootless, rough, careless men and women who drifted through life."[20] The rich set their sights on communities lining the Lake Michigan shore north of Chicago, "all far upwind from factory smokestacks."[21]

Mable Tresesder's travel diary gives a glimpse of what life in Evanston was like in 1893. Tresesder describes Chicago as ridden with want, misery, and crime, including gambling and prostitution. By contrast, she was thoroughly impressed by the suburbs, which struck her as an "ideal combination of city and country."[22] The landscapes were pastoral, yet the comforts brought by technological progress were present: "paved streets, gaslights, water mains, sewage lines, and eventually electricity."[23] During an excursion to Evanston she noted: "We saw the most beautiful stretch of country which was as fresh and green as sun and rain could make it. Farms were ideal with everything present necessary to make them so, the houses being complete with all conveniences and barns and sheds well built and painted."[24] Evanston had "clean air, quiet domestic seclusion, and little chance that rich and poor would rub up against each other in a threatening way."[25]

The suburban ideal was based on exclusion. White elites with the resources to reorder the material world to their needs created a strict segregation of class and function. They established their home life in bedroom communities, commuting to Chicago for work. Middle-class women were especially affected by the new dichotomy of work and family life. Suburbia exalted their role in the family as wives and mothers, but it also segregated them from the world of power and productivity. To function, these newly formed towns required a workforce to live and work nearby. Black southerners eagerly filled these positions, but their labor was virtually invisible to commuters who did not work where they lived, and did not view those who shuttled back and forth between segregated residential neighborhoods as contributors or political actors. The exclusion of labor and industry from the social milieu revealed a deeply buried fear that translated into a hatred of others.

Technological innovations in transportation accelerated population growth. But the relatively high cost of train travel insulated bourgeois peripheries like Evanston from lower-class invasion.[26] The first charter for a railroad through Evanston was in 1851. To this point trains had been used to move goods in and out of the city; now they helped middle- and upper-class Chicagoans remove their residences from the "crowds, noise and pollution of the downtown and factory areas. The result was Chicago's extraordinary suburban growth in the decades following the fire."[27] By 1883, improved rail service provided convenient transportation. By 1891, the Chicago and Northwestern Railway ran thirty-five passenger trains daily between Evanston and Chicago. By the end of the century, Evanston's population had grown to 19,259. It was transformed from a college town of 4,200 in 1880 to a busy commuter suburb of 25,000 by 1910.[28] The university set the dominant tone. Residents were attracted by its influence.

A Classic Town

In her memoir *A Classic Town: The Story of Evanston by "an Old Timer"* Frances Willard praises the city's natural beauty and advanced technology, including a "system of supplying an abundance of pure water."[29] The accolades of this early booster emphasize religious and moral values inextricably tied to Northwestern University. Founding fathers infused the growing town with many of the qualities that it is still known for today. Religion shaped politics, forming the issues and the rhetoric. Education was at the core. Religious fervor and intellectual discourse attracted wealthy white families, who affectionately called Evanston "the Athens of the Northwest."[30] The dreams of early settlers were transparent in their reference to the ancient Greek city. Garrett Bible Institute and the Woman's College put Northwestern at the forefront of an emerging modern higher education.

The university encouraged an abstract pursuit of knowledge, offering courses such as art and philosophy. The curriculum also reflected a moral code of righteous living, which in turn shaped the social and political life of the town. A school of oratory where preachers and ministers were trained to spread the gospel opened in 1878. The first of its kind, the department was financed with money donated by meat-packer Gustav Swift, whose wealth came at the expense of limbless workers. Recruited from St. James Episcopal Church in Chicago, Peter Christian Lutkin developed the nation's first music school and was named dean in 1892. Lutkin believed that students needed to be educated in a "proper" atmosphere: "In large cities there is, unhappily, a tinge of the moral laxity prevalent in European capitals among professional men. . . . The wholesome surroundings of Evanston offer a marked contrast. Its churches and Christian associations, its freedom from saloons and questionable resorts, together with its educational facilities and attractive location, make it an ideal home for the pursuit of a musical education."[31]

The Woman's College had special significance during a time when men dominated public life. On October 29, 1855, the Northwestern Female College took its place as one among a trio of schools. "Evanston has thus been, from its first hour, a paradise for women," wrote Willard.[32] In 1870 the name was changed to Women's College of Northwestern University. Students took classes in departments of art and music and ran a small kindergarten. Appointed dean in 1873, Willard was a professor in the department of aesthetics. She boasted that "a woman's college course equal to that arranged for young men was unheard of, except at Oberlin and Antioch, Ohio. . . . Yet Evanston was to be the classic suburb of Chicago, the western Athens, with its face to the future."[33] Years later John Evans, one of nine founders of the university, and a member of its board of trustees, would happily tell Willard that it was his wife Margaret who gave the final form to the name of Chicago's classic suburb. "I know you will rejoice that a woman named the Woman's paradise," he said.[34] No one seemed to mind that she named it after her husband.

The university was also dedicated to practical and utilitarian goals. An 1855 amendment to the university charter called for "no spirituous, vinous, or fermented liquors" to be sold except for medicinal, mechanical, or sacramental purposes.[35] Teetotaling Methodists, the trustees had an earnest hatred of gambling and alcohol and demanded abstinence from all vices. Willard could not have been more proud:

There is a celestial Evanston, there is a terrestrial Evanston, and there is a diabolical Evanston. They intersphere at every point and every moment of the day. But we all think the celestial Evanston is in the ascendency, and one of my reasons for the belief that is in me is Evanston's noble stand against the evil of strong drink. The happiest thought of those good men who founded our classic village was to incorporate in the university charter a provision that no intoxicating liquors should ever be sold within four miles of the college campus. The very announcement of this fact was the magnet to draw hither a class of people who were total abstainers and who desired for their children the surroundings of sobriety. Owning most of the land on which original Evanston was located, the university trustees placed a clause in every deed of transfer, declaring a lapse of title in case intoxicants were ever vended. Moreover, so soon as the village was incorporated a local ordinance was passed in harmony with the university charter, and now that Evanston has become a municipality of twelve thousand souls, the provisions of this ordinance have been steadily strengthened until it is iron-clad.[36]

To attract a particular pedigree of student, the school's catalog for the academic year 1858–59 informed parents that the community's atmosphere was "strictly moral and religious." Young people would be "placed at a distance from temptation and brought under the most wholesome influences."[37] Students came from upstanding families. They were children of railroad barons, attorneys, and industrialists. Recruitment was clearly discriminatory. The first black student matriculated in 1880 but transferred to another school before graduating. It wasn't until 1903, some fifty years after Northwestern was founded, that the school graduated its first black student.[38]

Victorian activism expressed itself in temperance work, a specialized expression of morality. A movement devoted to upholding prohibition, the Women's Temperance Alliance, formed on March 17, 1874. Following the university's rigid policies, the organization launched its crusade against liquor. On May 1, 1875, the society changed its name to the Women's Christian Temperance Union (WCTU) and joined local auxiliaries around the world. The group made house visits and held public meetings circulating a pledge of abstinence. To all of this was added the "impulse of fervent prayer."[39] Beginning in 1879, regular Sunday afternoon meetings were held where hundreds of men "signed the pledge and sought the lord."[40] A free kindergarten designed to intervene before it was too late had as its motto "Give us the children until they are six years old, and we will risk the rest of their lives."[41] Pastors from every church were "champions of prohibition; certainly all have believed in it for Evanston."[42]

Willard was the organization's president for nineteen years, beginning in 1879. Her Victorian white-framed home, located just blocks away from Northwestern, served as the international headquarters for the organization and as a boarding house for WCTU workers. As dean of the Woman's College and an activist in the temperance movement, she took an important feminist stance for the period. However elitist and racist (she barely mentions the working class, Native Americans, or blacks in her memoir) her history of Evanston is, it offers some insight into early class-based and racial politics. Ties between temperance work and racial hatred have been well documented. Alcohol and other vices were associated with foreign-born immigrants, blacks, and the poor; banning one effectively banned the others.[43] Willard all but admitted this when she wrote, "The freedom of our town from saloons also does much to render it unattractive to thieves and thugs."[44] Following the repeal of Prohibition in 1933, the WCTU persisted. Its work paid off: Evanston was dry until 1972.

Although black and white reformers occasionally worked side by side, more often than not women's clubs were racially segregated. They united around temperance and suffrage, although these took on racially specific meanings for each group. A politics of respectability, or effort to uplift and reform the race, would have driven black women to found their own temperance society, which they named in honor of Frances Willard.[45] Black women's involvement with temperance long preceded the WCTU's founding in 1874. Free northern blacks embraced temperance as an idea and a movement before the Civil War. Clergymen often related temperance to abolition in their sermons. When the war ended, abstinence continued to figure in programs for black education and advancement. Moreover, racial segregation was written into the WCTU's bylaws. Black women resented white women's singling out of black men for criticism. Antilynching activist Ida B. Wells confronted Willard on her racial views, especially lynching and her belief that black men threatened white women's safety in the South. Nevertheless, Willard's temperance ideas were compelling to black women who were working for racial uplift. They honored her by naming clubs for her, taking great pride in their leadership in the worldwide movement against drink.[46] Willard explained the divide a bit differently: "It has been the latest work of the W.C.T.U. to organize the colored women of Evanston into a local auxiliary. They were invited to belong to the original society, but preferred to form one by themselves, and they have been kind enough to name it the Willard W.C.T.U."[47]

Philanthropist Clyde D. Foster moralized Evanston's storied landscape in his collection of essays titled *Evanston's Yesterdays*. According to Foster, it was religious revelry that inspired the invention of a famous dessert in 1914. Chicago's godly neighbor Heavenston (a nickname that had been given to the city by Willard) was so pious that it resented the dissipating influences of the soda fountain on Sunday. Thus activities as mundane as sipping an ice cream soda were forbidden by city ordinance on the Christian Sabbath—that is, Sunday. An ingenious clerk at Garwood's Drugstore complied with the law by serving ice cream with syrup but no soda. With the dangerously "scintillating" soda water removed, the nation got a respectable treat. The sodaless dessert instantly became popular on other days of the week as well. Naming a dish after the Sabbath would have been blasphemous, though, so the spelling of Sunday was changed to "sundae."[48]

Other local legends contributed to the town's principled social character. Bowling, trick-or-treating, and even skipping, seen as a sign of public drunkenness, were purportedly prohibited. While there is no evidence that city ordinances banning these activities ever really existed, they were part of the discourse of morality that shaped the town. The accumulation of local culture is a matter of time, and these stories were repeated so frequently that they came to be accepted as fact. There was material evidence to support them: Evanston did not have a bowling alley, and trick or treating was limited to three hours on Halloween day. Furthermore, other prohibitions were a matter of record. Spitting was illegal, and so was noise: yelling, shouting, hooting, whistling, and singing were prohibited between the hours of 11 p.m. and 7 a.m.

Lincoln Republican Evanstonians were sympathetic to abolition and black civil rights. The Vane Family bought Maria Murray, a plantation slave from Maryland, out of slavery at age sixteen. She came to Evanston with them in 1855 and worked as a domestic in their household. One of the most influential Northwestern leaders, Grant Goodrich, devoted time to advocating repeal of the Fugitive Slave Act. He also founded the Freedmen's Aid Society, a Methodist organization that assisted blacks during Reconstruction. The society established schools and carried out missionary work throughout the South. Other university officials actively participated. Robert M. Hatfield, a Northwestern trustee from 1878 to 1891, was a staunch abolitionist and served on the society's board. In a speech given at the General Conference of the Methodist Episcopal Church in May 1860 in Buffalo, New York, Hatfield denounced slavery as "sinful, an offence against humanity."[49] The Honorable Harvey B. Hurd, a law professor at Northwestern University, also an ardent abolitionist, participated in the Underground Railroad and played a prominent role in the Kansas Conflict of 1856, a bitter fight between proslavery and antislavery forces.[50] His house, located on Evanston's near west side, was the one that I grew up in one hundred years later. Finally, the Reverend Miner Raymond, professor of theology and a pastor at the Methodist Church, became fed up with an inane dinner conversation about women's rights and their impropriety and is said to have responded, "*If she can do it well*, I am willing to see a colored woman president of the United States."[51] The relationship between Northwestern and the Freedmen's Aid Society suggests a link between Evanston and southern blacks that functioned to inform migrants about the town.

Hurd escorted Abraham Lincoln when he visited Evanston on April 5, 1860. The two traveled by train from Chicago, where Lincoln had given his famous Cooper Institute speech opposing slavery. They sat together in the railroad car next to the stove. In Evanston, Lincoln was taken by carriage around the village before arriving at Julius White's house, located on the corner of Ridge and Church. That evening the tall and lanky Lincoln gave a speech from the front porch to townspeople who gathered on the lawn to meet the distinguished political orator. They were eager to shake the hand of the man they hoped would become the next US president. The rising hope of the new Republican Party was nominated and elected the following year. Lincoln must have thought fondly of Evanston. When the Civil War started, he made White a general in his Union Army.[52]

Nearly one thousand people were living in Evanston when news of the surrender of Fort Sumter reached it in 1861. "No town in America met the shock of the Civil War more bravely than our own," boasted Willard. As she remembers it, the news came on a Sunday and was delivered by a minister at church:

Nothing could have been more incongruous with the soft air of that spring day or the sweet peace of our idyllic village. A *war* meeting in Evanston! The congregation walked homeward in the solemn hush of great sorrow; there were so many young men in Evanston, dear by ties of kindred or of heart to almost every home, and if there must be a war then *they* must go! Perhaps the most fervent prayers that ever went up to God for courage and for resignation pierced the sky that Sabbath day, when the sunshine was so golden and the great lake so blue and calm.[53]

Northwestern students demonstrated loyalty by leaving school to join the Union Army.

Women were at the forefront of the emancipation effort. Well aware that Lincoln had visited friends in Evanston before the war, the women may have felt a certain familiarity. "It was an Evanston woman who suggested a movement that would have rolled into Abraham Lincoln's office a petition with more names of women than were ever before attached to any paper, if his official pen had not anticipated its advent and issued the Emancipation Proclamation," writes Willard. Once the Civil War started, the ladies of Evanston were "active in aid of the soldiers in the field in various ways, holding frequent meetings, sending hospital supplies, such as bandages, lint, hospital garments, mittens and bed clothing, and in assisting the Sanitary Commission in Chicago."[54] Together these acts created a sentiment about the city's racial politics and receptiveness to blacks.

Southern migrants, meanwhile, created a growing market for black professionals, including physicians, dentists, and a lawyer. Entrepreneurs offered services to black and white clientele. Henry Butler and William Twiggs grew substantial businesses with good reputations. Butler came to Evanston in 1878. He worked as a coachman before building a thriving livery service at the turn of the century. His entrepreneurship was tested when cars began replacing horses. Butler acted on this technological shift and converted his business to a taxi service, becoming one of the city's wealthiest men. Invoices archived at the Evanston History Center record this evolution. A receipt from 1898 has a drawing of a carriage drawn by two horses on it. By 1922 the carriage had been replaced by a Ford Model T. A prominent citizen, Butler was included in Harvey Hurd's *History of Evanston*, published in 1906. Hurd writes that Butler "led a life of exceptional personal purity, having never made use of tobacco or intoxicants, nor indulged in profane language."[55] Twiggs was also well regarded; in 1895 he opened a printing shop, where he printed Evanston's first black periodical, *Afro-American Budget*, in 1889 and later published the *Reporter and Directory*.[56] As of 1930, black-owned businesses were found largely within the city's west side. While these achievements are a testament to the perseverance of certain individuals, the most available sources of income for blacks remained in domestic service and unskilled labor.

The black church was the soul of the community. The first churches reflected class stratification within black society. Decades later, pastors from these institutions would be important leaders in the civil rights movement. Established in 1882, Ebenezer AME (African Methodist Episcopal) Church was the first black house of worship to be recognized in Evanston. The congregation consisted of middle-class and wealthy blacks, including Twiggs, who was a trustee for close to fifty years. In 1908 the facility relocated to Emerson Street from Benson, following its congregation as blacks were pushed farther west. Black members of the mostly white First Baptist Church broke away from it, establishing two more black churches in Evanston. Working-class blacks had a different mode of worship and had felt constrained by academic over-tones at First Baptist. Like Ebenezer AME, Second Baptist was organized in 1882. Happy to accommodate separatism, Northwestern University granted the church a twenty-year lease on a building on Benson Avenue near campus.[57] In 1894, Mount Zion Baptist on Clark Street became the third black church to make Evanston its home.

Between Evanston and Waukegan to the north and Cook County to the south, there were no hospitals that would regularly admit Negro patients. Blacks suffered from inadequate access to healthcare, and Isabella M. Garnett was determined to do something about it. Born in Evanston in 1872, Garnett grew up to attain remarkable achievements. At a time when neither blacks nor women became doctors, she earned her medical degree at the College of Physicians and Surgeons (later the University of Illinois College of Medicine) and practiced medicine on Chicago's South Side. In 1907 she married Dr. Arthur Butler from Savannah, Georgia, a graduate of Northwestern University. Using money earned in their private practices, they opened their home on Asbury Avenue to treat patients and train black staff in 1914. In this small center named the Evanston Sanitarium, Garnett delivered babies while Butler performed surgeries. After his death in 1924, Butler was eulogized by W. E. B. Du Bois in *The Crisis*. In 1926 an interracial council determined what everyone already knew: blacks needed a larger facility. The council didn't think to convince existing hospitals to change their policies by hiring black medical personnel and treating black patients.

White donors like Clyde Foster supported campaigns to establish separate facilities for blacks, providing aid while reinforcing segregation. Paradoxically, they reformed while actively maintaining social arrangements. Whites acted out of a sense of unfounded fear and obligation. They worried about contagious disease. Blacks and whites came into contact every day. Moreover, blacks worked in white homes. The participation of white elites mimicked broader patterns of race relations in the suburb: white philanthropy and paternalism, or aiding the black community, while reinforcing segregation and dependence. Beyond public charity work and aid, private paternalism was commonplace. The relationship of paternalism and deference was symbolized through domestic service. White employers often gave gifts to the blacks who worked for them rather than increasing their wages.[58] When the stock market crashed in 1929, a new hospital building became all the more unlikely.

The Evanston Sanitarium's operations were moved to another private home on the west side in 1930, and the name was changed to

Community Hospital. Garnett was named superintendent. With eighteen beds, the facility was larger but still overcrowded and inadequate. It would take another black woman to step into the breach. Dr. Elizabeth Hill, also an alumnus of the College of Physicians and Surgeons, joined the staff in 1931. Hill organized a women's auxiliary in 1939. The primary function of the group was to raise funds for a new hospital. Black women went door to door collecting money and organized a series of campaigns, but the annual Garden Tea was the main fundraising event. Dedication and hard work materialized into a new hospital building opening in 1952. Program covers for the dedication ceremony read: "The Dream Comes True."

Meanwhile, with modern conveniences more typically found in large cities, monumental buildings marked Evanston's downtown. City Hall, dating from 1892, was in the style of a French Renaissance château. The public library, whose gray limestone structure was built in 1906, had been founded in 1871 and was one of the first free libraries in the state. Reference use was free, and "any resident of Evanston could draw out books on the payment of an annual fee of five dollars."[59] As of 1891, the library boasted a collection of 9,609 volumes. The city was home to two other libraries: those of Northwestern University and the Garrett Biblical Institute. The Post Office began free delivery service in 1887.[60] The Works Progress Administration (WPA), a federal agency created in 1935 to provide jobs and income for those left unemployed during the Depression, funded numerous construction projects downtown, including a new post office also made of limestone with art deco designs and New Deal sculptures, adding further charm to the city. At the center was Fountain Square, surrounded by department and dime stores and restaurants.

Material culture supported a narrative of progress despite the fact that during the building boom of the 1920s entrepreneurs wrote segregation into the metropolitan fabric more effectively and comprehensively than ever before. A new genre of children's toys reflected the construction boom of the period, introducing young boys to the field of engineering. Culturally familiar to audiences across the country, construction toys were an overnight success. In New Haven, Connecticut, a Yale Medical School graduate invented the Erector Set in 1911. Containers included small metal beams with holes for nuts, bolts, and screws that could be assembled into skyscrapers, bridges, and railways. Three years later in Evanston, Charles H. Pajeau and his partner designed the Tinkertoy Construction Set. Pajeau, a stonemason, developed the toy after seeing children building structures with pencils and empty spools of thread. Lincoln Logs also originated from the Chicago area. John Lloyd Wright, son of the notable architect Frank Lloyd Wright, created the toys in 1916. Box sets included windows and doors to make the buildings more realistic and instructions on how to build cabins for both Abraham Lincoln and Uncle Tom. Lincoln Logs invoked the history of the American frontier, resonating with the nation's ethos of rugged individualism. In Illinois, where the moniker "Land of Lincoln" signified the state's antislavery stance, Evanston's children must have been eager consumers.

As Evanston's population expanded, so too did the town's infrastructure and need for labor. On the outskirts, factory workers found jobs in the many industries taking advantage of available land and a cheap workforce. The Mark Manufacturing Company, which produced well supplies, opened in 1900. The American Steel and Tube Company, the only large industrial plant in Evanston at the time, was the largest employer of blacks during the 1930s. Rust-Oleum Corporation built a twelve-acre manufacturing plant in 1939. In 1948, Hibbard, Spencer & Bartlett built the largest hardware warehouse in the world, employing 650 people. Downtown pink-collar workers were hired by department stores. Marshall Field & Company opened a branch in 1926, giving residents "the best of retail options" outside of Chicago's Loop. Finally, white-collar workers took advantage of positions in the city's private sector. In 1936 Washington National Life Insurance Company became one of the city's largest employers.[61] By 1961, Evanston had earned another nickname, "headquarter city," as it was home to flagship offices for numerous national and international organizations, associations, and foundations.

City of Homes

With growth came a demand for landscapers and architects. Evanston's gardens and homes idealized the countryside and stood in contrast to Chicago's gray and polluted urban environment. Architects captured and repeated images in brick and mortar, deliberately designing homes in a less formal style. The boxy rooms of the typical Victorian dwelling were eliminated to create a relatively open plan that flowed from room to room in replication of the suburban landscape. Interior designs exalted the family while demoting the help. Ground floors were divided into a few large rooms, providing togetherness for the family. Gone were rigidly segregated spaces for men, women, and children.

The downstairs area found its focus in a central fireplace symbolizing family unity. Domestics were separated from their employers by back stairways that connected them to the kitchen, servants' quarters, and rear entrance. A prominent architect in the American Picturesque Movement, as defined by the Prairie School, Andrew Jackson Downing believed that suburban homes reflected the class of people living in them. His designs aimed to encourage the honest practice of social virtues, a sense of duty, and character development.[62] Frances Willard's house was patterned after a Downing model. Linking hygiene with morality, living quarters were built with separate bathing rooms, and pantries separated kitchens from dining rooms to keep odors from reaching diners. By the end of the nineteenth century, Evanston had a new nickname: "The City of Homes."

As the town grew, efforts to protect it intensified. The city sat next to the lake and had plenty of light and clean air. The university charter prohibited the sale of liquor within a four-mile radius. With downtown Chicago twelve miles away, "temptations afforded by saloons" and other "contaminations" were at a safe distance.[63] In 1917 the *Plan of Evanston*, a published report from the Small Parks and Playgrounds Association, warned that population growth was threatening Evanston's natural and social assets.

We saw the big yards subdivided, the vacant squares built upon, sporadic solid rows of houses, and the flat buildings appearing here and there, without asking where our children's children were to find playground space. We drained our sewage into the lake and drank its water, without reflecting that the process couldn't go on indefinitely. We went on confiding in our isolation from Chicago, without realizing that the distance was getting shorter year by year.[64]

The report laid out strategies to protect Evanston's "material and moral advantages" for the "sort of people to whom these advantages appealed."[65] It operationalized exclusion and inclusion in the lived environment. To stop haphazard growth and beautify the lakefront, traffic and sewage were redirected to the west side.

Anything that threatened the shoreline was diverted west. Sheridan Road followed Lake Michigan's coast from Chicago to the suburbs north of Evanston. It was crooked, congested, and unpaved, "a disgrace in its present haphazard condition."[66] But it would be a mistake to repair it and make it a through artery for vehicles moving rapidly between Chicago's urban center and suburbs farther north. Instead, city planners suggested rerouting traffic west to a boulevard along the sanitary canal.[67] Running through the center of town, Chicago Avenue was also badly congested. The committee proposed rerouting commercial vehicles west to Dodge Avenue. The drainage canal on the west side became a dumping ground for the city's sewage. Its excavation provided landfill to expand lakefront property for the wealthy.

To further beautify the shoreline for boating and cycling, the city laid plans for an elaborate park system. Extra land that was not needed for production purposes symbolized Evanston's wealth. Parks were also emblematic of the marriage of town and country espoused by the American Picturesque Movement. Increasing green spaces, "the lungs of a city," benefited air quality and public health.[68] Recreation areas were said to deter criminal activity and "play gone wrong."[69] Bathing beaches, a harbor, and a yacht club would meet the needs of an emerging aquatics culture. Eighty percent of the population lived within one mile of the lake. It was less accessible to the other 20 percent. Officials recommended building a swimming pool for west side residents, hoping to deter undesirables from the lakefront. A golf course, predicated on exclusive open-air exercise and beautifully planted grounds, would be the most perfect realization of the cultural ideal of the picturesque. Strictly private nature would become an "instrument of social snobbery and of racial and religious prejudice."[70] To maintain Evanston's reputation as a center of high culture, the city would add a new auditorium and art museum. No stone was left unturned. The committee recommended covering alley entrances with vine-covered archways to "conceal the ugliness beyond and light up dangerous places at night."[71]

Evanston earned another nickname: "Best Shaded City in the West." While the lakeshore was the city's greatest physical asset, trees symbolized Evanston's domestic charm. Willard said as much: "The peculiar glory of the village is its trees—its long avenues bordered with wide-spreading elms and maples and grand old oaks."[72] The planning committee wanted to preserve the double rows of "immemorial elms." Towering branches arched over the streets resembling the "pointed arches in old Gothic cathedrals of Europe."[73] Shaded streets, broad open lawns, and substantial houses set back from sidewalks reflected the union of nature, property, and family life and created the illusion of parks in residential areas. They suggested that the city build a nursery, hire a tree expert, and require permits to cut down trees. Drawing class distinctions, they noted Evanston was "fortunate in possessing a class of citizens who had a clear vision of the future in tree culture" and should be cautious of ignorant contractors known to strip an "entire lot of fine old trees simply to build an apartment house."[74] According to the report, planting trees was the single most important civic act.

Evanston was the first to take advantage of an Illinois state statue that permitted cities and towns to regulate land usage. By establishing separate residential and business districts, Evanston could maintain its character as "primarily a city of individual homes."[75] On January 18, 1921, the city council passed a zoning ordinance to classify, regulate, and restrict the location of trades and industries, to limit the height and bulk of buildings, to limit the intensity of use of lot areas, and to establish the boundaries of districts.[76] The ordinance zoned for commercial use almost every block where blacks lived outside of the west side. Poor and working-class people were hard hit as this directly affected the construction of apartment buildings. Over time, public and private redevelopment demolished dozens of black-occupied housing units in these areas. Race restrictions began appearing on deeds and leases. Whites responded to black settlers with restrictive covenants, zoning regulations, health and safety ordinances, and building codes governing the cost of new construction and the uses to which it could be put.

Racial Covenants

The American South had a lower degree of residential segregation than the North. Both laws and a social custom of separation eliminated the possibility of equality. Communities that formed before industrialization usually were more integrated. Residential segregation proved inconvenient to whites, who preferred to have black domestics close at hand. The North relied on restrictive covenants to do the work of Jim Crow. Rare before 1920, when a small black population was more easily controlled, such covenants multiplied during the Great Migration, until the US Supreme Court ruling in *Shelly v. Kraemer* found them unconstitutional in 1948.

Evanston's blacks, once scattered in clusters throughout town, were systematically forced west. Drawn up by developers or neighborhood associations and defined as a network of agreements between neighbors, covenants prohibited blacks from buying or renting in white neighborhoods. Agreements were formalized by adding racial and ethnic clauses to property deeds. The 1937 Burnham Park development was prototypical. Located near Lake Michigan between Dempster and Forest Streets, Burnham plots were prime real estate but were sold on contingency. Before the land could be purchased, a buyer had to agree to abide by a lettered list of restrictions running from A to H. Two provisions ensured that only moneyed whites could own and occupy the property:

A. Not more than one single family dwelling house, costing not less than $15,000 may be erected on any said lots.

G. Only persons of the Caucasian race may own, lease, occupy or use any of said lots, except that any persons may be employed on said premises as domestic servants or chauffeurs.

Provision A addressed social class by ensuring that multiple-family homes and boarding houses were not erected. Provision G restricted properties to whites with the exception of black service workers. The National Association of Real Estate Brokers' complicity in such matters was formalized in its 1928 code of ethics. Article 34 deemed it improper to introduce members of another race into a neighborhood because it might be detrimental to property values.

Across town, homeowners formalized pacts through neighborhood associations. In 1922 the West Side Improvement Association formed to "protect the neighborhood from encroachment of all kinds, and particularly, to preserve it as a place for white people to live." Wesley Avenue residents worried that blacks might cross Emerson Street, a recognized division between black and white neighborhoods. They pooled their resources to keep the neighborhood white by bribing neighbors or, if they were too late, buying property back from Negros. They hired an attorney, Mr. Wing, to prepare a covenant. A total of six agreements were signed. When in 1933 a home at 1844 Wesley was about to be sold to Mr. and Mrs. Walden, a Negro couple, Wing was sent to dissuade them. Mr. Walden protested: "We are respectable people, and we will keep our house in as good looking condition as the other people in the block."

It made no difference to Wing, who stood firm "This is not directed at you individually. . . . It is purely a matter of property values."

Rightly assuming that the attorney was a religious man, Mrs. Walden asked, "Well, Mr. Wing, what do you think is going to happen when we get to heaven? Are we Negroes going to be separated from the whites?" Her question called into question Willard's pet name for the town, Heavenston. Certainly the Waldens would not have used biblical terms when referring to their hometown. "Where can we live?" a distraught Mrs. Walden asked Wing.

The attorney replied, "There are plenty of places in Evanston where you can live, and particularly there are some very good residences west of here, west of the railroad, and along Emerson Street. There is no difficulty with that."

The neighborhood association brought the case to court, the sale was reversed, and the Waldens were evicted. They hated to leave their new home.[77]

In 1948 the National Association for the Advancement of Colored People (NAACP) challenged racial covenants in the Supreme Court case *Shelly v. Kraemer*. By demonstrating that social ills wrought by overcrowding in the ghetto resulted in no small part from discrimination in housing, the legal team developed the same logic it would employ during *Brown v. Board of Education*. Lead attorney Thurgood Marshall (who would also argue *Brown*) utilized sociological data showing the debilitating effects that covenants had in creating the biggest ghettoes in history. When the court ruled unanimously that covenants were unconstitutional under the Fourteenth Amendment, the *Chicago Defender* rejoiced: "Let Freedom Ring."[78] There was, however, one caveat: covenants were legally written *private* agreements, and if they couldn't be legally enforced, they could be upheld voluntarily.[79] Advertisements in the *Evanston Review* running well into the 1960s illustrate the continued use of covenants. The paper listed homes for sale or rent under the designation "colored." Restrictive covenants were not the only means by which residential segregation and discrimination were enacted. There were other mechanisms to contain and control the growth of the black community. The aim was not to entirely exclude black residents. Blacks were relegated to the west side, but within city limits nonetheless.

According to Andrew Wiese, unlike those of other suburbs on the North Shore and around the country, Evanston's city planners and real estate establishment played key roles in the growth of the black community. Elites resorted to segregation in large part because they could not stop black migration to their communities. By containing black residential space, they established segregation while (and by) expanding a notion of integration. Not unlike their southern counterparts, white residents wanted service workers living in close proximity. Separation was a powerful and visible indicator that blacks were subordinate to whites. The psychological dimension to separation reinforced negative ideas about blacks. Separation made ordinary interaction between blacks and whites difficult, if not impossible. Contained, blacks were mostly invisible to whites unless they were servicing them. Exposure was key to undermining racist ideas, but Evanston's geography of race prevented contact. Most Evanstonians knew each other not as human beings but as symbols of blackness and whiteness. As a result, white power was difficult to challenge, and whites had more room to be tolerant.[80]

Just Like Heaven

Historians would call it the Great Migration. Beginning with the First World War and over the course of most of a century, some six million black southerners would leave the racial caste system of the South. Growing out of unmet promises made after the Civil War, this mass act of independence would help push the country toward the civil rights movement in the sixties. While sheer numbers ebbed and flowed, momentum increased with the production demands of two world wars. The curtailment of European immigration during World War I and Executive Order 8802, signed during World War II, all but guaranteed work to new arrivals.[81] Desperate employers sent agents south to entice blacks, but direct recruiting was not necessary for long. As word spread through "race papers" and social networks, eager southerners left sharecropping and perpetual debt for blue-collar occupations that paid a wage.[82]

The black population of Chicago, one of several "receiving stations," rocketed from 44,103 in 1910 to more than a million by the time the flow ended in 1970. Less is known about the substantial number of southerners who settled in the surrounding metropolitan ring.[83] These suburbs were also "significant sites of paid labor," distinguishable by their dominant sources of local employment.[84] The steel and railroad industries employed workers in the manufacturing satellites of Harvey, Aurora, and Joliet, Illinois. Upscale residential suburbs employed service workers.[85] Blacks performed labor essential to creating the cultivated landscapes and leisure class that epitomized bourgeois suburbs. Taking advantage of rail and trolley lines, white elites separated their home life even further from Chicago's manufacturing core, and Evanston became a domestic service hub for other far-flung communities.[86]

While the wealthiest suburbanites employed whole staffs of domestic workers, middle-class residents depended on some form of black servitude as well.[87] Trains, responsible for Chicago's incredible economic growth, helped wealthy beneficiaries remove themselves from the big city. While domestic workers at first had resided in the homes of their employers, the introduction of streetcars made live-in help unnecessary, and by the turn of the century, these workers had left their servant quarters.[88] The separation of work and community was essentially a mark of class privilege, for low-paid black workers and their families, jobs, and residences remained closely joined. Evanston's west side was cheaper and more convenient to employment than most black neighborhoods located within Chicago city limits. Black women traveled from the west side to the expensive lakefront properties on Evanston's eastern border: "the daily migration of black women from west side to the east side and back again was one of the familiar rhythms of Evanston life."[89] Those who did not reside in Evanston waited each morning for the northbound train to take them away from Chicago and deeper into the suburbs.[90]

The promise of work spread quickly, reaching migrants in the deep South where advertisements on buses read: "Come to Evanston, Haven of the Negro."[91] As early as 1910, the *Chicago Defender* featured regular news columns about Evanston, and by 1911 these headlined entire pages. Favorable reports circulated among blacks wherever the paper was distributed. Black literary figures like Richard Wright, who arrived in Chicago from Mississippi in 1927, gave voice to the fears of fellow migrants. Wright's classic novel *Native Son* is set in Chicago, but he singles out Evanston as a more desirable location. The novel's protagonist, suspected murderer Bigger Thomas, struggles to evade capture. As the police close in, he laments not leaving Chicago earlier to go to "perhaps Gary, Indiana, or Evanston," both of which he considers safe places for a Negro to live.[92] Less vulnerable to racial violence in the North, blacks found suburbs like Evanston even safer than urban centers, where they became targets of white violence during periods of labor unrest.

When government contracts dried up after World War I, Chicago's job market tightened, unemployment rose, and tensions between laborers swelled. During the summer of 1919, a combination of isolation, restricted movement, and economic deprivation incited frustration. When a black boy drowned after being bullied in water adjacent to a whites-only beach, a full-fledged race riot broke out. Black workers bearing the brunt of white anger sought refuge in communities outside the city. According to census data, Evanston's minority population grew precipitously.[93]

Andrew Wiese writes about Evanston's early history. Smaller and more intimate than Chicago, Evanston was generally a safer destination for black women traveling alone. Pioneers in domestic service, such women became anchors for continuing chains of migration, sending information about the city and its employment opportunities to relatives and friends down South. Working women recruited siblings and other female kin to help care for their children and assist with housework. Both parties benefited, as "unpaid work in the homes of relatives often served younger southern women as a period of 'apprenticeship' before they found paid housework of their own."[94] This process began a self-perpetuating cycle of kin-based female migration and recruitment into domestic service.

Osceola Spencer's story is representative. In 1912 Spencer's aunt left West Point, Mississippi, to marry a Chicago man, and the couple settled in Evanston. Several years later, she recruited Spencer's younger sister to care for her children so that she could work outside the home. Soon Spencer's parents and another sister joined them. During their visit they "found out how much liberty there was in Evanston compared with what it was in West Point. . . . They said 'just like Heaven'" and decided to stay permanently.[95] Like Willard before them, Spencer's family described Evanston using biblical terms. They would have prayed to be reunited with relatives much as in the afterlife. No longer would they endure the indignities they faced living in the South, Jim Crow laws and the racial violence that enforced them. Up north they could start over, own a home, and make a decent living. Furthermore, the move would secure advantages for children and grandchildren, especially in the realm of education, which were all but denied them by the state of Mississippi. By the time Osceola Spencer became pregnant in 1918, her closest female kin had all moved north, so she traveled to Evanston from Mississippi to stay with her mother and sisters.[96] She felt blessed when her husband joined her soon after.

Whereas black women represented one-third of the workforce nationwide in 1920, they often made up 40–50 percent of black employees in affluent suburbs.[97] By 1940 "domestic and kindred service workers actually formed a larger proportion of the population in Evanston than either professional or managerial employees, the two highest categories of white collar work."[98] Female domestics outnumbered male professionals.[99] Blacks who were not directly employed in white households often worked in private clubs, restaurants, or hotels. There were also various black-owned businesses that served white clients such as caterers, movers, and painters, all of whom were "equally bound to the economy of residential affluence."[100]

Fraternities and associations including the Masons, Knights of Pythias, and Old Settlers Association provided material aid to black men. Most black men worked in domestic and kindred services rather than in the industrial work available in Chicago and nearby factory suburbs.

Chauffeur, porter, and janitor headed the list of men's occupations. Some worked in personal service jobs, as gardeners or elevator operators; others as common laborers, shoveling, sweeping and maintaining city streets or carrying loads in coal and lumberyards. Jobs were generally short term, poorly paid, and subject to economic fluctuation. Like other black communities of its size, the black community of Evanston included a small professional elite as well as a number of skilled workers and local entrepreneurs.[101]

Early migrants left their imprint most conspicuously in the social geography of black and white neighborhoods. Designed to secure black inequality and white privilege, suburbs provided a clean slate for development and played a key part in the movement to "racialize urban space, that is, to link specific places to an evolving hierarchy, limiting access, cementing advantage and disadvantage, and defining locations and their residents in separate and unequal terms. . . . As the suburbs boomed, white people purchased not merely homes but a concept of space in which racial segregation and white superiority were taken for granted." [102] Patterns of race relations in Evanston, based as they were on a foundation of domestic and personal service, affected geographic and historic settlement, home building, and interracial cooperation. Domestic servants enhanced rather than detracted from elite status, so whites favored housing for blacks. Physical separation helped to rationalize the psychological and cultural distance that whites clearly tried to maintain.

Blacks in domestic service in suburbs across the country were far more likely to own a home than those in central cities, according to Andrew Wiese. Despite their occupational status in the service industry and the low income that accompanied it, they had unprecedented opportunities to own homes in Evanston, albeit within strict geographic limits, in the least desirable areas, and at a cost well above market value.[103] Two factors supported black homeownership in Evanston. First, there was a seemingly endless amount of available land. Although landowners had subdivided the area into building lots before the turn of the century, the far west side remained undeveloped through the 1910s because it was far from public transit, prone to flooding, and isolated from downtown by black neighborhoods to the east. Second, whites made no concerted effort to block home ownership for blacks, as long as they stayed on the west side. Rather, they participated in the process by lending money to black homebuyers through mainstream institutions such as banks and professional real estate and mortgage brokers as well as through individual loans.[104]

Like other suburbanites, blacks ventured north seeking security and autonomy in homeownership, but they were set apart by the value they placed on their homes. Workers favored use over commodity value.[105] Families often built their own homes, starting small with one or two rooms until they could afford to add on. Homes were means of preserving and reconstructing black families in the midst of migration. By renting out rooms or apartments, many of these families generated income to pay the mortgage.[106] In the 1920s four hundred new housing units were built in Evanston's west side. Two-flats were the specialty of the suburb's leading black construction firm. By 1930, 40 percent of the town's homes were occupied by two families. By sharing costs, extended families provided protection against hardship and a foundation for upward mobility. Moreover, domestic production contributed to the welfare of the family. A house with land to garden and on which to raise small livestock promised shelter and sustenance in the face of unstable employment or retirement without pension.[107] Greenery filled stomachs, not lungs.

Excluded from white clubs, black women formed their own. A particular type of organization, social uplift clubs, developed as a collective response to migration from the South and increased discrimination. A local affiliate of the National Association of Colored Women (NACW), the Iroquois North Shore Community League organized in 1917. Incorporating the national organization's motto, "Lifting as we climb," as a guiding principle, established black women reached out to young southern girls seeking domestic work in private homes on the North Shore. The group's motto reflected its commitment to improve the welfare of all black people, regardless of social class.[108]

With the help of white churchwomen, the Iroquois League purchased a three-story building on the corner of Garnett Place and Ridge Avenue, opening the Northshore Community House as a residence for young black women in June 1924. A member of the city's black elite, Cora Watson, wrote that the Iroquois League thus helped to solve the problems of colored girls who came to Evanston with no place to stay.[109] The home served several functions. It addressed one of the most pressing issues facing new arrivals, a lack of housing. It also schooled them on northern customs, fast new ways of speaking, and the hard-to-decipher rules of de facto segregation. Further, it provided a safe and supervised place for live-in servants to visit and socialize on their days off. "Thursday night was the night the colored people went out to have a good time, because the maids were off then," recalled Caldonia Martin.[110] The club's Christian values provided a steady influence, with respectable home life taught and modeled. Endorsing white Victorian ideals, members were concerned with "all things pertaining to the elevation of the home."[111] Like those of their white counterparts, Iroquois members' actions were grounded in middle-class values, particularly the importance of the home and women's moral influence in it. Club women believed that the first step toward racial uplift was the solid foundation of a good home. These concerns dovetailed with job training. Young ladies living in the Northshore Community House received practical experience through upkeep and assigned chores. This gave them an advantage when looking for employment.

Chicago, as noted earlier, was at the forefront of retail trade. Montgomery Ward and Sears Roebuck sold goods to rural communities through mail order and catalogs. Goods were shipped via railroad. Modern retail was introduced by Marshall Field, an upscale store on State Street that offered impeccable customer service. Catering to the upper classes, the store did not hire black sales clerks and sometimes even refused service to colored women. An Evanston branch opened in 1928 with the promise of "routine procedures and type of service to customers being identical with those maintained at the main establishment."[112] Indeed retail stores, restaurants, and other downtown Evanston businesses were segregated. Because it was inappropriate for blacks and whites to socialize, recreation and entertainment facilities, including beaches and especially movie theaters, were off limits to blacks.[113] They were forced to sit in the balconies at the Varsity and Valencia Theaters. Exclusionary practices and segregated neighborhoods thus required the formation of black-owned businesses, and the influx of migrants provided a ready-made clientele.

Blacks responded by building their own institutions and electing leaders to represent their interests. In 1931 women helped Edwin B. Jourdain Jr. become the first black alderman in Evanston. Representing the Fifth Ward, Jourdain was a Harvard graduate who had come to Evanston to attend the Medill School of Journalism at Northwestern. At the time of his election, he was the managing editor of the *Chicago Bee*. W. E. B. DuBois visited Evanston to publicly endorse his candidacy. Jourdain was one of the few blacks running for office at the time. DuBois spoke at a NAACP meeting held at the Evanston Masonic Temple on March 18, 1931. Politically aligned, both men were integrationists. Jourdain served on the city council for sixteen years. While blacks actively campaigned for access to the white economy and political structures, they also maintained strong commitments to racial solidarity through community organizations and historically black institutions. Community Hospital and the Iroquois League were sources of immense pride, but it was the colored branch of the Young Men's Christian Association (YMCA) that elicited the most sentiment.

Evanston had two YMCAs. The whites-only Grove Street facility was off limits to Jews, Catholics, and blacks. Even if they were allowed inside, chances are blacks would have felt unwelcome. In the 1930s and 40s, the High-Y boys' club staged minstrel shows. White performers wore blackface and played characters based on exaggerated and offensive stereotypes. Teenagers met friends in the Plantation Room. Known as the Plant Room to successive generations, its etymology was insulting. Every year between 1955 and 1962, the Y held a fundraiser called Aunt Jemima Pancake Day, named for the mythical slave nanny. Later the popular event's name was shortened to Pancake Day.[114]

On July 5, 1914, the same year Garnett and Butler opened their sanitarium, the Emerson YMCA became one of eighty-four colored divisions nationwide. Separate did not necessarily mean equal. Grove Street facilities were larger, offering more varied activities and programming. Still, operating on a fraction of Grove's budget, Emerson established an active schedule and became an "anchor to the social and civic life of Evanston's black community," a home away from home for blacks of all ages.[115] One of the only places where blacks could socialize, it quickly became a focal point. The neighborhood was a vibrant area in its heyday. Ebenezer AME Church was across the street.

The Y's facilities were not always big enough to meet the needs of the community. The Question Box Club invited lecturers to discuss issues vital to black American life and regularly had to seek larger spaces. On March 18, 1931, DuBois gave a talk titled "The Future of the Negro in America." Expecting a large crowd, the club arranged to hold the lecture on a Monday evening at the First Methodist Episcopal Church on Hinman Avenue. The Emerson Street Y was also a site for women's clubs and salons where members gathered to discuss books written by eminent authors such as Booker T. Washington. Mother's Day was always a special occasion. Men competed in chess and checker tournaments.

The Emerson Y also serviced black youth. In the 1940s and 50s, working women with nowhere to take their children took advantage of a daycare center operating there. As a socializing institution, the Y provided mentorship and espoused Christian values. Supervised activities played an important role in the development of young people. Low wages made it necessary for both parents to work, and many boys lacked adult supervision. With nowhere to go, black youth were "con-

FIGURE 1.1 Ladies dressed in their finest for Mother's Day at the Emerson YMCA. Shorefront Legacy Center.

tributing to 50% of Evanston's delinquency problem, and, out of all proportions to their numbers, to the problem of Associated Charities. They are found to be somewhat troublesome in the schools, and the matter of their conduct on the streets is often a thing of which we are not proud."[116] With a sense of urgency, the organization undertook a fundraising campaign to expand its facilities in 1928: "Today, hundreds of colored boys stand, so far as their recreational program is concerned, homeless in a city of homes."[117] The Emerson branch was able to expand a year later, although its financial resources never approached Grove's.

The impact on people's lives was enormous. Former members recall the father-son banquet, where children whose parents could not afford to take them to restaurants were given a rare opportunity to go out to dinner with their fathers, dressed in suit and tie. It was an exciting night out. But daily programs also drew crowds: anxious kids lined up well before 4:30, when afterschool programs started—boxing and judo lessons, opportunities to play Ping-Pong and pool.[118] Clippers basketball games were popular community events. The Clipperettes cheer-leading squad embodied team spirit. Limited to playing other colored teams and excluded from professional clubs, however, talented athletes were not able to fulfill their promise. Friday-night dances were crowd pleasers where boys looked forward to meeting pretty girls from Fos-ter School. High school proms were segregated, and the Y stepped into the breach. On June 13, 1935, Nat Cole's Orchestra (later known as Nat King Cole) provided the music for one set of lucky seniors. The Y also hosted parties for black Northwestern students.

Both high school and university students used the facilities for physical education, as their schools did not allow blacks in gymnasi-ums with whites. Excluded from dormitories, black college students had several options: commute from Chicago, board with black families in Evanston, or lodge at the Emerson Y. In at least one case a black student lived in a janitor's closet. Perhaps the most famous resident, Ralph Bunche, resided at the Y during the fall semester of 1936 while he was a postdoctoral fellow in anthropology at Northwestern. Bunche had come to the university to work with Professor Melville Herskovits for a semester. The two men became fast friends.[119]

During the 1960s teens frequented the Orbit Room, where walls were decorated with planets and stars twinkled on the ceiling. They listened to soul records by James Brown and the Temptations. Former patrons still talk about Mr. Boyd, a swim teacher who must have set an example to emulate. Segregation was a one-way process: Emerson Street was always open to whites, but the opposite was never true. Whites had freedom to move about in black space, but blacks didn't enjoy a recip-rocal freedom. My mother sent me to the Emerson Y to learn to swim. Another young mother, Alice Kreiman, who would lead the fight to save Evanston's controversial school superintendent, also brought her children to that Y for swimming lessons.

Even though a national YMCA policy of segregated facilities ended in 1946, it would be almost a decade before an interracial committee was formed to oversee the desegregation of Evanston's two facilities. In 1948, the same year Truman issued his executive order desegregating the nation's armed forces, the Varsity Theatre opened first-floor seating to blacks. Nine years later, in 1957, Evanston's Ys began to gradually de-segregate. Grove Street claimed to be fully integrated by 1963. Member-ships were automatically transferred, but when they expired, fees in-creased from $7 to $24 a year, making membership too costly for some black families. Unable to pay the higher fee, some youth counted on a "worthy boy and girl" program to help cover expenses. Nineteen resi-

FIGURE 1.2 Segregation was always a one-way process. White children took swimming lessons at the Emerson Y. *Evanston Review,* January 23, 1964. Shorefront Legacy Center.

dents were moved as soon as rooms became available. Excited about the merger, executive director Douglas Donahan told news reporters that all members would now have access to the same caliber of service.[120] But some staff disapproved of mixed swimming, socializing, and residential facilities. They also expressed concerns that white membership would drop as a result of integration.

With its membership drained, the Emerson Y fell into disrepair, lost clientele, and was forced to close its doors on March 15, 1969. This closing caused mixed emotions in the black community. A documentary film, *Unforgettable: Memories of the Emerson Street Branch YMCA,* records these sentiments. Some blacks thought closure was long overdue, a symbol of racial prejudice and Jim Crow. Others were resentful and wondered why the black community always bore the burden of desegregation. By this time Community Hospital had closed and the all-black Foster School was integrated. Why close the Emerson Y when it was "one of the last things we could call our own?" asked a former member.[121]

Today there is no trace of the once vibrant African American community that frequented the eastern edge of the black triangle. Integration has its advantages, writes Dino Robinson, but at the same time it has cost the black community several important institutions.[122]

Migration Stories

Excessive attention is placed on the earliest phase of the Great Migration. Less has been written about the post–World War II movement north. Ignited by the war, the nation as a whole enjoyed general prosperity, incomes rose, and unemployment was relatively low.[123] Pressure from civil rights organizations for a share of expanding public employment also unlocked limited opportunities for black workers in civil service and private-sector clerical work.[124] Evanston's black middle class increased as a result. Still confined to the city's west side, by 1960 the black community had grown to constitute 12 percent of the city's population, or 9,126 out of 79, 283. There were virtually no black people living north of Evanston. In neighboring Wilmette, census data recorded a Negro population of *less than* 1 percent. It would be a distortion to assume that "white flight" had generated Evanston's demographic makeup. Two factors combined during the 1960s to ignite the city's civil rights activism: a sizable black population, many of whom had lived in Evanston for two or more generations and were deeply concerned with questions of housing, schools, and jobs, and a growing number of white liberals who had been attracted to the racially diverse city because of their political views.

Whites lived on the east side near the lakefront. Blacks settled west, in an area often referred to as "the black triangle" because of its shape —the darkest area on the map, demarcated by a sanitary canal and train tracks. There were mixed areas such as the neighborhood where Nichols Middle School was located (marked 16% Negro) and where most of the black teens in my photograph lived. Larger units of measure give the appearance of integration but can be deceptive. A single number cannot sum up the complexity of a neighborhood's racial integration.[125] While the black population in this neighborhood was proportionate to that of the larger city, black and white homes were not

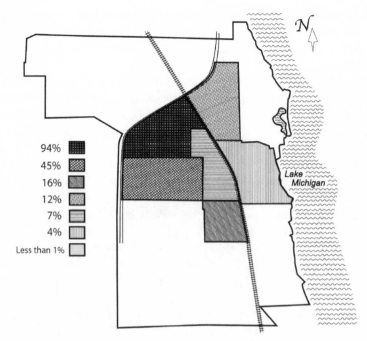

FIGURE 1.3 Map of Evanston's Negro population circa 1960. Ron Crawford.

evenly distributed; black families were clustered along railroad tracks and around Nichols, where their children joined white students from adjacent residential areas.

Geographically, the west side was not very big; it ran north of Emerson and west of Green Bay Road, extending to the banks of the sanitary canal, Evanston's Mason-Dixon line. The boundaries were easily traceable and in the shape of a rough triangle. Inside looking out, to the east black neighborhoods halted at a high embankment of railroad tracks, with the exception of one small node, which projected eastward on two streets to the tracks of the "L" train. At the center, the high school marked a dividing line between blacks and the Polish neighborhood of southwest Evanston.[126] Children attended the all-black Foster Elementary School. The community functioned like a village or big family. Everyone seemed to know everyone. News spread through a neighborhood grapevine. Adults watched out for the children: "If you got good grades, everyone knew about it and someone would likely bake you a cake or rolls."[127]

This was the Evanston where my parents and my friends' parents raised their families. None of us were "old Evanston" elites or long-settled black families. But old Evanston shaped our experiences as youth. With their family's best interests at heart, our parents moved to Evanston to pursue a middle-class lifestyle, including homeownership, safe neighborhoods, and good schools. Evanston was more affordable than the rest of the North Shore, and homeownership was a realistic possibility for couples just starting out. It was also a safe place to raise children and give them a good education. Born and raised in the North, white parents were part of a pattern that was drawing young liberals to the area. Moving from a gradually desegregating South, black parents rejoined family members who had migrated north before them. Integration carried different meanings for blacks. Whites wanted their children to have black friends. Blacks moved to Evanston hoping to expand their children's life opportunities with the vast resources (private and public services) available in predominantly white areas. They associated educational quality with the resources and high expectations characteristic of predominantly white schools. They also wanted their children to grow up around other blacks.

Jobs played a large role in the decision-making process. Most of the white couples had met while attending college in the late 1950s and early 60s. After obtaining professional degrees, men moved for career opportunities, bringing their wives and children with them. Some sought a commuter suburb in close proximity to Chicago, while others established professions in Evanston. Once they arrived, they settled close to Evanston's lakefront. With one exception, parents of the black youth in my photo did not attend college. Without university as a life marker, their children were less sure about where their parents had met. Domestic work and manual labor were the two most common positions available for unskilled workers without high school or college diplomas. These parents hoped to find jobs in Evanston's service sector, or in a nearby suburb where they would have been denied housing. Service and factory jobs were enticing to both elite whites and poor blacks. The first would benefit from the labor of the second, and the latter would find work that required few, if any, credentials. Black adults supported elite lifestyles by working in the service and manufacturing sectors. These couples gravitated toward an increasingly vibrant black community for support and settled on the city's west side.

White men were the traditional breadwinners of the period. Carla's parents met when they were undergraduates at Bates College in Maine, before they went to graduate school. Carla's mother's career came second to her husband's. When he was given tenure at Northwestern, her job was to find a new home and arrange for the move. In 1969, when Carla was eight, the family loaded up the car and drove to a "wonderful house that was cheap and right across the street from the lake" in Evanston.

A prestigious firm in Chicago quickly hired my father when he graduated from Harvard Law School. Living in Evanston put him in proximity to his first job in Chicago's Loop. A commuter, each day he would ride the Northwestern Railroad to work and back. Like other neighborhood children, I waited at the corner to greet him on his walk home from the train station. My parents had met at Grinnell College in Iowa. Moving to Evanston brought them back to the Midwest, where they had both grown up.

Candy's parents embodied the values of their Christian faith. They attended college but didn't meet there. Her father, Roger, "felt the call" and spent most of his life working as a layman for the church. He met Donah through the "written word" at a youth conference on temperance. Roger's job with the Health and Welfare Ministries of the Methodist Church brought the family to Evanston from Washington, DC, when Candy was six or seven. They bought and restored a large Victorian house on Evanston's far east side.

Divorced women sought acceptance in an era that looked down upon them. Regina's parents had met at the University of Kansas. They started their new life together in her mother's hometown, Oak Park. When they separated, it was especially hard on the children, who felt shunned at church and school because apparently "you don't get divorced" in Oak Park. Everyone was Irish, while Regina's mother was Italian; "in those days Italian was almost like being black or Mexican." When Regina was nine, her mother remarried and moved the family to Evanston, where she hoped people would be "more accepting," a characteristic associated with the city's "diversity" and "the fact that it was integrated." Enticed also by the arts community, her mother was all too happy to leave behind Oak Park, a place where she had felt "contained." A "freethinker," she was inspired by installation art popular during the period to completely cover their home's living- and dining-room floors with sand carted from the beach.

Barbara's parents had met while her father was attending Northwestern Law School. They married, had three children, and moved to Skokie, a predominantly Jewish suburb neighboring Evanston to the west. When her parents separated, Barbara's mother felt free to find herself. She changed her name to Ricki and moved the kids to a big house in Evanston, where she told them the crowd would be more "laid-back." She wanted to raise her kids to be independent and non-conforming. There were "a lot of love beads" and there was Janis Joplin and Jimi Hendrix music playing around Barbara's new house. Ricki didn't work or even worry too much about what the neighbors thought. She never mowed the lawn. Instead she'd have friends over to smoke pot. They'd "roll it out on the table, and they'd all get high." If they needed paraphernalia, they could walk down Dempster Street to any one of a number of places selling pipes, rolling papers, candles, and incense. She passed on her liberation to her children, practicing a permissive parenting style. Barbara was allowed to skip school two days a month with no questions asked.

When Jennifer's parents moved in nearby, they did the same. Ron and Sydney had met at the University of Miami. A professional artist and independent filmmaker, Ron fit in well with the local art scene. More than anything else they prioritized diversity. "The last thing they wanted was for us to live a sheltered life," Jennifer told me.

Class advantage enabled most white women to stay home until their children were old enough to go to school. When they did enter the workforce, they held jobs near their homes. Candy's mother waited until her daughter started school before she decided to return to her secretarial job at the Methodist Church's headquarters, located less than a block from the family home. The proximity made her readily available if her family needed something. In some cases, women went back to work after their divorce and put their degree to practical use for the first time. After Carla's parents separated, her mother started working as a psychologist. When my parents divorced, my mother was able to capitalize on her elite liberal arts education.

Contrary to the white suburban norm, a large proportion of black families relied on dual breadwinners throughout the postwar period. More than half of all black women in Evanston worked outside the home, the majority of them laboring in domestic work or commercial laundries.

Prince's family was part of a historical pattern of migrants moving north from the South. His family had left Spartanburg, South Carolina, sometime around 1957 or 1958 to join his mother's brother in Evanston. "My understanding was, she was the first one to move to Evanston; she moved up with my uncle and watched their kids during the day, while they worked," Prince told me. The invitation to work in her brother's home served as an apprenticeship of sorts for Prince's mother, who later took a paid position as a domestic worker. Four sisters and their children, including Prince's cousins Jesse and Earl, would eventually follow. Before long the entire maternal side of the family would relocate. Prince's grandmother was the last to arrive.

As a child, Prince must have felt that white children usurped his rightful position in relation to his mother when she left him and his siblings to do "day work" for a doctor and her family. His worst fears were realized when he was too sick to attend school and accompanied her to work. It was on these days that he learned that black people were relegated to either the kitchen or the basement, where he would watch television and "hang around until she was done." Prince wondered, "Why is she coming here to clean their house?" The fact that it was a "huge house" made an impression, teaching him the relative wealth of whites: "They had money, we didn't." Norms regulating the interpersonal relationships between blacks and whites were underscored when Prince saw his mother being treated as a second-class citizen. Around 3:00–3:30 the children came home from school, and they were "calling my mom by her first name, and that was kind of unusual for me." He watched while "she would be fixing 'em snacks and making sure they get changed from school clothes to regular clothes," only to be ignored by the white children she cared for. "It was kind of weird because I knew they were there, they knew I was there, and we never had any kind of conversation at all. I knew their names, and I assume they knew mine, but I never had a conversation with them at all or never really sat down and played with them." When Prince was in seventh grade, his mother quit this job to work on an assembly line at "MC Powers" with her sister, Jesse's mother.

Jesse's parents wanted him to have "better opportunities than they had had in the South." "I guess they just feel that city life offered more up north, better jobs, better pay, better education," he mused. "They wanted us to have better than what they had." Jesse has no idea how they met, "but I know my mom and dad been together since they's ten years old." In South Carolina they worked outside: "chop wood, go pick cotton, pick cherries and peaches." A segregated and unequal school system meant that both of his parents had to "get up early in the morning and walk miles and miles to school." Their schooling suffered: "My mom only had a freshman education and my dad only got a sophomore education of high school." They chose Evanston as a destination because his mother's sister "migrated already, up north to Chicago, and they told us to come up, and we followed."

Earl's mother also married young, when she was just fifteen years old. She had her first child a year later, when she was sixteen. And then she, too, joined her sisters, Prince's and Jesse's mothers, in Evanston.

Jesse's mother's work history is representative of these early migrants. She moved north to join her sisters, who had come before her. Limited by her lack of formal education, she worked as a domestic. She "would work at people's houses" in order to "make ends meet." Later she found employment doing laundry at National School Towels, which serviced all the area's public schools. Located around the corner from the Emerson YMCA, "they did nothing but towels." Kinship networks functioned as sources of news, spreading information about job openings. When relatives were hired at Powers Regulator Company (MCC Powers), Jesse's mother left her housekeeping job and began working on the assembly line. The factory's proximity to Evanston's west side made jobs convenient for many of the city's black working class. For thirteen years she worked at Powers during the day and National Towels at night. The work was brutal and likely played a part in her early death. When she "passed," Jesse's "faith wavered." He wondered in his prayers, "Good as she was, she was only sixty years old—why would you take her and all these other mothers are still living?" Jesse questioned why the God he deeply believed in, a source of moral support throughout his life, would "have to take my mother, the only person I had." Jesse's religious beliefs justified an economic system that routinely exploited black workers. "You can't question God," he told me, "so I had to reach back inside myself and ask God to forgive me for questioning him."

While black men held a wider range of jobs than women, they also had greater difficulty finding stable and well-paying work in the suburbs. Jesse's father found employment at Golf Mill, a mall "out there in Des Plaines." He worked as a cook, preparing the homemade southern "specialties" that his mother had taught him—"just certain things that he could make that other people couldn't do, and his boss wanted him to make hams and cakes and stuff like that." At night, after the mall closed, he had a second job cleaning it. Social networks at church led him to his next job when a fellow parishioner referred him to Wyeth Laboratory, a pharmaceutical company. Wyeth provided a "better job" with "better pay," and "he didn't have to work long, long hours, and he didn't have to work two jobs because he made enough money where he could support his family." The job entailed "fixing machines to keep the assembly line, like a mechanic on the machines, that brought [the products] down the belt." He worked for Wyeth until he retired. His family's first home was on the west side of town.

To make ends meet, Jesse's parents held card games and sold dinners on Friday and Saturday nights. Relatives and coworkers attended; "they loved to play cards for money." There was always a good turnout:

"they'd have two or three tables with card games going" at a time. The events were successful for another reason. "My mother was real lucky, my mother would win all the time." She would use her earnings to buy her son the essentials he needed to participate in sports; "when I needed baseball cleats or a mitt she would win." Exuberant at her good fortune, she would call out his name: "Jesse!" During "intermission" she and Jesse's father sold chicken, spaghetti, and catfish dinners to their guests. A typical meal included a main dish with coleslaw and bread or french fries. Neighbors would also stop by to purchase food; they'd "grab three-four dinner plates." Jesse's friends loved her cooking. They'd beg: "'Miss Floyd when you going to have some more catfish?' 'Miss Floyd when you cooking some more spaghetti?' 'Miss Floyd you make the best cornbread.' She didn't use the Jiffy mix cornbread, she made it from scratch, and a lot of people up north didn't know how to do that, but she learnt all those recipes from my dad's mother, 'cause she was a real good cook." Separation of work and community was essentially a mark of class privilege, but the reverse could also be true.

White homes too were used as sources of income; the difference was that these families did not rely on their business ventures in quite the same way. Revenue generated from the home was not essential to the livelihood of the family. Divorced white women, supported by alimony and child support from their ex-husbands, rented rooms to Northwestern students to generate income from existing assets. Barbara's mother earned extra cash by taking in boarders. When I was young we rented rooms on our third floor and, in one case, my sleeping porch. For others, the decision to work at home was just that, a choice, rather than a necessary supplement.

Flexibility and autonomy were the chief advantages to working at home. Child support gave Regina's mother the latitude she needed to start her own business, manufacturing and selling small painted ceramic broaches, from her new house. Working from home gave her the flexibility she needed to take care of her seven children while simultaneously earning an income. Later, when her children were older, her business provided income for them when they were unemployed or in between jobs. When Regina moved home after her own divorce, her mother hired her.

Jennifer's parents converted a coach house in the backyard into a film studio and started their own company, Fat Film. Their skills were complementary: Ron was the filmmaker "doing the art" while Sydney "was sort of running the business" by "keeping track of the books." Both parents were present to care for the children. When Jennifer was older and needed a job, her parents provided one. During high school she painted animation cells and earned school credit. With no boss to answer to, Sydney and Ron had time to monitor their children's schooling.

Perkey and Bernie's father, Robert, had met his wife, Jackie, "somewhere between Michigan and Ohio." Born in Virginia, Jackie was the only black parent of the group to have attended college, although she left Michigan State University before she graduated. Bernie told me, "I think Dad might have been painting," because he "went all over painting." He was from Toledo, Ohio, but had relatives in the Chicago area. Thinking back, Bernie told me, "From what I know, my aunts, my father's sisters, were here first, and they decided that it was a good place to live. . . . I know his brother lived in Rockford." His parents settled on Evanston's west side "sometime in the 60s or late 50s." Bernie was the youngest child of nine, and after he was born the family moved to Hovland Court, an early subdivision that provided affordable housing to blacks on the west side.

Teaching became a significant route for black entry into middle-class professional work, particularly for women. Jackie was the only black woman of the group to escape common labor and enter the professions as a teacher's aide in Evanston's public school system. She worked for Head Start and used insider knowledge to her advantage when she enrolled her son Bernie. Since a car was prohibitively expensive, she traveled to work with him on the school bus each day. Jackie was the only black parent to own her home.

Robert worked as a "painter all of his life." The work was temporary and therefore unreliable. When he found work, he helped maintain some of Chicago's architectural landmarks. Bernie was awed by his father's industrial painting jobs, including "big sky scraper buildings." He'll never forget the day his father painted the Chicago Planetarium and brought the children along to watch. As a child, Bernie would not have understood that the low wages associated with semi-skilled labor might have been partially responsible for his father's alcoholism. Instead, he saw the situation in reverse and blamed his father for periods of unemployment: "When he wasn't drinking he had lots of good painting jobs." Unemployment, associated with temporary low-wage work, was a constant threat.

Ray's father was the "number-one man for detailing cars" at the Rolls Royce dealership on Davis Street in downtown Evanston. Ray and Jesse helped wash and wax cars on weekends, quickly learning their place as workers servicing the upper classes. Ray's father taught them to clean cars, and Jesse was grateful for the income and the training. "That sustained me for a long time for getting my school clothes, 'cause I knew how to do cars." These skills helped him make extra cash on the side. "I would do anybody's car I could think of; I would go by the car wash and recruit people: 'You want your car done'? and I'd say, 'Well, how much are they charging you to wash and wax your car? I'll do it for twenty-five dollars.'" Ray's and Jesse's experiences are typical of black Evanston teenagers who worked to contribute to the family's income.

Prince spoke to his father only once, when he was in fifth or sixth grade. The call was no more than a quick hello from a prison telephone. Years later, when his mother gave him the news that his father was dead, he debated with himself about going to Washington, DC, for the funeral. "Why should I go? I never knew who he was. I don't want to go," he told his mother. Convinced in the end to do the "right thing," Prince went but was left heartbroken by the experience. First, his father's remains did not look familiar. "I go up and view the body—no recognition at all of who this man is." Next, after taking his seat in the third row, he opened the program to find a list of survivors. "I notice that one of the names says 'Prince Williams Jr.' and then the other one says 'Little Prince Williams Jr.'" At this moment Prince realized that his father had "another kid that he named my exact name. I was just floored. It made me feel as if I never existed." I thought it might be a compliment, but Prince was quick to correct me: "I took that as this, the Prince Williams Jr. that you first named Prince Williams Jr. is no longer there, and was never there, and this is who Prince Williams Jr. is . . ."

Prince's father's choices are significant. Passing his name to his sons was a way of responding to high mortality rates for black males. Jesse and Chip did the same. Jesse named his first two sons after himself, "because [that way] I always got to have another Jesse," he told me. Chip, whose real name is Darian, gave the name to two of his sons "because one was here in the United States and one was in Germany. And legacy," he explained. Relatives had given Chip his nickname because he was like his father Thomas, a "chip off the old block."

Thomas typifies another trend among black migrants. He came north having secured work before his arrival. Born in Augusta, Georgia, he lived in Tennessee as a young adult. A white man "had seen some of his work" and invited him north to work in his auto body shop in Glencoe, Chip told me. Thomas had left the South with no regrets; actually he was in a little trouble, "so it was best that he left." "My pops and his two brothers were—I wouldn't say rough characters; they just didn't take too much stuff." He met his wife Tempie when her car broke down in Glencoe. Unlike other black women in the group, she worked in suburbs farther north. Prohibited from living in Glencoe and Wilmette, she made her residence in Evanston.

Tempie must have been proud when she graduated from DuBois High School, named for the great civil rights leader, in Wake Forest, North Carolina. Like her future husband, Tempie secured employment before moving to Evanston. She was in her early twenties when a former Wake Forest resident hired her as a maid. Tempie preferred the more dignified term "day work." It is unclear who came first, but by 1940 Tempie and her sisters had all moved to Evanston to work in the private homes of the well-to-do. Later, Tempie found work in nursing homes and as a switchboard operator. Chip's friends called her Mamma Sweets because she was always looking out for them. Like that of Jesse's mother, her hard life probably contributed to her early death at age sixty-four. Black parents had a tougher time during their retirement years than white parents, and they died earlier. They relied more heavily on social security and had less wealth than their white counterparts.

Black children's life chances were altered because their parents made the hard decision to leave their homes in the South for an unfamiliar world up north. Educational opportunities provided an impetus to both sets of parents. Evanston's public schools were known to be some of the best in the nation, and there was a strong community commitment to integration. Many white parents moved to Evanston because they believed that their children would learn something essential by going to school with blacks. Once our families settled into their new homes, our parents quickly enrolled us in one of the city's twenty elementary schools.

TWO

A Salt-and-Pepper Mix

A school bus with black and white children gets turned on its head in proudly
bigoted South Carolina. A school system with black and white children in it
gets turned on its ear in uneasily progressive Evanston.

DAILY NORTHWESTERN[1]

Following the Supreme Court's 1954 decision in *Brown v.
Board of Education,* and under pressure from federal authorities, southern districts started the slow process of
reassigning black students to formerly all-white schools
(though not vice versa).[2] Attorneys from the NAACP expected the court's mandate to even the playing field. Educational resources had always been unfairly distributed,
and integration would require state governments to start
spending more money per black pupil.

On the other side of the Mason-Dixon Line, where geography did the work of Jim Crow, northern schools were no
less segregated than their southern counterparts. Rooted
in racially segregated housing arrangements, elementary
attendance areas were organized so that small children
could walk to school and back home. As legal and political
pressures for integrated education spread north and west
in the 1960s and 70s, local activists drew on the momentum. Educators in progressive cities, including a number
of college communities, executed relatively peaceful and
voluntary plans.[3] School districts followed a familiar pattern. Methods used to desegregate presumed that black
schools had no value and that black students were served
best by being assimilated with whites. A magnet-school

desegregation plan privileged white interests by breaking up a black school.[4]

Evanston's nationally acclaimed desegregation plan came at the expense of black children. It called for the elimination of the all-black Foster School and the redistribution of those students to institutions in white neighborhoods. After its attendance area was eliminated, Foster was then transformed into a laboratory school with a revised and innovative curriculum. Students from across the district were allowed to apply and, if admitted, voluntarily enroll. While some black students won admission, most boarded buses to schools across town where they were alienated from white children. Elementary schools had been built without cafeterias because city planners assumed mothers would prepare lunch at home. Which children could walk home for lunch was as much an issue as whether a lunch and a mother were waiting for them. At noontime, white children went home for a hot meal while their black classmates were left behind to eat cold sandwiches.[5] When the school day ended, black children were transported back to their homes on the west side of town. Busing and school lunch policies thus hindered interracial friendships and stigmatized black children.

Citizen Advisory Commission on Integration

On the eve of desegregation, Evanston's school system was divided into two districts servicing close to eleven thousand pupils. District 65 oversaw twenty elementary schools, including three educational institutions in the neighboring village of Skokie. Primary schools enrolled students in grades kindergarten through sixth and manifested considerable racial imbalance due to segregated residential patterns. As a result, they were the focus of desegregation efforts. Drawing from larger segments of the community, student bodies at the middle and high schools were already relatively integrated. Seventh- and eighth-graders attended one of the district's four junior highs. All students continued their education at Evanston Township High School in District 202.

Black children could attend any school they wanted but often faced "friendly persuasion" to go to Foster. Aggravated by natural or man-made boundaries and a "neighborhood school" model that placed elementary institutions within walking distance of children's homes, the racial makeup of student bodies mirrored that of their residential area.[6] As a result, nearly all blacks went to either Foster or Dewey, while enrollments at College Hill, Orrington, Timber Ridge, and Lincoln-wood were predominantly white.[7] Foster School was a continuing symbol of isolation from mainstream society. Generations of black children didn't have white classmates until high school. Foster was also severely overcrowded.

With support from the NAACP, black parents pressured School Superintendent Oscar M. Chute to do something about it. On October 21, 1963, he appointed B. J. Chandler, dean of Northwestern's Department of Education, to chair the newly formed Citizens Advisory Committee on Intercultural Relations. The committee was charged with evaluating the problems of de facto segregation brought on by housing discrimination. Its recommendations would guide the board in its efforts "to provide the best education possible for all of the pupils attending its schools." In December 1964, ten years after the 1954 Supreme Court's landmark decision, Evanston's board of education voted to gradually end de facto segregation, and a target date of September 1967 was set for a fully integrated school system. However overdue the corrective measures were, Chute hoped that they would give white children the advantage of learning to live in a world that was becoming increasingly diverse and that integration would advance the academic performance and self-esteem of their black peers. The school board outlined its philosophy: de facto segregation was a community problem that both white and Negro children suffered from; if they remained isolated from one another, they would fail to live and work together as adults. The board's agenda was admirable, but the existing racial housing pattern and the uneven density of the school-age population complicated its task. As the community was preparing to desegregate its school system, the North Shore Summer Project (NSSP) was planning to take action against discriminatory housing practices. The two issues were inextricably tied.

The board of education was not required to hold a referendum. Instead Chute visited schools to promote the idea of integration and prepare parents. Frank Whiting, president of the Northwest Evanston Homeowners' Association, attended Chute's presentation at the all-white Lincolnwood School in July 1965. Several months later he wrote a long letter asking the superintendent to clarify his stance on fifteen separate issues raised at the parent meeting. Under the guise of concern about budgets, children's welfare, and the democratic process, the Northwest Homeowners were clearly opposed to integration from the start. Whiting gave himself away when he asked what was being done to control the influx of Negroes from Chicago and elsewhere who lived with relatives for the sole purpose of attending Evanston schools.[8] Determined to move forward, Chute answered each question in turn in a letter dated December 1, 1965.

Overall the city's major institutions and political leaders demonstrated their good intentions by supporting initiatives to integrate the public schools. Local news sources endorsed community efforts, emphasizing long-term effects: "Integration of the grade schools will prepare students better for mixing in the junior highs and the high school and for working together as adults in a mixed society."[9] Across town, Reverend Charles Eddis urged his parishioners to be active supporters by referencing Martin Luther King Jr.'s 1963 "Letter from Birmingham Jail": "Do not hide your family under a bushel. Do not be polite and discreet. Be a thermostat, not a thermometer."[10] The metaphor provoked his audience. A thermostat transforms society's mores, whereas a thermometer simply records ideas and principles.[11] The reorganization of junior highs to include sixth-graders and a student transfer program were already paving the way for full-scale integration.

Before a formal plan to desegregate was developed, sixth-graders joined seventh- and eighth-grade classes to constitute the new middle schools. Reorganization into a three-year sequence made educational sense. Expanding the junior highs would ease overcrowding at the elementary level, allow for an easier transition between the lower grades and high school, and expose students earlier to a more intensive and broad curriculum. The three-year plan was gaining acceptance across the country. Donald V. Grote, director of curriculum and instructional services for District 65, opined that the "present day 11-year-old is, on the whole, ready for varied and advanced experiences which junior high school can offer," such as encountering different teachers and separate rooms for science and foreign languages.[12] A report released by the educational consulting firm hired to assess the capacities of school facilities concluded that a "special advantage can be noted in Evanston. Moving the sixth grade to the junior high school adds a grade to the schools serving wider geographic areas with a consequently heterogeneous population and takes another grade out of the schools which predominately serve one race or creed."[13] The three-year plan would place children in integrated school environments one year earlier than was presently the case. Restructuring the junior highs incited little, if any, opposition from city residents, who were aware of the pedagogical benefits that came from reform.

The required transfer of 448 black students from Foster to less crowded facilities was another precursor to district-wide integration.

FIGURE 2.1 School transfers board bus to go home for lunch. *Evanston Review,* September 23, 1965.

For the three academic years preceding integration, students voluntarily transferred out of both Dewey and Foster to alleviate overcrowding.[14] Because transfer students did not live close enough to their new schools to walk, the district was responsible for providing transportation—including for lunch. Each day transfer students made four separate bus trips. Historian Jack Dougherty has uncovered similar routines in Milwaukee. During the 1960s the city regularly practiced "intact busing," or transporting entire classrooms of elementary students to nearby underenrolled schools, where they were kept "intact." Classrooms were bused in the morning, back to their sending school for lunch, again to the receiving school for afternoon instruction, and finally back to their sending school at the end of the day. "The two round-trips per day not only curtailed instructional time but heightened the stigma of racial separation."[15] Similar practices in Evanston yielded similar results. Transporting black children in and out of schools not only thwarted social interaction during the noon hour but also hindered friendships after the academic day ended. These problems would be exacerbated by district-wide desegregation. Concerned with jump-starting an integration plan, Superintendent Chute overlooked warning signs. Speaking to the *Evanston Review,* he emphasized positive aspects of the transfer program: "considerably more integration of the district" with the added benefit of using limited space in the best possible way.[16]

To develop a desegregation plan and provide a smooth administrative transition, Chute appointed the Citizen Advisory Commission on Integration (CACI). The group held its first meeting on October 5, 1965. CACI was comprised of civic and business leaders, none of whom represented any particular group, but all of whom shared the common belief that integrated education was quality education. By the end of the decade, CACI chair Mrs. James Moran and members including Mrs. Helen Cooper, Joseph Hill, and Robert Marks would become household names. By virtue of their official positions, Chute and his successor, Gregory C. Coffin, were ex officio members. CACI was given two years to execute a student reassignment plan that would depopulate Foster and Dewey with a minimum of disruption to existing attendance areas. By the 1967–68 academic year, Evanston schools would reflect the city's demographics—21.9 percent black and 78.1 percent white.[17] Moran was committed to a democratic process. CACI went "into the field" to gather input from the community through parent-teacher associations (PTAs) and other neighborhood groups.[18]

The creation of a kindergarten center served as a trial prior to the elimination of Foster as an attendance area and its transformation into a laboratory school with an innovative curriculum. White parents were asked to voluntarily transfer their children in from five overcrowded schools, and Foster parents were simultaneously asked to transfer their children out, the goal being an equal number of black and white children in each kindergarten classroom. On February 18, 1966, CACI sent parents a survey to gauge interest. Its members were pleased when they received applications representing children from every school in the district. Parents unwilling to transfer enumerated the advantages of "neighborhood schools." Children walked to and from home, especially for lunch, played with classmates, and were in close proximity in case of an emergency.[19] Some parents said that the decision to purchase their home was based solely on the school attendance area. After the experiment was run at the kindergarten level for a year, Foster was scheduled to desegregate with the rest of the district.

Several measures were taken to entice white applicants. First, the school's name was changed to the Laboratory School (LAB), in part to "eliminate the image of Foster as an all Negro school and also to better convey the concept of an experimental school."[20] Second, educators developed an innovative curriculum. Smaller class sizes allowed teachers to practice a pedagogy that included project-oriented learning and field trips. Specialists in creative drama, music, and art were hired to assist teachers.[21] Foreign languages were offered in all grades, including kindergarten. A reading program was added at the kindergarten level.

FIGURE 2.2   Recess time at the newly integrated LAB School. *Chicago Sun Times*, September 7, 1967.

The school would operate using a nongraded class structure so that children could learn at their own pace instead of moving along according to chronological age. Finally, admitted kindergarteners and their siblings received first priority when the regular magnet school opened the following year. The district promised to provide transportation and give students lunch privileges.

The red brick building with the jungle gym in front was no little red schoolhouse. With financial assistance from local, state, and federal agencies and the support of nearby universities and colleges, LAB School became a model for the nation. Northwestern's Department of Education was invited to weigh in on the curriculum. College students were used as tutors. Teachers and administrators evaluated educational techniques, methods, and materials before they were implemented in other schools in the district. The board issued the following statement:

The objective of the lab school is to demonstrate the effect of an integrated school environment on the learning of children. We hope to create a microcosm of the district representing the racial, socioeconomic, achievement and ability levels represented in the district. So that the lab school will be a kind of proving ground not only for integrated education, but for the educational process itself. The many new innovations that have come into education during the past few years will be tried out in the lab school and then of course the information from them will be disseminated into the other attendance areas.

A racial mix was key but was not the only component of integration. A representative number of Negros as well as students from a cross-section of socioeconomic groups, pupil aptitude and intelligence groups, and district-wide geographical distribution would help to create a truly integrated classroom.

White advantage may have been a driving force behind the magnet school plan. A strategy that least disrupted the power structure would be the most likely to succeed. Documentary filmmaker Larry Brooks recorded the monumental event. His interviews with parents reveal racial tensions. When asked why she submitted an application to LAB School, a white woman said that she felt it was her responsibility and called integration an "exciting and spectacular thing." Another white woman found the offer too attractive to turn down. She believed that the district had handled the plan "very wisely," having sent out a brochure citing the advantages of the kindergarten center. In particular, she was drawn to a program that introduced children to reading earlier than at other schools. She liked the inclusion of art, music, industrial arts, and creative dramatics. Small student-teacher ratios and extended hours were also an incentive. She was not "terribly happy" to watch her son board a bus to the kindergarten center at Foster but decided it was a sacrifice she could make. She preferred that he stay in the neighborhood so that she could watch him walk down the street and into school, where she knew he would be safe. She changed her mind because her son liked the school bus and thought it was fun to ride. His older sister was kind of jealous that he got a ride to school while she had to walk.[22]

Some black parents felt the kindergarten center showed a clear preference for children outside the Foster attendance area. The Foster PTA vigorously supported the LAB School plan, however, and the community had substantial representation on CACI. Few black parents preferred to retain Foster as a neighborhood school, but some felt deceived. A black mother said she had been "perfectly satisfied" with the integration plan, including the transformation of Foster into the LAB School, until she found out that her child would not be attending the school anymore. Another woman believed that the black community had

been misled. She assumed that Foster children would be given preference the following year, when the entire school was desegregated, and
was surprised when they weren't. She conceded that there was nothing in writing so it might have been an innocent misunderstanding.
When she brought her concerns to school authorities, they explained
that "white parents outside of our neighborhood were influenced to
bring their children in to the district." Conflicted, she believed in integration but was not convinced that Foster School should be closed.
Given its location in "an all Negro district, I imagine this would be the
only way," she decided. Placing the burden of desegregation on black
shoulders was a form of racism itself.[23]

Announcing his retirement after twenty years of service, Chute conducted a national search for his replacement. Gregory Coffin, a progressive and like-minded educator willing to promote integration, was
hired. Comparative studies of desegregation reveal that elected school
officials, in contrast to those appointed, have been far less willing to
promote integration because if they do they tend not to get reelected.[24]
Chute selected Coffin, and an elected school board approved the appointment. Ultimately the board had the authority to hire or fire the
superintendent. Several years later its members would vote against renewing his contract.

Coffin came from Darien, Connecticut, an "all-white and mostly
Protestant" suburb of eighteen thousand where he had been superintendent of schools since 1961; that system enrolled 5,100 students and
had the highest per-pupil expenditure and teacher salary schedule in
Connecticut.[25] Coffin was best known for introducing a student-teacher
exchange program with Harlem schools. Proud of his accomplishments, he believed that everyone involved considered the program to
be a "tremendous success." Those who criticized it had only "superficial knowledge" of the program, he said. A self-proclaimed integrationist, Coffin believed the process involved "more than mixing numbers."
Unlike those who think that "schools should reflect society," Coffin
said, "I feel they should shape society. Attitude training is not apart
from academic and skill training." Emphasizing an educator's responsibility to "inculcate moral attitudes that are healthy and generally accepted," Coffin said he looked forward to "a lot of healthy experiment-
ing" in District 65.[26]

Before he left Darien, Coffin wrote a letter to Martin Luther King Jr.,
congratulating him on being selected for the Nobel Peace Prize on
January 4, 1965. He used the opportunity to tell King about some of
his initiatives in Darien, including his Harlem exchange program. Cof-

fin had had a speech that King gave in Stamford, Connecticut, filmed. He was showing it in social studies and public-speaking classrooms throughout the district. These efforts were part of a broader program for improving civil rights education. King was impressed and wrote back. He prayed for Coffin's success in breaking down the walls of segregation and discrimination in Darien. The civil rights hero ended the letter with words of encouragement: "May you remain steadfast in your struggle to secure freedom and equality for all Americans."[27]

Coffin's professional experience was impressive. It included superintendent positions in North Reading, Massachusetts, and the Narragansett regional school district in Templeton. He had been principal at Woodstock Academy in Connecticut and a teacher in Massachusetts at both Middlesex School and Marblehead High School. More recently, he had held positions as an assistant professor at the University of Massachusetts and was a visiting lecturer at the University of Bridgeport, Connecticut. Coffin's credentials were also notable: he had earned an AB from Harvard, a MA from Boston University, and a PhD from the University of Connecticut. Given his accomplishments, one could see why he was selected from among eighty-three candidates to succeed Chute in a unanimous decision by the board. In a statement to the press, Coffin said, "I have had a high regard for the Evanston school system for many years. The current problems of the Evanston schools are as challenging as those in virtually every section of the country."[28] He traced his stand on integration to his schoolteacher parents, who were both nonconformists.

Coffin did not threaten Evanston's social imagination. An article in the *Review* titled "Coffin Family, Cat Make Themselves Comfortable Here" introduced the superintendent, his wife, and their four children to the public. "Typical New Englanders," the family was "fondest of lobster." They loved to ski and sail. Coffin himself had been a member of the rowing crew at Harvard and belonged to the Darien Yacht Club. The Coffins' children included Gregory Jr., called Gig, age fourteen, who had "lost no time in rigging an intercom between his third-floor bedroom and his mother's domain, the kitchen"; Geoffrey, age twelve; Cynthia age nine, known as Bindy; and Emily, age eight. The superintendent's wife, Nancy Coffin, adhered to the conservative gender roles that were still popular in Evanston; she was an "attractive brunet with Jacqueline Kennedy features, who is third cousin of her husband." Mrs. Coffin was an avid cook who used to bake all of the family's bread, until Gig was able to eat an entire loaf by himself. She was working on a master's degree in education but had "no plans to teach until the children are older." She made it clear that she intended to "leave the problems of District 65 to her husband." According to the article, she had seen little of Coffin during his orientation to the school district and had kept busy fixing up their new home, where she "spent two days refinishing an antique hutch."[29]

Not everyone was impressed. Signs of serious trouble coincided with Coffin's arrival.

Coffin's commitment to integration was immediate and intense. He set about achieving what he called a "salt and pepper" mix in the schools through redistricting and a massive busing program. His focus was on large-scale change: swift appointment of black personnel to essentially all white schools and the central administration, federal and foundation funds for aides in all classrooms, and securing outside funding for equipment and added personnel. He understood that to be successful, integration had to be embraced by the community at large. Several programs prepared the public. First, a buddy system paired students with children from the school they would be attending the following year. Next, "exchange programs" made it possible for pupils to visit their newly assigned schools prior to their enrollment. Third, parents were made to "feel at home" in their new school through social events sponsored by PTAs. Finally, the board reached out to its constituents, communicating through surveys and mailings.[30]

Funded by a $123,000 grant received under Title IV of the 1964 Civil Rights Act, the Teacher's Institute, a five-week summer program held in 1967 and again in 1968, was perhaps the most noteworthy initiative of all. It prepared faculty for the "cultural and educational problems associated with teaching in integrated schools." Workshops in human relations offered instruction for diverse classrooms. The overarching aim was to identify things teachers did unwittingly to perpetuate invidious racial distinctions. Teachers learned about the cultural differences and similarities between Negroes and whites. They were instructed to modify techniques of classroom management, individualized instruction, student counseling, parent interviews and involvement, and academic motivation, which might have different effects on Negro and white children. By providing instruction on how a teacher should deal with black children, district leaders revealed their preconceived ideas about these youth. When two school board members, Mr. Carver and Mr. Farquharson, urged the institute to include instructions on disciplinary procedures, they reinforced a racialized stereotype that associates black youth with deviant behavior. Farquharson defended his stance: "Student behavior has been a great concern to me, and the integration program could fumble if the teachers are unable to cope with discipline problems."[31]

Some teachers and staff felt insulted by a requirement of sensitivity training for all. Still, over three hundred, nearly half, of the district's teachers and administrators participated in the program. They simulated classroom situations, visited the homes of black and white students, and viewed films on closed-circuit television. Speakers were eminent and varied, and included scholar John Hope Franklin, chair of the History Department at the University of Chicago, and author Jonathan Kozol. Teachers divided into small groups to discuss ideas and issues raised by speakers and to talk about race relations. Frank conversations regarding race were difficult to have. According to one attendee, his small group "had taken 2 ½ weeks of polite discussion before they laid their cards on the table." "It's not easy," another participant added; "we don't even discuss openly and frankly other simpler things that don't have the implications of integration." At the end of the five-week period, the institute was declared a success by the local media: "When school opens next month District 65 teachers will be better equipped for teaching in a multicultural classroom."[32]

Busing

Redrawing elementary school boundaries in order to accurately replicate the city's racial proportions was CACI's final logistical step. In March 1966, group members met with advisers from the Illinois Institute of Technology (IIT) to discuss the use of computers in the redistricting of elementary schools.[33] After several meetings, convinced that technology could heal the city's social wounds, the committee requested funds from the school board to pay for computer-generated redistricting. CACI member Quaife M. Ward explained how the computer would determine changes. A technician entered a code card for each student in the district: "It would give the student's race, age, and grade, and the enrollment capacity of each school by grade. The computer would return alternatives for redistricting that would take into account such factors as racial composition, available classroom space, and travel time to school."[34] The goal was to assign every boy and girl to a school within one mile of home, taking account of geographic barriers and safety factors. The use of technology gave the illusion that redistricting was objective and impartial. Human oversight would mediate technological solutions, however. Parents were reassured that

FIGURE 2.3 Using technology to heal social ills, an engineer maneuvers an oscilloscope to determine the even distribution of black and white children in Evanston's schools. *Chicago Daily News*, October 22, 1966.

boundaries were flexible and would be reviewed annually. Redistricting maps were presented to the city council on October 17, 1966, and made available to the public that same day. Changes were carefully documented and were based on seemingly colorblind criteria such as school capacity, traffic routes, and industrial barriers.

A nearly equal number of black and white children were reassigned.

In grades 1–5, 1,365 of 6,171 pupils would be transferred to different schools. Of that total, 700 were black and 665 were white. Pleased with the results, the board announced, "The new boundaries will recreate, as nearly as possible, the 21 to 78 Negro-to-white ratio in the school district."[35] Children who did not live within one mile of their school or whose route was considered hazardous would be bused at district expense. Federal courts had already mandated busing to achieve integration throughout the southern United States. Due to residential segregation, nearly all of the 450 students who would undergo busing were black; fewer than 20 were white.[36]

Two types of bus service were required: charter buses for black students traveling to the five schools to implement integration, which was paid for by the board, and parent-paid charter buses for LAB students and pupils enrolled in schools within walking distance from their homes. The black community would bear the financial burden of busing, paying out twenty-five thousand dollars for each ten-month school year for 450 black children. These were not the children being bused at board expense to five outlying schools; these children lived

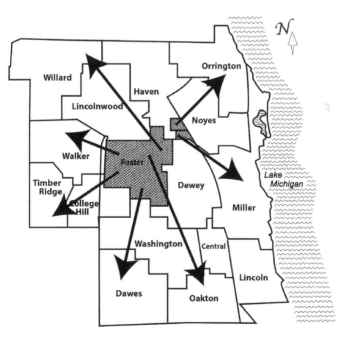

FIGURE 2.4 Elementary school desegregation map, including the three Skokie schools. Based on map in the *Chicago Daily News*, October 14, 1966. Ron Crawford.

less than one and a half miles from school, the state legal limit required for the board to supply transportation, and were bused on "tripper buses." Some 250 white children also rode these buses. The Evanston Bus Company provided four of the ten needed, and the black-owned Robinson Bus Service provided the remaining six.[37] The district deliberately chose a black-owned bus company.

Opponents questioned financial efficacy. They wondered why money that could be used for new textbooks would be spent on buses. A resident who also opposed a recommended high school bond referendum complained, "If the school board can find $65,000 or more per year to squander on busing children to schools miles from their homes, I do not think they need any more money."[38] The legality of busing was questioned by Mrs. Paul E. Meves, referencing Title IV of the 1964 Civil Rights Act, which clarified several of the Supreme Court's original definitions in *Brown* and included a statement that "desegregation shall not mean the assignment of students to public schools in order to overcome racial imbalance."[39] Meves signaled one of the most controversial aspects of school desegregation when she called into question the use of racial balance quotas, which had replaced neighborhood and other geographic means as a way of assigning students; she said that any plan to change boundaries for reasons of race, religion, or nationality was subject to legal question because it was openly based on differences between children. *Brown* called for the assignment of children to schools without regard to race, yet it used race as a measure for overcoming segregation.

Others incited fear over a too-powerful school board, invoking Cold War politics as a scare tactic. The ideals of Republican Motherhood insisted that children be educated at home by mothers and by teachers in neighborhood schools. Some of the more hyperbolic letters printed by the *Review* likened the integration plan to a communist conspiracy. "The destruction of our neighborhood school system is part of a larger scheme to take children away from the influences of their parents," wrote one resident, who called integration "'Sovietization.' Russia has done it for years."[40] As noted earlier, three schools in Skokie, a predominantly Jewish suburb bordering Evanston to the west, fell within the boundaries of District 65. Prevented from buying or renting homes in Evanston, members of this community may have felt taken advantage of. Charges were made that the integration plan was rigged to make Skokie schools a "place to transport Negroes."[41]

Busing to the new LAB School was voluntary. Busing for blacks was not. CACI held a series of informational meetings to address parent concerns. Because virtually all of the children who attended the all-black Foster School would be dispersed to other institutions, it was the site of the first meeting. In the beginning reservations amounted to little more than concerns about greater walking distances. Objecting mostly to the distance many of their children would have to walk because they did not meet the criteria for busing, some parents expressed willingness to pay for transportation. John Haugabrook, the parent of a child attending Foster, received enthusiastic applause from the audience when he declared, "We would like to see our kids transported, and we are willing to pay for it." Mrs. R. A. Doolin believed transportation was the parents' responsibility: "These are your children and mine—not theirs, it's up to you to see that your child gets to school."

The question of public and private responsibility would divide the community as the desegregation process moved forward. District officials expected parents to oppose busing and were surprised when instead they worried about children walking. Although he was sympathetic, Joseph E. Hill, Foster School principal, believed that "whenever it is practical and possible, children should be allowed to walk to school." Hill had the foresight to understand that children "have a more difficult time becoming an integral part of a school when they are taken in and out on a bus schedule. Interaction between classmates is what brings about meaningful integration. It may be a little sacrifice but a mile is not as far for children as we may think." Coffin placated parents by promising to discuss paid routes with bus companies where there was sufficient demand and to consult the police department about the possibility of increasing the number of crossing guards.[42]

Urging black parents to support integration and approve busing, the NAACP, along with other civil rights groups, circulated flyers reminding parents of sacrifices being made in southern states. "Remember the children of Granada, Mississippi walked to school in spite of all opposition," one such flyer read.[43] Most blacks supported busing, according to a survey of families living in Foster and Dewey areas. Approximately two hundred families were surveyed, and 92 percent of respondents whose children would be bused to integrate schools expressed no objections to the plan. Those who opposed busing said they preferred that their children walk. They also worried about the lack of lunch facilities. When, with overwhelming support, the board voted to approve the transportation plan, CACI's final task was complete. By the middle of the first year of Coffin's term, an integration plan in place,

FIGURE 2.5 Assistant Principal Bob Dawkins assists children off the bus at LAB School. Bernie is pictured on the far left. Courtesy of Bernie Foster.

the commission was dissolved. The superintendent praised CACI: "I have never before worked with such a dedicated group." He called it a "gratifying experience."[44]

Every morning Bernie and his mother Jackie waited on the corner of Elmwood and Crain for Robinson's yellow school bus. Jackie enrolled Bernie in Head Start, a federally funded preschool operating out of LAB.[45] She worked at Head Start, but couldn't afford a car. Her family met the federal guidelines for the program, and she knew the difference it could make academically for her son. When the bus arrived, she'd take his small hand and help him board. Before they took a seat she'd greet the driver, Jesse. The Robinsons were Evanston royalty; "their whole family drove most of the buses." Bernie felt her love but was also embarrassed by their routine. "I remember people teasing me 'cause I used to ride the bus on my mother's lap." Jackie's workday ended later than Bernie's, so she didn't make the return trip with him. Instead she relied on Jesse to get Bernie and his sister Tina to a neighbor's house:

I used to have to go a half a day, so they would bring me home on the bus, and they would take me to a babysitter that was around the corner from us. Tina and I, we both had to go to the babysitter, and we didn't like it, so we would jump out of the window and run home, and our bus driver realized that we didn't like it. One day we snuck out of the window as soon as we got there—the bedroom window. Because she would make us go in there and lay down, we'd open the window and climb out. Jesse was the one that told my mom that we didn't like this daycare, and we told her we didn't like it 'cause the lady's kids used to pee in the bed and then she would try to make us go lay in it and we'd go, "Oh no." When the bus driver caught us that day, I think he took us back to school, or he dropped us off at our house and made sure we got in, and then he told our mother the next day; she eventually got us out of there.

Bernie would have preferred playing with school friends, but residential segregation and the busing employed to circumvent it limited these relationships. Children were permitted to use school telephones to arrange after-school visits, and they were allowed to ride to friends' homes on the bus. Still, white parents remained reluctant to allow their children to play in black neighborhoods. When the school bell rang, "we got on the bus and came home, and we played in our own neighborhood," Bernie told me.

Carla's walk home from Miller took her in the opposite direction from her black friends, who lived on the other side of the tracks. Fred sat at the desk behind Ronny's in a third-grade classroom at Dewey. They became fast friends. Fred was his "very best friend for many, many, many years," Ronny told me, but there were limitations to the friendship. During the week they couldn't spend time together because Fred "lived far away" on the west side, "way over by the high school." They didn't "hang out until the weekends . . . when maybe he'd sleep over or I'd sleep over at his house." At Central, Prince had trouble making white friends because they lived in different neighborhoods. The only time they socialized was during structured activities like Cub Scouts. "Every once in a while I would go to their house and play," he said, but that didn't happen often because it required a plan and parental approval. Socializing with black children was more spontaneous and natural for Prince: "I would actually go to their house and play ball, whatever." He didn't have to prearrange play dates with black classmates; "it was just anytime you go by, and most of the other time it was like 'Can you come over?'"

Jesse expressed a deep trust in what school authorities were calling a "unique experiment." Transferred out of Foster to Orrington, Jesse explained, "I fit the profile of one of the guys that would be easy to come into the integration because I got along with pretty much anybody, so they asked my mom if it would be okay." Jesse believes his chances in life improved when he was singled out: "They thought I was one of the gooder kids, so they wanted me to have a better chance so they bused me out over to Orrington School." Traveling on the bus gave Jesse a rare opportunity to leave the west side. "I got to leave the neighborhood and then go to another neighborhood, and then I would come back to the neighborhood once school was over." He thought the learning environment was better at Orrington. "It wasn't as much distractions in school. I had a lot of kids in my classroom at Foster that disturbed the class a lot, and you really couldn't learn; a lot of kids they wasn't getting the upbringing that I was getting from my mom and dad, because their parents either were out of the house or just didn't care."

Chip had one year left at Foster School before authorities decided to transfer him to Willard for fifth grade. He remembers arriving at his new school on the first day. "I kind of felt like we were—I wouldn't say caged animals, but the white kids and their parents were out there, and the buses pulled up, and everybody's mouths are closed, but their eyes are wide open, and they're looking." In the end it went smoothly—"No riots," he joked. During the late 1950s, southern schools had erupted in violence over school desegregation. Thus Evanstonians viewed the absence of conflict in their hometown as a sign of northern antiracism. School lunch policies would prove them wrong. While busing was stirring controversies in Evanston, it did not generate the same fury that was beginning to unfold over school lunches.

Noontime Jitters

Compact cities along with a deep belief in the domestic ideal explains why elementary schools in the North were built without cafeterias. An expansion of public education during the 1920s increased the number of schools, but most were designed using the neighborhood model. Structure supported ideology when city planners by and large assumed that mothers would prepare lunch at home for their school-aged children. Originating during the Depression under informal arrangements, urban school lunchrooms were marked by a class divide. They were housed in separate buildings and were operated by women's charities to feed the working poor.[46] The presence of malnourished youth prompted President Harry S. Truman to establish the permanent, federally funded National School Lunch Program in 1946. The program provided free or reduced-cost meals to needy children.[47] President Dwight D. Eisenhower increased the school lunch budget in 1954 and added the Special Milk Program for children outside of meal plans. In 1966 President Lyndon B. Johnson signed the Child Nutrition Act (CNA), establishing funds for the Free Breakfast Program and extending the milk program. These compensatory programs were moot, however, in communities with schools that didn't have lunchrooms. Under government provisions, federal funds could not be used to construct, expand, or rent food service facilities.[48] Furthermore, the federal government refused to intervene in municipal affairs. Local officials, left to decide whether or not to take advantage of programs, often did not, choosing instead to preserve community tradition. Northern liberals understood these programs as expansions of New Deal social safety nets. Civil rights activists made school lunches a public policy issue. Where they were not provided, black children and their mothers, who often held jobs outside the home, suffered disproportionately. Tight budgets, the high cost of land, and unavailability of federal funds all contributed to the reluctance of local authorities to build additions onto schools. Like other middle-class suburbs where white women did not enter the workforce in large numbers, Evanston preferred to uphold conservative customs.

Evanston's school boards resisted requests for lunch programs at elementary schools for many years. They went so far as to ignore the United Community Services Study of the Latch-Key Child (1964, updated 1967), which uncovered a serious need for them. With integration, however, they couldn't afford to ignore it any longer. Black pupils in grades K–5 lived too far from the five bused schools to go home for lunch. They would have to bring sandwiches to school in lunch boxes or brown paper bags. Both parents and teachers asked the school board to come up with a more substantial and inclusive solution. When the issue, an unanticipated side effect of busing, was raised during informational sessions, Coffin tried to stifle further inquiry, insisting that the board make a "deliberate attempt to keep the lunch issue separate from integration."

At least one parent wondered why the board was compartmentalizing the lunch issue: "I can't think of a better way to integrate the world than to sit down and eat together."[49] Presumably Coffin understood that school lunches called for a deeper commitment to integration than busing, and a change in policy might hurt larger efforts to desegregate.

In search of a solution, the board approved a trial sack lunch program at Central School for the academic year prior to integration. Seventy-three black and white children who did not have supervision during the lunch period participated. Volunteers from the PTA monitored them while they ate. Temporary facilities were furnished with card tables and folding chairs that were easy to assemble and break down for storage. According to the school's principal, Francis S. Vogel, "The children were well behaved and the time spent setting up and cleaning after lunch was less than anticipated."[50] Most important,

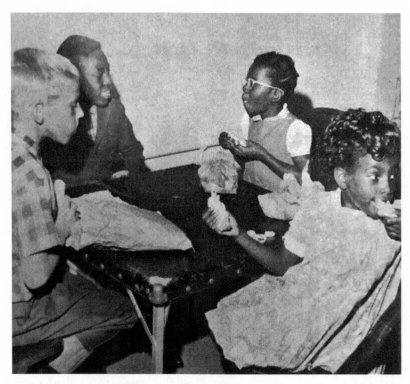

FIGURE 2.6 Children sit at card tables eating sack lunches because elementary schools were built without cafeterias. *Evanston Review,* September 21, 1967.

according to board stipulations, the program did not interfere with normal school activities and did not inconvenience teachers. Good reviews turned bad later that summer, however, when the Central School PTA issued a contradictory report that attempted to dissuade the board from expanding the program. "The advantages of this program greatly outweigh its disadvantages," the report admitted. But, it immediately asserted, "we do not feel this program should be open to everyone. The problems would be multiplied many times if that were the case."[51] The report foreshadowed the extent to which some members of the community would try to contain school integration.

Loy Landers, Miller School principal, supported a more open and inclusive lunch plan. Like other administrators, Landers wanted to accommodate elementary school students who lived more than three-fourths of a mile away from school: "This is quite a distance to walk, and we also hate to see bused children forced to eat alone."[52] Carla and

Earl, who were both Miller students, would benefit from his perseverance. Several years later, when Carla's mother started working outside
of the home, her children would need to take advantage of the sack
lunch program. Earl, too, utilized the program, and while we can only
assume, it's probably true that he preferred the company of his classmates to eating alone.

Both students actively participated in school programs. Two years
after desegregation, Earl and two of his classmates were chosen to represent the newly integrated student body. Dressed in a shirt and tie,

FIGURE 2.7 Friends Sally, Earl, and Amy pose for a picture at Miller School. *Evanston Review,*
May 22, 1969.

Earl must have been proud to be featured in the paper with his class-mates Sally and Amy. They posed holding a poster promoting a school fair. Miniature train rides, refreshments, movies, and games would keep children occupied while their parents purchased baked goods and plants and attended a white elephant auction and art show. Certainly Principal Landers would be present to enjoy the day with the students he cared deeply for.

Like Landers, editors of the *Review* endorsed an open lunch plan. An op-ed piece published in February 1967 argued for a program that would take into account practical problems such as working mothers and inclement weather.[53] The following week the paper's editors went further, favoring expansion to all schools for the upcoming academic year.[54] District 65 parents concurred: 2,500 of the 3,000 respondents to a PTA questionnaire indicated that Evanston children would benefit from a supervised lunch program at school.[55]

The school board remained unimpressed. Power rested in the hands of a white conservative majority: four of seven members were from a non-black, non-poor, non-young ward in northwest Evanston. At one time or another, three of these four had served as board president. Thus, notwithstanding institutional and public enthusiasm, the school board voted 5–2 against a more accessible plan.

While states had always appropriated money for buildings, teacher salaries, and textbooks, lunch had been considered a family responsi-bility. Some believed that communal feeding was part of a dangerous triumph of socialism. A lunch program might weaken the spirit of in-dividualism, or so some members of the board thought. Government interference in private matters was among dissenters' chief concerns. Feeding children in school, they claimed, would be a first step in the intrusion of government into citizens' kitchens. Parents, not schools, were responsible for serving meals.

Donald H. Farquharson stated emphatically, "I am not in favor of sack lunches for everyone."[56] He added, "The fact that some children have no adequate supervision at home at noon is a personal problem, not a district concern. The fact that the five school lunch programs will be segregated should have been thought of when we considered break-ing up boundaries."[57]

John J. Carver agreed: "These things snowball. We will see the ex-pansion of this program in short order, and it will be a babysitting bur-den on the taxpayer, teacher, and administrator."[58]

Farquharson and Carver voiced concern about the district's legal re-sponsibilities for children and lunchroom volunteers. The board's only black member, Allwyn H. Gatlin, abstained from voting for a plan for bused Negroes. He, like others, understood that the board's objectives should link larger educational goals with integrated lunch programs: "We believe that the education of children includes their intellectual, physical, emotional, and social growth."[59] Lawrence Lavengood voted reluctantly for the limited plan, submitting that any program short of his proposal for opening the program to everyone would "discriminate by schools or race or both."[60]

The goals of integration went beyond racial balance in the schools to include enhanced interpersonal relationships. Eating lunch together would give students the opportunity to socialize, talk over morning events, and form friendships. There were other benefits to be had. Education encompasses the development of the whole child. The lunchroom could indoctrinate children in social customs, teaching manners, conversational skills, and housekeeping duties. Lunchroom volunteers might pique an interest in social service and civic duty.

The *Review's* Public Forum section reprinted letters from the community. Mr. and Mrs. Paul Brummel wrote, "A policy of integrating Negro children into the academic program but segregating them during the social lunch hour is self defeating." Another resident wrote, "We have fallen short of our obligation to children being bused to the five receiving schools. These children are now relegated to a segregated lunch hour. How does this improve their emotional or social growth? What does this do for the Negro child's self image?"[61] With no practical resolution in sight, the buses rolled out on September 7, 1967. The media covered the momentous occasion: "A milestone in Evanston history was passed quietly last Thursday as nearly 10,000 children attended their first day of classes in 20 fully integrated primary and junior high schools. . . . For about 435 Negro children, former Foster and Dewey students, the day began with a ride on one of 11 buses to Dawes, Lincoln, Oakton, Orrington, or Willard schools." Mothers dressed their children in "sweaters or light jackets to keep out the chill in the early morning air," then waited with them until they were safely on board. Students reportedly rode to their new destinations in silence. They weren't as anxious about integration as adults. These children were excited by their bus ride and the cartoon characters—Dick Tracy, the Green Hornet, the Man from U.N.C.L.E.—pictured on their "brightly colored metal boxes."[62]

Interviewed at the day's end, Coffin said he was "delighted with the smooth opening." "Now that physical integration has been accomplished, the removal of barriers between the races, or psychological integration, will be the next major goal for the district." Referring to both children and their parents, Coffin said, "In many cases, whites are making Negro friends for the first time in their lives." When asked by a reporter whether he expected children to educate their parents about integration, Coffin replied that he hoped for some "rub off" here too. Joseph Hill, newly appointed assistant superintendent, added: "Attitude changes are expected to precede any changes in academic achievement."[63]

As predicted, the detrimental psychological effects of segregated sack lunch programs were exacerbated by district-wide integration. "Appalled," Mr. and Mrs. Townsend wrote a letter to the paper: "Our son's school (Walker) receives busloads of Negro youngsters in the morning. They attend classes, eat in a ghetto-type room while their white classmates go home for the 'warm meals and break in the school day' that are the ostensible reasons there is no school lunch program, and immediately after school they are bused away."[64]

The following week, the school's PTA president corrected the Townsends' allegations in the local media. Apparently Walker was busing black children home for lunch. Those who were eating at school were part of a "special services class."

The Townsends apologized for the misunderstanding but did not back down from asking for a comprehensive lunch program. Fed up with thinly veiled excuses, they wrote: "Please don't answer with that 'neighborhood school system,' 'healthy walk,' 'teachers wouldn't like it' series of excuses." Other published letters asked the board to reconsider its position because of the busing costs being incurred by parents and the dangerous traffic on routes that some children walked to get home.[65]

Racially segregated sack lunch programs raised a number of class-based issues. The integration plan had been in operation for less than a month when white parents who thought both busing and lunch policies were discriminatory against their own children inundated the board with letters, phone calls, and postcards.[66] Some genuinely needed their children to stay at school for lunch; others thought integration policies amounted to nothing more than reverse discrimination. Suddenly, components of the integration plan had become rights that were being denied to white citizens. An editorial piece in the *Review* warned that exclusionary procedures might jeopardize school desegregation: "Parents of pupils who are not permitted to bring sack lunches are likely to become antagonistic toward the integration plan, feeling their children have been slighted in favor of the bused pupils."[67] The paper printed the following letter from a disgruntled resident as an example:

This busing of children to integrate is definitely discriminating against white chil-dren in poorer neighborhoods. We are taxed for our schools by assessed valuation of our property. Why shouldn't those living in more expensive neighborhoods be getting a better education for their children? They are paying more for it. And why shouldn't the white children living in poorer neighborhoods be bused to a better school? If we are to have busing then it will become necessary to revise the taxation for schools to be fair to all residents.[68]

At a special board meeting held on September 25, Mrs. Paul Stein, chair of the Citizen's Committee for an Adequate Lunch Program steering committee, presented a report to the board: "We feel the present lunch program can only fill community needs if it is expanded to include children of working mothers, if safety and distance factors are taken into consideration, and if the present lunch program is integrated."[69] Stein's report indicated a growing awareness of the increasing numbers of working women.

The community's patriarchal belief in the nuclear family was being shaken by meals served outside the home. Enmeshed in the rise of a "culture of domesticity," some residents were adamant that a woman's place was in the home, and by extension the neighborhoods they de-fined as they walked children to and from school. Diluting traditional gender roles was a slippery slope that might culminate in the state's taking over all childrearing practices. Elite perspectives cut across ra-cial boundaries. A CACI committee member, Helen Cooper, stated in her letter to the *Review*, "We agree that it would be best if every child could go home to a mother, or to a maid, who has prepared a good lunch for him. This is what happens in many district 65 homes." A member of the black elite, Cooper privileged homemakers as children's primary caregivers, with working-class women as an acceptable alter-native. She didn't consider where the maid's children ate. Black—as op-posed to white—women's labor outside the home was deemed accept-able in another letter: "Many Negro mothers have to work and should be encouraged to do so in order to promote values of independence and self-help long regarded as necessary to overthrow the dependency fostered by welfare programs."[70]

Harking back to the ideals of Republican Motherhood, a concept de-veloped by clubwomen at the turn of the century, one woman insisted that home-cooked meals transmitted democratic values from mother to child and were a part of the education and socialization needed to form good citizens:

I believe home lunches to be a wonderful thing for children 6–10—one of the advantages of a neighborhood school system. Home lunches are an excellent opportunity for unburdening problems that develop during the morning with classmates, teachers, or schoolwork. The walk home gives youngsters an opportunity to burn up energy or restlessness stored up during classroom sitting. Linking a sack lunch program to integration is a mistake. I see no connection. Mothers who don't want responsibility of being home for lunch surely cannot justify it by linking it with integration. Ideally, bused children soon will be invited to homes of children in the neighborhood. A home lunch together would be of much greater benefit to both children.[71]

This contributor also relied on a paternalistic definition of school integration. She implicated working mothers, accusing them of using integration as an excuse to seek employment outside the home. Her opinion was representative of a segment of the community that could not be easily dismissed. Another letter, written by a former elementary school teacher, added to this perspective: "The child who goes home at lunch is a far more teachable creature each afternoon than the child who has spent his noon hour in the company of 50–200 peers."[72]

Because there was a contradiction between the community's social imagination and the reality of everyday life, children fell through the cracks. The United Community Services Study of the Latch-Key Child found that hundreds of youngsters went unsupervised during lunchtime. These findings were published in the *Review*, revealing the conditions some children were facing: "The 'lucky' ones go home. They are the ones whose mothers trust them with a key to the house or apartment, or who leave the door unlocked. Others go to a neighborhood restaurant or a food store where they fill up on potato chips, candy, and bubble gum. Some just wander around until it is time to go back to school." One youngster ate lunch on his back porch. Working mothers, too, were paying the price for a stubborn community: "The mother who is forced to work to support her family could stop fretting between noon and 1:00 p.m. about whether her child remembered (a) to be careful when pouring his hot soup; (b) to not answer the doorbell to strangers when he's alone; and (c) to turn off the gas." Women bore the brunt of responsibility. The article also included tales of a widow who had to work, a mother forced to work evenings so that she could be home with her child during the lunch hour, students who ate at their mother's office, and relatives or neighbors who were paid to watch schoolchildren during the noon break.[73]

Children without noontime provisions were stigmatized when they were accused of "breaking the law" by bringing their lunches to school "illegally." An article printed in the *Review* focused on two schools where these alleged activities were taking place. Robert Gilbert, the principal of Kingsley School, opted to defy authorities when he decided not to "send the children, mostly Negroes, home to empty houses." Instead, he allowed them to eat on the stage of the school's auditorium. David Haggstrom, Willard School's principal, was also making do under less than ideal circumstances when he used Kendall College students to help supervise bused black students who had to stay at the school to eat their lunch. According to Haggstrom, "The students eat in three, approximately 20-minute shifts. While one group is eating, the Kendall students supervise the others on the playground."[74]

With pressure mounting, school authorities agreed to hear testimony from concerned parties. One resident stressed academic success as impetus: "During class time, attention must be given to the teacher and to the work at hand. Clearly, the founding of friendships can best flourish over the lunch table."[75] A psychiatrist claimed that a comprehensive lunch program would increase the likelihood that "students would eat a more nutritious lunch"; other benefits listed were "relaxation and pleasure, rather than walking and rushing to get home and back to school; and development of social interaction skills."[76]

Convinced that some change was necessary, the board agreed to broaden the sack lunch program, making individual schools responsible. Parents submitted applications. Children whose school attendance areas had been changed and whose distance from home to school was increased due to integration were given priority, as were "children of working mothers and those with impaired health."[77]

Finally, one and a half months into the first integrated academic year, the school board endorsed an expanded version of the limited sack lunch program by approving 757 applications. Redistricting, parental employment, and serious health problems were the top three reasons given by parents seeking lunch privileges for their children.[78] The onus was placed on PTAs to develop, implement, and support programs for their individual schools. The board agreed to pay $7,731 to cover the cost of card tables, chairs, garbage cans, and salaries for lunchroom supervisors.[79] This wasn't enough to cover all costs, so programs relied heavily on volunteers. With experience from the trial period behind them, parents from Central School were the first to submit a plan to the superintendent. Lincoln and Dewey Schools followed suit. Editors at the *Review* supported the initiative: "Like the integration plan, the sack lunch program is an idea whose time finally arrived in Evanston. We are pleased that the school board recognized this and added a new dimension to its goal of meeting the changing needs of the community."[80] By December, the school board had approved nine new or expanded programs. The *Review*'s headline read: "1,712 Pupils in District Carry Lunch."[81]

Board members who voted against the expansion protested that "the problem with children not being supervised when sent home was a community problem and should be taken care of by some other agency." They suggested that parents invite children needing a place to eat lunch into their homes. Alternatively, churches, community centers, and other institutions adjacent to schools might develop lunch programs for students. Allwyn Gatlin, who had abstained from voting for a limited program earlier in the year, called the idea of white parents taking black children into their homes for lunch "paternalism." He resented that black children were being blamed: "The problem was not entirely one of integration, because white children of working parents also have the problem."[82]

Had the community compromised its values? Could mothers continue to fulfill their expected roles despite being separated from their children at the lunch hour? Suggested menus that appeared in the newspaper reveal an unrealistic assessment of family budgets and mothers' time. Stressing variety, creativity, a balanced meal, and the importance of "little touches," the paper published recipes for sandwiches. The middle-class ideal of domesticity called upon women to instill the virtue of proper eating in their families. "Mothers know that lunch should be interesting, tasty, and nutritious. But sandwiches to make five days a week for one or more children can be a defeating challenge to even the most conscientious mother," so the paper enlisted experts including home economists and nutritionists from the Milk Foundation and the American Institute of Baking. A photo showed homemakers how a proper lunch should be presented: a sandwich, frosted cupcake, and bottle of milk were displayed on a doily, along with the suggestion that mothers add "a colorful napkin for fun."

An image of a white schoolgirl carrying her books in one hand and a sack lunch in the other adorned the decidedly bland Anglo-Saxon menu. The image chosen by the paper's staff is illustrative of how cultural hegemony works. Antonio Gramsci argues that through the era-

sure of the dominated group, in this case the black community, one social class can dominate a culturally diverse society by imposing culture
(values and norms) so that its perspective is viewed as normal.[83] The
choice to use a picture of a white girl was incongruous with lunch controversies centering on black children. Furthermore, the girl's happy-
go-lucky demeanor belied the reality of the situation. Needless to say,
not every mother and child fit so neatly into Evanston's model of the
ideal nuclear family.

On some level children must have known that adults were bicker-
ing, but it was the day-to-day strain on their friendships that made
the most impact on their lives. Chip made his first white friend, Brian,
at Willard School, where he was bused every day from the west side.
While Brian went home for lunch, Chip stayed on school grounds to
eat. One day Brian invited Chip over for lunch. When Brian's brother
told him that he was the first black person to eat at their house, Chip
felt awkward. When recounting the incident later he said with a rueful
smile, "Probably some had worked there." Chip liked school, especially
science and math. At Willard and later at Haven Middle School he took
music lessons. His mother didn't allow him to play with friends until he finished his homework. She really "cracked down" during the
school year. "After you do your homework, you can go out," she'd tell
him, "and when the street lights come on, you'd better either be putting your foot on the stair or already be in the house." One weekend
night she let Brian sleep over. The tables were turned: "I believe he was
the first white person that had come and spent the night at my house."
The next morning Brian's parents came to pick him up. They lived too
far away for their son to walk home.

Escalating divorce rates in the 1960s were partly responsible for
drawing white middle-class women into the workforce. Carla remembers that eating lunch at home was always accompanied by her
mother's humor. "I'd come in and it would be like 'beans and hotdogs.'
I'd go, 'Just what I wanted,' and she'd say, 'My hand was going for the
one can . . . and somehow I was drawn to . . . I just . . . I could sense it!'"
When Carla's parents divorced in 1971, her mother entered the paid
workforce. She promptly enrolled her daughter in the school lunch
program. Eating lunch together gave children the chance to laugh and
have fun. Gianna, Carla's friend, always had a "good sandwich" and a
"garlic dill pickle." Kids gathered around Gianna; "everyone loved the
pickle, and she would cut this pickle into little pieces and give everybody a piece."

With little effort Candy crossed her backyard, and the alley behind it, arriving at her elementary school on time every day. Her house was adjacent to the schoolyard. At lunchtime she went home to eat a hot meal prepared by her mother, who didn't have to work outside the home. Energized, she was ready to return for afternoon classes. She recalled, "When I heard the bell ring I knew I had to dash out my back door and get to school." When the day ended, Candy's friends came over to play without leaving their neighborhood or the school vicinity.

Earl's parents were members of Evanston's working poor and struggled to provide food for his midday meal. While the number of subsidized lunch programs was growing in other regions of the country, free or low-cost meals for the poor were still a long way from coming to fruition in Evanston. Children from economically disadvantaged backgrounds had to fend for themselves. His cousin Jesse describes Earl's experiences:

I really wasn't a bully to the extent of my cousin Earl—now Earl was [a] bully. Earl used to take kids' lunches because there was six kids in their house and . . . [they had] problems with food, and so he get hungry, and he go to school and all these kids eating these nice lunches and they got a little treat in their lunch box and Earl would take it. He was a good kid, but he was a bully so he would take stuff. I never took too much stuff from anybody, guys just liked me, and they see I didn't have much and they be like "Well, Jesse, you can have this extra sandwich," or "You can have this apple or banana—I don't like it, if you want it you can have it."

Evanston's school integration plan failed Jesse and Earl. Forced to intimidate other children so that he could eat lunch, Earl was learning his value from a school system that was reluctant to create an equal playing field for all its students.

On the front lines of integration, teachers urged the board to participate in the National School Lunch Program. Studies had concluded that students performed better in school if they were given a nutritious meal.[84] Hungry children like Earl and Jesse "alternate between being listless and weary and frustrated and angry. They are often discipline problems."[85] Coffin worried that these issues might undermine the positive effects of integrated academic spaces. He told the media that he supported a "federally-supported hot lunch program so all children can get good balanced meals."[86] Busy mothers as well as children who would no longer be obliged to carry a lunch bag would benefit.

The American Food Service Association estimated that at least 6.5 million poor children, mostly in cities and rural areas, still had no access to free lunches in 1968. Opponents of a national program warned against "inculcating in little children at the most impressionable period of their lives the idea that they can get something for nothing from Uncle Sam."[87] Most urban schools still had no cafeteria or kitchen facilities, and few had budgets that could encompass a free meal program. For school districts struggling financially, undertaking school lunch programs gradually was, in part, justifiable. Evanston, a wealthy suburb, could not make these claims. Lunch programs were associated with relief or public charity and carried a stigma that Evanston's boosters discouraged. Distinguishing itself, Evanston did not immediately take advantage of federal assistance to offer subsidized meals or milk to schoolchildren.[88] Social services were antithetical to the suburban ideal.

Before the end of the first year of integration, Martin Luther King Jr. was shot dead. While Evanston was mostly sheltered from riots that erupted around the country and on Chicago's southwest side, Prince, who lived across the street from Nichols Middle School, remembers an angry mob setting fire to the building: "I just remember the fire trucks coming and seeing the place burn. What I was hearing was that they shot Martin Luther King and Memphis was a bad place to be, they hated black people." The institution was a symbol of wealth and power in the midst of a disenfranchised community, and therefore a target for discontent. As a young child, Prince was learning about his place in the racial hierarchy.

Educators scrambled to relieve racial tensions and help children cope with and understand the evils of racial prejudice. In Riceville, Iowa, a third-grade teacher divided her class using eye color to distinguish between privileged and oppressed groups.[89] In Evanston officials developed Project Prejudice. LAB students were the first to experiment. Children were divided into two groups and wore colored ribbons to designate their affiliation. A green group was given preferential treatment. Those in the blue group were treated like second-hand citizens. They were ignored and the last ones to be admitted to class. After the first day, children went home "angry, bewildered, or discouraged." The next day the groups exchanged ribbons. At the end of the week, children discussed and wrote about their feelings. Reportedly, some students did not object to being ostracized because "they got attention, and it was better to get attention by being bad than to get no attention at all." This phenomenon was common, according to a psychiatrist assisting the program: "It is important to work with Negro children at an early age so they do not feel there are rewards for being bad. . . . Ghetto children must be highly rewarded for being good so they will feel it is more worthwhile to achieve than not to achieve." Again black children were not only being asked to assimilate but being cast as the problem.[90]

The following month a similar exercise was conducted at Central School. Also progressive, Central had abandoned grading altogether. More than three hundred students were divided into blue and orange groups, with an equal number of students from each "race." Students wearing blue ribbons were given privileges. They enjoyed candy, recess, and freedom to move about as they pleased. Drinking fountains were marked "For Blue Only." Both teachers and students openly discriminated against those wearing orange ribbons. Members of the orange group "learned a lesson the painful way" when they had to be accompanied to the washroom and were not trusted with books. Some teachers went so far as to tear up papers and break pencils belonging to orange group members. The next day, the two groups switched places. For two days the pot boiled at Central. Playground fights and racial name-calling increased. Children went home crying to their mothers, refusing to return to school. During the last three days of the week, they were "debriefed" and encouraged to talk about their feelings. One pupil stated, "I hated every minute of it."

Prince was in third grade when he participated in the program:

Some of the kids had on an orange ribbon, some of the kids had on a yellow ribbon, and the kids that were with the orange ribbons were treated real nice by the teacher. And the other kids—everything they asked to do was "no." Then I remember coming back to school the next day and that was reversed. I remember asking the teacher why that was, and she said to me, "We're just trying to show you guys how things are different for one group of people and another group of people, when you pick out a certain group of people."

Using empathy as a pedagogical tool, the district hoped to teach children a difficult lesson about discrimination and prejudice.[91]

Black history and culture was employed to correct the district's Eurocentric curriculum. Bernie described LAB as a "big mixing pot." The diverse student body was the "experimental part" of the school, not the curriculum. He was partly right. As a young boy he saw the difference between his school and others. LAB was "trying to do things that other schools weren't," he told me. "I don't think the classes were as big as the rest of the schools; they spent more time with you," he added. The school was eventually renamed for Martin Luther King Jr., and Bernie associated the change with the curriculum. He learned black history and "a lot about the civil rights issues." His class took the train to Springfield, Illinois. The field trip lasted all day; "we went that morning and then we came back that evening—it was pretty neat. I remember going to Lincoln's house." The hometown hero had lived in Springfield with his family until he was elected president in 1860. Three years later he freed the slaves. At the time Bernie wasn't impressed; he was more interested in "bothering the girls" on the train.

As the first integrated school year drew to an end, the argument against lunch programs shifted to economics. The sheer magnitude of demand no longer made a volunteer-based operation feasible. Parents were "unable to provide the continuity and reliability of personnel which are essential to the success of the program."[92] The school board narrowly approved a budget of $22,500, but this amount was not enough to staff lunchrooms and subsidize milk.[93] Tables and other lunchroom equipment needed to be purchased. The board also agreed to pay for a bookkeeper and added the federal milk support program, but the bulk of the cost was still borne by participants for the 1968–69 school year. A *Review* article published outlining these expenditures held "bused Negro students" responsible for increased costs. Black families were disproportionately carrying the burden of integration. Because of residential segregation their children had no choice but to eat lunch at school. White families also benefited from lunch programs. The next year, a two-hundred-page report titled "Change and School Building Needs: A Study of the Interrelation of Educational Processes and School Facilities" made even grimmer predictions. The study estimated the cost of adding lunchrooms to the sixteen elementary schools at well over two million dollars.[94]

With one year of integration behind it, District 65 organized its second summer institute. Central School principal Laval Wilson was named director. The board rejected a request from Coffin that all principals be required to attend. Participants received a stipend. Unlike the previous year, this time the primary focus was on a new curriculum and preparation of integrated resource materials. Ten crucial race issues were identified. Participants were divided in to small groups of five or six. Each group was assigned an issue and an expert consultant to help develop materials on the assigned subject. They produced two teacher's manuals: one containing main ideas, objectives, and bibliographies for staff, and the other a guide for teaching the topic using simple language for students and containing lesson plans and film suggestions. Groups also prepared a third manual; known as a unipac, it was a self-instructional activity book for students.

Experts from around the country participated. All points of view on race relations were represented. Thomas Sutton, president of Operation Crescent, characterized the conservative and right-wing perspective. Sociologist James Coleman epitomized the moderate middle. John Hope Franklin was back for a second year and cotaught "The Negro in American History" with Beatrice Young, director of education services for the Illinois Commission on Human Relations. Like the other experts, Franklin made a two-hour presentation to provide background information for all participants. Lectures were filmed so that teachers could watch them again and discuss them throughout the school year. Franklin and Young then served as consultants to six teachers responsible for writing history manuals and unipacs. Franklin also put the most crucial concepts into a thirty-minute film. Materials were developed to plug holes in the "white curriculum." So, for example, "Afro-American History" was not a unit in itself but a guide amending the social studies curriculum. This form of integration was considered extremely important. Jonathan Kozol, a teacher in Newton, Massachusetts, and the author of *Death at an Early Age*, cotaught "Black Power and Its Effects on Racial Integration" with Russell Meeks, a Black Power advocate and community leader on Chicago's west side. Parents were invited every Wednesday night to hear presentations.

The resulting teacher's manuals and unipacs were filled with innovative assignments and activities. Students were asked to discuss the meaning of vocabulary words such as *whitey, riot, militant, power, soul, brother, Tom, inferior, sister, honky, reactionary, Negro, Black Power,* and *conservative*. They were asked to define *busing, integration, segregation, desegregation,* and *de facto segregation*. Homework assignments included the following: "Look at everything around you at home and school and notice everything black and beautiful. Make a list" or "Listen to soul music." The manual gave teachers examples of active learning assignments such as producing a skit about SNCC and voter registration or having children eat lunch with a different person each day for a week. Civic engagement exercises were also incorporated. Teachers could invite a Black Power speaker to school or have students interview an African college student. Ideas for field trips were added, including visiting the Wall of Respect in Chicago.

Just as it had a year ago, in early September 1968 the *Review* covered the first day of school: "435 Negro children, former Foster and Dewey pupils, began the day with a ride on one of 10 buses to Dawes, Lincoln, Oakton, Orrington, or Willard schools." Doting mothers waited with their children for the buses. But this year's opening was different.

FIGURE 2.8 Social dancing was part of the innovative curriculum at Miller School. Photograph by Arnold Kapp.

Now the rides were routine. On the bus to Orrington, "five boys talked about last year's fights and their chances for becoming patrol boys this year. Last year, the 60 children on the bus rode 12 minutes practically without saying a word."[95] Jesse, who had transferred to Orrington from Foster, was more than likely on the bus. He would have been excited to leave his neighborhood again and have the world open up a little more.

Eventually the board was forced to recognize community needs and assume the total cost of lunch supervision, but this was not until a year later, for the 1969–70 school year. During the spring and summer of 1969 black families expressed concerns at a series of community meetings. The burden of school integration had been firmly placed in their laps. Small children had to walk long distances and cross dangerous streets to go to school. Children with poor diets were not reaching their full academic potential. Family income was determining safety and nutrition. These were some of the concerns expressed by parents of both races, along with educators and welfare officials, at meetings in the spring and summer. The district's Pupil Services Department translated them into a number of different proposals for consideration in the 1969–70 school year budget. At meetings held on June 23 and July 28, the school board responded by approving expanded programs to meet lunch and transportation needs: $143,055 to pay for busing of all elementary school children where enrollment was voluntary (with the exception of the LAB School) and $52,500 to pay the wages of lunchroom workers and supervisors for all twenty elementary schools and a program coordinator paid for by the district. Additionally, the district would take advantage of the federal Class A lunch program. The middle schools would offer hot lunches for 45 cents, and reduced-price or free lunches would also be available. Pupil Services made applications available to parents.[96]

The community gestured toward integration by busing black students to previously all-white schools but stopped short when it did not allow those same children to eat lunch together. A flawed lunch plan made desegregation look worse and function less well than it would have otherwise. Still, Evanston's desegregation plan was thoughtfully planned and carefully executed. Certainly some aspects were quite successful, such as the addition of innovative teaching, curriculum, and programming in the schools. Despite obstacles, black and white friendships were made and had lasting effects. Liberal elites did not abandon their schools by either fleeing Evanston or moving their children from public to private schools. Escape hatches like these were being used in other parts of the country, including Chicago, but not in Evanston.

Scattered throughout the school system in the years from kindergarten to fifth grade, our group would finally meet at Nichols Middle School, one of four in the district—but not before a year-long battle to save Gregory Coffin's job and, by extension, meaningful integration. Coffin hired and promoted black staff, recruited teachers eager to work in an integrated system, applied for Title IV funds for summer institutes, implemented sack lunch programs, and revised curricular materials, including tapes and films for parents, faculty, and classroom use, and in-service training manuals. This exhaustive set of activities didn't sit well with everyone.

THREE

The Coffin Affair

Evanston's star, it seemed, had never been higher. But then, a not-so-funny thing happened on the way to integration. The community-or a sizable element of it-got off the bandwagon.

JUNE SHAGALOFF, NATIONAL EDUCATION DIRECTOR, NAACP

By the summer of 1969, Evanston had desegregated all of its elementary and middle schools. Under Superintendent Gregory Coffin's watch, District 65 was well on its way to integrating. Coffin oversaw the elimination of an all-black school and achieved racial balance in the others. He applied for and received federal Title IV funds to run summer institutes preparing teachers and administrators for integration. He hired and promoted an impressive number of black administrators, teachers, and staff, not as a token of white liberalism but because they were qualified and talented. Sack lunch programs were in operation in all twenty of the kindergarten through fifth grade schools. The board had unanimously approved complete financial support for lunchroom workers and supervisors at each school as well as a program coordinator.[1] Coffin had materials revised to incorporate black heritage and provided in-service training programs for school employees. Under his leadership the number of extracurricular programs was growing and facilitating interracial friendships. Local supporters, civil rights groups, and dozens of educators around the country called him dedicated, courageous, and innovative.

Evanston was making incredible strides toward a fully integrated school system when the superintendent's performance was called into question. Coffin never had had the unqualified support of everyone. The city's schools were second to none, but some people thought he was ruining them. There were unspoken assumptions that racial mixing meant lower educational standards, good students weighed down by poor ones, and increased discipline problems. Opponents described Coffin as abrasive and incompetent. They accused him of mismanaging funds.

A Turtle Only Moves Ahead by Sticking His Neck Out!

Balding and potbellied Coffin was a chain smoker who wore bright shirts, plaid sports coats, and loafers to work. He spoke in a direct manner, his sentences uncluttered by school jargon. On occasion he was outspoken and impatient. Coffin was the first to admit that he was no diplomat, but directness was his way of getting things done. More than a dozen turtle figures could be seen on shelves in the superintendent's paneled office. The turtle would become the symbol associated with the movement to save his job. Coffin's favorite was carved out of wood and sat on a pedestal bearing the statement "A turtle only moves ahead by sticking his neck out." It was a reminder that if he wanted to make a difference he would have to take risks.

With the national spotlight on Evanston, Coffin's celebrity status was rising. Evanston's school system had earned a reputation for being one of the best in the country. Its primary schools even had libraries with trained librarians. *Who's Who in America* honored the superintendent for his significant contribution to society calling him "very much a man of the hour."[2] The citation was the only one that *Who's Who* awarded in the field of education. *Nation's Schools* magazine, too, commended Coffin for Evanston's integration plan, including "initiating parent operated sack lunch programs for the bused children."[3] The more attention Coffin received, the more irritated his detractors became.

Behind Coffin's back, people whispered that he had come to Evanston for personal aggrandizement or to make a name for himself. Yet Coffin never claimed to be the author of the desegregation plan and always credited the citizens who had initiated and designed it. He did, however, deserve credit for developing and implementing full integration. Alderman Quaife Ward, a former CACI member, went to the local media to set the record straight, embarrassing the superintendent in an open letter to the public:

Dr. Coffin was not on the District 65 scene when the Board of Education made the key decision to integrate the schools; he played a partial and secondary role to Dr. Chute and the Citizens Advisory Commission in developing the integration plan; he played a major role in its presentation to the District 65 Board of Education and a vital role in implementing the plan. In the interest of giving credit where it is due and with all deference to "Who's Who," I cite Dr. Oscar Chute, former superintendent of District 65, the District 65 Board of Education, the Citizens Advisory Commission, Dr. Gregory Coffin, and the citizens of District 65 for "a significant contribution to society.[4]

Criticism of Coffin's personality was a smokescreen for anti-integration motives. It was a backlash against the Coffin stamp: rigorous implementation, including hiring and promoting black staff, curriculum revision, a teacher's institute, and a lunch program.

Because of the district's pioneering role in school integration, Coffin was now in demand as a speaker. In November 1967 he delivered a speech at a conference sponsored by the US Commission on Civil Rights in the nation's capital. His lecture, "How Evanston, Illinois Integrated *All* of Its Schools," explained that Evanston was essentially conservative and not especially virtuous. Coffin summarized the frequent excuses people had for doing nothing about de facto segregation. Money was always at the top of the list, along with the claim that segregated schools were really just a housing problem. The thrust for integration, Coffin emphasized, came from people outside the white power structure. History demonstrates that people never willingly give up power or begin to share it. While Evanston's mayor and city council remained aloof, civil rights organizations demanded change, ultimately influencing the board of education.

The superintendent was severely criticized in the *Review*'s Public Forum for his remarks. Resident H. S. Sandler demanded an apology:

I do object to the tone of Dr. Coffin's remarks, to downgrading of the Evanston community spirit, and the particular innuendoes in his remarks, and specifically to the misstatement of the conditions existing by reference to the Mason-Dixon Line and ghettos. The colored citizens of Evanston have been here for many years, they do not live in ghettos, and the majority live in pleasant, well-kept surroundings. They always have had equal school opportunities in Evanston, with equal teacher qualifications.[5]

Ill will came to a head on June 23, 1968, when the school board sent a private censure to the superintendent, warning him to change his behavior or face consequences. Board members accused him of being arrogant and abrasive. They said he was uncooperative, unwilling to "play ball," and moving too fast. His job was in jeopardy because of it.

Several months later, the board members expressed their commitment to the integration plan but unhappiness with the superintendent. They extended his contract for just one year beyond 1969 and gave him a small two-thousand-dollar raise. They warned that his performance would come under review again in June. The superintendent was not happy with the terms, which he and others understood as an invitation to resign. Rumors that the board was out to stop integration increased. School board president John Carver tried to dispel them. Indeed the accusation was hard to prove, because the board had adopted the integration policy before Coffin was hired. Carver defended the small scale of Coffin's raise, citing the district's financial situation and a deficit of $750,000. A portion of Evanston was delighted with the announcement. Another portion, nearly all black residents, was appalled. They argued that underlying prejudices motivated efforts to remove Coffin from office. For this group, Coffin and quality integration were indivisible. There was little middle ground. The board was unprepared for the assault on its judgment.

Bennett Johnson, who had faced indignities in his youth at the segregated Varsity Theatre and YMCA, called Coffin the "symbol of Evanston's integration plan." Johnson, president of the Black Business and Professional Association (BBPA), claimed Coffin was being punished for appointing qualified black administrators to key posts. As noted, Coffin had actively recruited a wide range of black employees, including administrators, teachers, substitutes, teacher's aides, and secretaries.

The real issue, of course, wasn't integration. Everyone purportedly was for integration. The real issue was power—the control, distribution, and exercise of power. Before Coffin, the number of black professionals above the rank of teacher in the district had been one. With Coffin, that number rose to twelve. The jump was significant. It gave blacks new power and participation in decision making.[6] Several of the district's principals were black, as well as the assistant to the superintendent, Joseph Hill, and the curriculum co-coordinator of math and science, Charles A. Martin. "Although racism may not be the main issue in this controversy, it is part of the mixture," Johnson stated. He called Coffin "the hero of the black community."[7]

With little discernible improvement in the everyday lives of blacks, violence was sweeping the nation. Coffin continued to make public appearances. Stressing the urgency of integrated school systems in the context of inner-city disillusionment, he addressed twenty-five thousand school officials in Atlantic City, New Jersey, in March 1969: "Without truly equal educational opportunities for all boys and girls we can never have law and order, no matter how many policemen we hire or how many national guardsmen we bring into the cities in times of crisis. I can't help but wondering if the President will advocate 1,000 more teachers for the Washington, D.C. public schools as readily as he called for 1,000 more policemen in Washington."[8] Coffin warned that the ominous predictions of the Kerner Report would be converted to self-fulfilling prophecies: "We'll have two separate and unequal societies which will end up shooting at each other."[9]

A year later he delivered a speech to a meeting of the American Association of School Administrators, also held in Atlantic City. Coffin's title for this speech was "The Black Administrator and the Nation's Schools." There still weren't any black superintendents in a major US city, even though black enrollment in some places was above 50 percent. Coffin called for a hiring campaign under a new set of rules. Tokenism in the old tradition of Evanston was no longer acceptable. "To be a real leader in the black community today, a black man must be black. He must think and act in terms of what's good for black people." Coffin was calling for black community control.[10]

Back home, a visit from the Office of the State Superintendent of Public Instruction illustrated the extent to which Coffin was being vilified. State officials found that five Evanston principals lacked "supervisory certificates." The administrators in question "came up through the ranks in District 65" and had been promoted to their present positions by Coffin. The superintendent defended his decision: "As I see it there is no question about the merits and qualifications of these people."[11] Although some had been trained in fields other than education, four of the five had master's degrees. All of them were enrolled in certificate programs to comply with new state requirements. Within the year they would be certified.

The report also cited the district for "illegally using teacher aides to conduct classes." The state required aides to have at least thirty hours of college credit, and not all of them did. Many of those under question were black. To the innovative superintendent, pressing educational needs were more important than guidelines. The administration had hired blacks to help move school integration forward. They provided a sense of familiarity and consistency to black children and set examples of respect and authority for white students. While aides may have been used to "help one or two children," according to Coffin, they were not conducting classes; mostly they were riding the bus or shepherding children from one place to another.[12] After the visit from state authorities, the position was reclassified from teacher's aide to teacher's helper.

Together these accusations were serious. District 65 risked losing both state recognition and financial aid. Critiques made headlines, while news that the visitors were "generally pleased" and were impressed by the integration plan and the development of the LAB School was set under the page fold.[13] Coffin's enemies were more than happy to take negative comments out of context.

The superintendent's tireless efforts fueled the movement against him. The ultraconservative Northwest Evanston Homeowners' Association fanned the flames, calling the situation a crisis: "We hear that there is district-wide concern over: threatened loss of state recognition, students' fears for their own safety and their personal belongings, a large turnover of well-qualified teachers, and the failure to implement a discipline policy."[14] It went so far as to reprint an editorial from a July 1965 issue of the *Darien Review* in its newsletter. The editorial called for the replacement of Coffin, in part because of his Harlem school exchange program. Emboldened anti-Coffin school board members Buck, Gagen, Seyl, and Zimmerman, who made up the majority, resolved to terminate the superintendent's contract. Without warning, on the weekend preceding the board's regular monthly meeting in June, they informed minority members Fitzsimmons, Gatlin, and Lavengood of their decision. The news spread like wildfire.

A crowd of fifteen hundred people jammed into the Unitarian Church auditorium on June 23, 1969 to support their soon-to-be fired chief. Angry supporters, confident defenders of the board's actions, a resentful board, and Coffin himself listened to more than fifty speeches lasting well into the night. All but ten of the speakers urged, cajoled, threatened, and pleaded with the board not to fire Coffin. They included school principals, teachers, and staff, and members of church groups and community and neighborhood organizations. Cynthia Whiting, the educational chair for the Northwest Evanston Homeowners' Association, was one of the few to speak out against the superintendent. Given her position, Whiting's comments seemed vague and uninformed: "I don't trust the man," she said. "There's too much going on that I don't understand."

As midnight approached, tension grew. One would have thought the community had expressed its will in no uncertain terms. All waited breathlessly for the revelation of the grounds for firing Coffin. It came down to this: the board had experienced some interpersonal difficulty in working with him, and the four members making up the majority deemed this sufficient grounds for firing him. Three minority members thought such grounds weak. In the dying minutes of the last possible board meeting, indifferent to community sentiment, members voted 4–3 not to hire Coffin beyond June 30, 1970. The search for his successor would begin immediately. Although Coffin held an appointed position, an elected school board had the authority to decide whether or not to renew his contract. Elected officials who vote to desegregate tend not to get reelected; in this case an appointed superintendent hired to spearhead desegregation was losing his job.[15]

The community was shocked, because the board had pledged to work out its differences with Coffin, who himself had taken seriously the criticism of his personality by modifying his administrative style. Accusations about personality conflicts were obviously an excuse. Both Coffin and his supporters knew he was being fired because he was succeeding, not because he failed. The board was willing to mix the kids, but it bristled when Coffin presented staff and teacher resource manuals endorsing Black Power and encouraging students to think black. "The school board wanted to reshuffle bodies, Gregory Coffin wanted to reshape minds."[16] The members of the board majority were treating the public in the same abrasive manner in which it accused Coffin of treating them. They were not responsive to the people they were elected to serve. They never said they were against integration; on the contrary, they said they supported it. Yet they opposed numerous plans, programs, projects, and personnel that were essential to make integration work. The main issue was not Gregory Coffin's contract; it was high-quality integrated education.

Coffin asked that the charges against him be put in writing. The stage was set for a major community contest. All political hell broke loose in Evanston.

This Is an Army, We Are at War!

Organizations and counterorganizations sprung up overnight. Within two days Donald Lawson of the Evanston Urban League formed the Citizen's Committee for Coffin and District 65 (renamed Citizens for 65 when it became apparent that Coffin's personality was not the real issue). Within the week, Roy Wilkins, executive director of the NAACP, pledged his organization's support; the Independent Voters of

Illinois issued a statement supporting the superintendent; and North Evanston West Property Owners Association (NEW) formed to "give another voice to Northwest Evanston," a notoriously conservative section of town.[17] NEW charged that the board's vote to dismiss Coffin was unrepresentative of the community at large. The League of Women Voters issued a statement urging retention. The Evanston Human Relations Commission asked the board to reconsider. Coffin received telegrams of support from school superintendents and state commissioners across the country. The Evanston Black Caucus formed. A grassroots organization, the Black Caucus took its name from the revered but undemocratic predominantly white General Caucus of Community Consolidated School District 65 (Caucus), which was used to handpicking school board candidates. Cochairman Ronald Lee said the district's schools were "integrated on white man's terms" and called for a redistribution of power to include blacks in the decision-making process. Northwestern faculty gathered signatures on a petition supporting Coffin. Jill Newberger, the thirteen-year-old daughter of an alderman, felt underutilized at Citizens for 65 when she was asked to do nothing more than sweep and fetch sandwiches. Frustrated, she organized a youth group named X.

Residents expressed support for the beleaguered superintendent in the *Evanston Review*'s Public Forum. In one such letter Coffin was compared to other civil rights heroes: "Well Evanston has done it again! . . . Dr. Coffin came from the area of the country where the Kennedys are. Would John and Robert have been treated so badly if they had come here? They were 'friends of all peoples' too, you know."[18] Convinced that Coffin was being punished for integration, another resident wrote:

The school board meeting was outlandish. American capitalism's critics have always maintained that it sets "property rights" above "human rights." Here was a man acknowledged by friend and foe as a successful school integrator—"too fast," his opponents charged—apparently brought to book by a self-appointed regional property owners group and several board members. The very idea that in Evanston a school administrator should be in trouble for successfully integrating the schools must raise eyebrows all over the country.[19]

Some citizens were confused by the board's decision: "When I attended the board meeting Monday, June 23, I believed that perhaps I would be enlightened as to the board's possible motivation. I was not. No speaker or board member was able to provide the slightest

FIGURE 3.1 Hoping to retain the superintendent, pro-Coffin marchers chant, "We demand Greg and refuse to beg!" during summer 1969.

justification for firing a man whom all agreed is brilliant, dynamic, highly talented."[20]

A series of marches and motorcades were held to show support for Coffin and dramatize the issue to the community. The Reverends Charles Eddis and Jacob Blake urged the board to reexamine its decision. Disrupting commercial business, marchers walked from the Unitarian Church through the city's two major department stores, Wieboldt's and Marshall Field, to Fountain Square. Young, educated, and vocal, the Black Caucus warned that the actions of the board were the beginning of a trend toward resegregation. In protest, they organized a march and rally for July 11, 1969. That evening a crowd gathered at the corner of Church and Dodge, in the heart of the predominantly black west side. Together they marched down Church to Fountain Square, chanting, "We demand Greg and refuse to beg." Additionally, the Black Caucus urged parents to keep their children home on September 10, declaring it "Keep Coffin Day." Active and motivated, the Black Caucus also sponsored a forty-car caravan to drive past the homes of four board members; it was described in the paper as a "gigantic mechanical snake dance at least half a mile long slithering through the streets of Evanston."[21] During the summer and fall of 1969 there were a series of crowded and vociferous school board meetings.

In mid-July, several weeks after the board announced its decision to terminate Coffin's contract, one thousand people (mostly white) attended a public meeting.[22] Citizens for 65 presented board members with a petition with over ten thousand signatures. Of the twenty-one speakers that night, eighteen demanded Coffin's reinstatement. Coffin listened but never spoke. With every statement it became clearer that his commitment to true integration had been his downfall. Avery Hill from District 202, which oversaw the city's high school, accused the board of attempting to "crucify a champion of the people, a man who's committed the sin of being farsighted enough to demonstrate his belief that integrated housing would help to solve our school integration problems. Because he dared to participate in open housing marches, he is unfit to be our superintendent of schools."

Hill raised a crucial point: Coffin's participation in the fair housing movement had made him more vulnerable to attack. He angered real-estate agents who could no longer allude to "good [white] schools" when selling a home. Coffin had known that his support might limit his tenure as superintendent. He had both professional and personal reasons for taking a stand. The district hired 130 new teachers a year but lost lots of promising candidates because moderate incomes and racial discrimination made the housing market especially tough for blacks. Thus Coffin marched in demonstrations for open and low-cost housing. He supported the passage of a fair housing ordinance and allowed petitions to be posted in schools. At the core, he believed that schools should be agents of social change. "After all, we must recognize that the housing patterns are a result of a whole cycle that begins with poor education," he said.[23] Dressed in a turtleneck and wearing a chain with a peace symbol pendant, he regularly held integrated social events at his home in northwest Evanston.

Near the end of the night the Black Caucus staged an hour-long filibuster. The board took its cue, absconding behind the closed doors of the school nurse's office to request an emergency meeting with the Human Relations Commission (HRC), a voluntary organization working to improve race relations. In the auditorium Ronald Lee read from W. E. B. DuBois's *Black Reconstruction in America*. The Black Caucus saw relevance in DuBois's words. After the Civil War, black and white laborers were driven apart by the propertied class, preventing them from joining together to overcome their oppressors. The crowd sang "We Shall Overcome," a renowned anthem of the southern civil rights movement. It wasn't until after midnight that Mrs. Robert Seyl, the board's new president, returned to tell the crowd that members had successfully arranged for a closed session with the HRC later that same day at 3:00 p.m.

As board members exited their chambers, citizens called them "racists" and "bigots" and shouted "Sieg Heil, Mrs. Seyl," an obvious reference to Nazi Germany. From that night forward Evanston police stood by to protect board members and to escort them home after meetings.[24] Both sides were guilty of harassment. Citizens for 65 received malicious calls threatening committee members and the superintendent's family. Schoolkids called Coffin a "nigger lover" to his children's faces. When the superintendent visited schools, he couldn't help but notice the "Oust Coffin" bumper stickers applied to student notebooks. Vile hate mail flooded his office. He was undeterred.

Coffin was calling for radical systemic change, and some people in Evanston weren't ready for it. Leaders of the Institute of Race Relations at Fisk University, a historically black school in Nashville, were so impressed that they extended an invitation to Coffin to give a talk. In his lecture he criticized what he called the "Dick and Jane" syndrome—the absence of black history and culture from school curriculums:

If you are not aware of the deeply imbedded white racism which pervades the curricular materials used in schools throughout this country, thumb through a child's school books, look at the illustrations, read some of the tests—not just the reading book, but the arithmetic word problems, the science book experiments, the history book heroes, the inventors, and discoverers. It's all white: not just white people, but white situations, white institutions, white frames of reference, and "white is right" conclusions.[25]

This theme recurred in other speeches delivered by the superintendent. During a lecture at Purdue University in January 1970, he described a white middle-class-oriented education thus: "A history punctuated with in-depth studies of American heroes—all white; national and state holidays commemorating three or four of these (Columbus, Christ, Washington, and Lincoln)—all white; school lobbies and corridors adorned with pictures of these same people, plus Jefferson, Franklin, Aristotle and Plato and dozens more—all white."[26] Materials developed in Evanston's teacher's institute more accurately reflected the student body.

Under enormous public pressure, the Evanston school board, along with its attorney, Louis Ancel, met with HRC to hammer out a compromise. On July 17, 1969, HRC released details of the plan that in effect delayed Coffin's firing. School board members were elected in staggered terms for three years without compensation. Terms were due to expire in April 1970 for three of the seven: Seyl and Zimmerman, both of whom were anti-Coffin, and Gatlin, who was pro-Coffin. Because of the gravity of the situation, the board decided not to seek a successor until new members were elected. A new board would decide the superintendent's fate. An election was set for April 1970, leaving the final decision to the people of Evanston. The winners would decide what to do with the superintendent—either renew his contract or unconditionally fire him. The board promised to discuss the turn of events with Coffin. The superintendent looked forward to the meeting. Board members also agreed to release a written report to the public within three weeks outlining their reasons for terminating the superintendent's contract. To ensure that all facts were correct, Coffin asked to review the report before it was released. The agreement left Coffin hopeful and optimistic.

Unhappy Coffin supporters didn't back down. Cast in the role as spokesman for the black community, Bennett Johnson confronted the board at its next meeting on July 28, 1969. He read a prepared statement telling members they should be praising Coffin, not firing him: "Coffin saved this city from racial strife and you ingrates should thank him, not fire him." Drawing an important connection, he reminded the board that pressure to integrate originated in the black community and was resisted then by the same groups that opposed Coffin now. Threatening to boycott the schools, blacks had been on the verge of filing a federal lawsuit in 1966, when the board ceded and hired Coffin. Johnson pointed out that although blacks had initiated change, they never received credit for it; instead white people were praised. "Instead of becoming the Selma of the North, Evanston became the bright star of the nation. [Coffin] should be your hero." Initially whites had accepted Coffin. "The confusion came when it was discovered that he actually believed in the legacy of 1776 and 1863," Johnson continued. "The personality conflicts came when it was discovered that he believed that Black is beautiful." Then came a demand: "The BBPA [Black Business and Professional Association] demands, not asks, demands that Mrs. Seyl move to rescind the previous action against Dr. Coffin tonight." Johnson ended his statement with a threat to prevent District 65 from passing a budget for the 1969–70 academic year: "We say no rescinding, no budget."[27]

There were other speakers during this somewhat chaotic meeting. Jill Newberger of X pleaded with the board to reverse its vote. Through tears, she screamed into the microphone in an effort to be heard amid the noise. Black Caucus member Ronald Lee read a four-page statement demanding the board rehire Coffin, pay for busing, and rename the LAB School for Martin Luther King Jr. Several months later, the group would insist that black architects be hired to renovate elementary schools and add lunchrooms. If the board refused to respond to lawful protests, the Black Caucus threatened to burn down the LAB School.

No one knew better than Donald Lawson that the HRC-board compromise amounted to no more than public relations gimmickry. On behalf of Citizens for 65, he read a prepared statement calling for a special election in September. The so-called compromise was a sham conceived under the guidance of a skillful attorney. There was no concession, only that the board wouldn't appoint a new superintendent until the next year and would wait to settle the matter at an April election. This was routine. He also knew that no candidate of any honor would want to deal with the board. Coffin, too, pressed for a September election, claiming he would abide by the results.[28] It seemed ridiculous to drag the battle out for another year. The new school year would start soon, and it would create an uncomfortable atmosphere for students. Whether the board had the power to call an early election was not the question.

Opposing a September election, former members John Carver and Frank Gagen said they wouldn't concede to intimidation. Carver, who lived in the infamous northwest Evanston area, blustered: "The four members of the majority have had the guts to stick to their decision in the face of intimidation that was damn near criminal."[29] Hoping to repair its deteriorating image, however, the board approved a motion to rename the LAB School in honor of the slain civil rights leader Martin

FIGURE 3.2 At a school board meeting on July 28, 1969, members of the Black Caucus demand that Coffin be reinstated. *Evanston Review,* July 31, 1969.

Luther King Jr. Other matters of business included voting 4–3 to retain the services of Stewart Diamond, an attorney who from that point on would sit dead center at the board table, on Mrs. Seyl's left. At times he would take over the role of chair of the meeting; at other times he was an advocate or defender of the majority. Coffin's supporters despised him.

The *Review* was a mouthpiece for the opposition to Coffin. Forceful demands raised its ire: pro-Coffin activists, one writer said, "believe that freedom of expression for those with whom they disagree should not be tolerated. They believe that the laws which are not to their liking should be ignored and flouted."[30] A board supporter wrote to the *Review*: "My anger mounts as days go by. My fears also. The fear that somehow they will get their way. That their tactics, the pressure and threats, will pay off and our system will be weakened further. I hope and pray the board will be able to withstand the coercion."[31] An editorial reprimanded "pro-Coffinites" for not being more appreciative of actions by the board thus far, such as approval of new sack lunch and bus programs, an increase in teacher salaries, and the renaming of the

LAB School in honor of King.[32] Now that blacks had asked for inclusion, there was suddenly talk of division, discord, and hate.

By contrast, the *Examiner* was a forum for Coffin's supporters. An editorial praised the actions of the Black Caucus for standing up to the board and demanding to be heard at the July 1969 meeting. The editors wrote: "We thank the Black Caucus. Their persistence without violence has brought into sharp perspective the real education issue. . . . The true fight is between those who would not disturb the status quo—who do not want to 'ruffle the water,' . . . and those who realize that Coffin is a symbol of progress in a restructuring society."[33]

Then, for the first time in history, a school board issued a report on the condition of Evanston's school system. Breaking its promise, it released the report to the public at a press conference in Chicago on August 26, 1969, only minutes after giving it to Coffin. The preparation and publication cost taxpayers $18,500. The *Report of the Board of Education on the Superintendency of Dr. Gregory C. Coffin* was divided in to two parts. The first fifty-seven pages consisted of accusations made by the majority. The charges were followed by a five-page appendix written by the minority. An attorney had advised and helped to prepare the document outlining opposition to the integration-minded educator. The lawyer, according to the *Examiner*, was a renowned segregationist. Majority members argued that school integration had been the board's policy long before Coffin was hired to further it, that this policy had not changed, and that integration therefore was not an issue. Thirteen charges were leveled against the superintendent. Most were ludicrous. They claimed that Coffin was not "effective as an educator because he has failed as an integrator." Coffin was cited for "mismanagement of funds," including directing teachers to prepare false vouchers for reimbursement and permitting administrative carelessness in handling funds and programs. The board seemed to want to quibble and nitpick. Purportedly Coffin had asked for manual covers to be reprinted so that his name would appear with the honorific "Dr.," and then had burned the old ones. He was faulted for an increase in teacher attrition rates and deteriorating pupil conduct. He was said to have an abrasive personality and "dictatorial handling" when dealing with personnel and the board itself.

The most serious charge was drawn from a still unpublished study funded by the Rockefeller Foundation. Comparing Educational Testing Service scores on standardized achievement tests from fall 1967 and fall 1968, the study found that scores had decreased. The two-hundred-page document concluded that "integration had no significant effect on the achievement patterns of the District 65 student body."[34] This was a highly emotional charge to make in an education-minded city such as Evanston. The truth was that the drop in eighth-grade performance tests could not be linked to Coffin, because students were taught by the same teachers and governed by the same instruction policies that had existed under his predecessor in prior years. Moreover, items on the exam were not specific to seventh- or eighth-grade course content, but rather covered information and skills learned in previous courses. That is, the eighth-grade scores reflected on a student's total prior education, only a small part of which had been under Coffin's administration.

More than five hundred people crowded into Ebenezer AME Church on September 4, 1969, to hear Dean B. J. Chandler of Northwestern University's School of Education discredit the majority report. His remarks were full of disdain and sarcasm. He wondered whether majority members were really qualified to make educational decisions on behalf of Evanston's schoolchildren. "Were I to read an undergraduate term paper of this quality I'd give it a failing mark," he said. The bias and "slanted" document made no effort to "present a balanced assessment of the problem." Eleven letters cited as evidence supposedly represented correspondence from the public to the school board. All of them were negative as well as anonymous or unsigned. Undated, they had probably been solicited. The perspectives of the many interested, intelligent, and concerned citizens who had sought to dissuade the board were missing from the report.[35]

A letter from Bernice Besore Hoffman exemplifies some of the failings highlighted by Chandler. For sixteen years she had been the principal of Lincolnwood School, located on Evanston's wealthy and conservative northwest side. She wrote that she had been frustrated with the district's new lunch policies:

I was often expected to assume responsibility for programs that were, without warning or any orientation on my part, placed in my hands to carry out. This particularly was true of the sack lunch program. When school opened on a Thursday in September 1968, about seventeen black children brought lunches. That day, I talked with every parent and there was agreement that we could work through this problem. However, without advising me, the two top Administrators met with the black parents on Sunday and told them that their children could lunch at school even though the administration had given the principal no indication of the possibility of a change in lunch plans for Lincolnwood. On Monday, forty children arrived with lunches, and despite the fact that there were no plans for space or supervision, I was expected to manage. I had been exploited; it was quite clear that the Administration knew that any objection on my part would be interpreted by the black parents as racial prejudice or as objection to integration.[36]

There are several problems with Hoffman's letter. First, it isn't dated. More than likely it was solicited and written after July 23, 1969. Second, by September 1968 all principals were accustomed to having black children eating in their schools. Finally, her language is hyperbolic—specifically her use of the word *exploitation*.

As noted, minority board members had been permitted to add a five-page statement to the end of the document. But they were not informed of the larger report's contents beforehand, and this made it impossible for them to comment on the charges against Coffin before the document was printed. Instead they took note of the superintendent's accomplishments. They praised his imaginative and innovative qualities in moving the district toward integration. They evaluated Coffin by the quality of the education system that he administered. "We judge Dr. Coffin's professional work in district 65 to have been, on balance, remarkably constructive," they wrote. Finally, they accused their opponents of acting to "slow down the pace of integration or maybe return to segregation."[37]

Not only was Coffin denied due process, but the board tried to destroy him personally and professionally by publishing a report on his employment record. The report was available to anyone who wanted to read it. More than likely no one would. Instead, sound bites would be used to shape public opinion. Coffin himself was blindsided; he had never before heard many of the charges. Furthermore, majority members prevented him from using public funds to reply to the report.

A full-scale response to the charges was called for, but it would be a long and tedious affair. In a press statement released on August 27, 1969, Coffin angrily denied allegations against him and called the majority report "full of errors, half-truths, and quotes out of context."[38] The charges were an "unsubstantiated, broad-brush attack on the administration," he said.[39] He regretted having to spend his time not merely answering charges about his performance but also trying to find out the nature of charges that no board member ever had the "courage or forthrightness to make directly" to him. He requested an open public hearing, welcomed a federal investigation, and asked for a legal adviser to help issue a reply.

Later that day the Community Education Committee (CEC) held a press conference calling for Coffin to resign. Organized on July 24, 1969, CEC was the right arm of the Northwest Evanston Homeowners'

Association, an all-white, ultraconservative group with a membership in excess of twenty-five hundred. Scare tactics and slick printed matter would manipulate public opinion against the superintendent. CEC claimed that integration was a "false issue injected by Dr. Coffin for his own purposes,"[40] a mantle in which he had wrapped himself to divert attention from his inadequacies. Choosing their words carefully, CEC leaders told the public that if high-quality integrated education was to be maintained, the divisive term of Superintendent Coffin must end. They accused him of polarizing the community and making it difficult for the board to carry out its duties. Complaining of Coffin's arrogance, they posed the rhetorical question "Wasn't he fired once?" Under the guise of restoring harmony, uniting the community, and reducing racial tension through "reason and with dignity," they sought to destroy the superintendent.[41] Well financed, they hired Martin E. Janis & Company, a high-priced Michigan Avenue, public relations firm to help embarrass and defame the superintendent. CEC chairman Howard T. Brinton directed the firm to "get Coffin." The company took on the challenge, using deceptive strategies and tactics. It distributed thirty thousand copies of the majority report as a "public service" to inform residents about the controversy. It regularly purchased advertising space in the *Review* to publish excerpts from the majority report. The CEC employed catchy slogans like "Oust Coffin, Vote Reason" and "Bye, Bye, Greg Baby." Members attached pink bumper stickers reading "Quality Education" to their cars. The community was flooded with mailed broadsides.

Demoralized by the report, Coffin's staff still stood firmly behind him. United Black Employees of School District 65 (UBE), composed of 135 black teachers, administrators, and staff from custodians to the highest-ranking black employee, Joseph Hill, leveled the charge of racism. A first-grade teacher, Ruby Murray, was named chair. Murray had "deep concern about the anti-black views of the majority members of the board."[42] Black perspectives had not been solicited for the report.[43] The report was interpreted to signal that since black children had been integrated into the system, the schools had "gone to pot."[44] UBE credited Coffin with making the district a model of successful school integration. "Before him it was only on paper," Murray said. UBE requested a public seminar with board members to discuss the racist undertones of the board's decision to fire Coffin. Its members threatened to walk out if Coffin wasn't reinstated.

An interracial group of principals and teachers formed the Association of Concerned Teachers (ACT). The executive committee included both William Hannan, the white principal of Dewey School, and Laval Wilson, the black principal from Central School. ACT was offended by implications that the school system and quality of teachers had gone downhill since integration. Hannan warned that the district would lose teachers if Coffin was not rehired.

Installed in late October, the new sign in front of the LAB School glistened in the sun. Standing out against the red brick building, the cast bronze letters read "Martin Luther King Jr. Laboratory School / District 65." A month before the renaming ceremony, Joseph Hill drafted a tentative program. Allwyn Gatlin, the only black school board member, and the one who had originally suggested renaming the school, was invited by the PTA to represent the board and speak at the dedication ceremony. At some point Seyl was added to the list of speakers. On the day of the event Corinne Schumacher, King LAB's new principal, and Robin Moran, LAB School PTA president and former CACI member, welcomed the crowd. Coffin made remarks. Seyl and Gatlin were scheduled to speak. Hill introduced Reverend C. T. Vivian, who had worked closely with King in the Southern Christian Leadership Conference. Reverend Vivian reminded the crowd: "If this dedication means you are committed to the philosophy of Dr. King, then you are worthy of the name." The audience was "joyful, and often tearful." Betty Washington, choir director at Ebenezer AME Church, sang "Lift Every Voice and Sing," the Negro national anthem. When it was over, the crowd of more than one thousand parents, teachers, and children was invited to tour the school.

Not everything went as planned. The program was interrupted when it was Seyl's turn to speak. There are differing accounts of what happened. According to the *Review*, a member of the Black Caucus, John Ingram, grabbed the microphone from Seyl. According to the *Examiner*, Ingram "courteously and firmly requested" that Mrs. Margaret Seyl not speak.[45] Either way, Seyl hesitated but then gathered her papers and moved to the side. Ingram then told a "hushed" audience why it "felt inappropriate" for Seyl to say anything.

It is our feeling that the speaking of Mrs. Seyl will be a disservice to the memory of the late Dr. King. Mrs. Seyl abstained from voting for the renaming of the King Lab School. More importantly, she has not supported those actions necessary for the implementation of the ideals for which Dr. King died.[46]

The Black Caucus was angry not only because Seyl had voted against the renaming of the school but also because her actions seemed

FIGURE 3.3 LAB students perform "We Shall Overcome" at a dedication ceremony honoring Martin Luther King Jr. The school's name was changed to honor the slain civil rights leader. *Evanston Review*, October 19, 1969.

antiblack. "We fail to understand why she would have the audacity to appear in the black community at an affair so important to the souls of black folk."[47] It was only two minutes of a three-hour ceremony, but it caught the attention of the press and overshadowed the real significance of the day.

Pro-board sentiment was increasing in response to each of the Coffin supporters' attempts to escalate the situation. Such sentiments were expressed in the *Review*. The father of a seven-year-old student who attended the event said he was filled with pride before the disruption that ruined it: "You've learned from us well, you blacks. If you don't agree with someone, don't let him speak. There was a smell to that move—it had the odor of mob rule—of a lynching almost. Just the thing you have been fighting against for so long."[48] Another said, "Preventing Mrs. Seyl from speaking because she held, or they thought she held, a different opinion than that of the Black Caucus smacks of

Nazi Germany."[49] The CEC purchased advertising space in the *Review* to print the speech Seyl would have given.

An outraged "establishment" and its mainstream media claimed the board president was denied her right of free speech, reported the *Examiner*. In doing so they failed to recognize that this day was

a Black triumph, a rich, historic and moving ceremony—a profound tribute to Dr. King in that at this moment in time, Black and white were sharing the power on equal terms. Moreover, together they were aware of its potential for themselves and for their children and that indeed, 'freedom of speech' was Black by right and by fitness of the occasion. . . . Mrs. Seyl's insistence can only be described as insensitive. . . . The Black Caucus more truly represented the philosophy of Dr. King than did those who were outraged at the denial of the president of the board.[50]

Scrambling to protect its reputation, the board reluctantly agreed to meet privately with UBE. The board approved Coffin's recommendation to hold a teachers' institute and give students a holiday on January 15, King's birthday. It was too little too late for Joe Hill. Maybe it was thirteen-year-old John Throop's statement that was the last straw. The young boy asked to be recognized during the November meeting and remained at the microphone until he was. When he finally spoke, he said that he had listened to adults in "horror and shame for five months" and accused the four majority members of "deafness in both ears." It's unclear if Throop was speaking as a representative of X or of Citizens for 65. His optimism unwavering, he penned "The Ballad of CEC" in April 1970: "But Citizens will triumph; / And CEC falls; / And black and white will live together once and for all."

Before Thanksgiving, Hill resigned his post as assistant to the superintendent. A native of Evanston, he had attended Foster School when it was segregated. He often recalled that experience when he spoke about the need for integration. Hill had been "shocked" when the board voted against renewing Coffin's contract. He was infuriated by the public release of the report on Coffin and was "deeply hurt" by its contents. The board's actions gave him "doubts about the Evanston in which I had faith" and "uncovered the seething wounds that have been festering in this community for years." Hill was especially bothered by the board's dictatorial attitude—"we have made a decision and that decision is non-negotiable." Hill accepted a position as assistant superintendent in Grand Rapids, Michigan.

His resignation was short-lived, however. Black organizations asked the school board to do what it could to retain him. In the midst of the crisis, the board gave Hill a counteroffer that included promotion to associate superintendent, which he accepted. Coffin was relieved—and then disappointed again when two weeks later Frank Y. Christiansen, director of personnel, submitted his letter of resignation. He found the present circumstances to be "beyond his comprehension." It was the board's actions, not Coffin's, that were creating tension and making work conditions increasingly difficult.

The *School Outlook* was the district's chief means for communicating with parents. To avoid "rumors, misinformation, and lack of information," the director of information, Delores Kaufmann, advised Coffin to document a "straightforward chronology" or timeline of the summer events in the September newsletter. Coffin added comments reassuring parents that the district would be "continuing without stop a program of educational excellence."[51] CEC responded by accusing the superintendent of misusing funds by publishing his side of the story in the *Outlook*. Howard Brinton called Coffin's account biased, slanted, and inaccurate. CEC threatened to file a lawsuit for misuse of tax funds intended for education if Coffin wasn't stopped. In his own defense, Coffin reminded his detractors that it was the board's policy to leave editorial and production responsibility in the hands of information services. He also pointed out that the list of events left out "more than a few items favorable to me."[52]

CEC may have been better financed than Citizens for 65, but it was less organized. A dedicated staff worked tirelessly to retain Coffin. Overseeing operations, Donald Lawson chaired the executive committee. Jeremy Wilson plotted block-by-block canvasses, organizing hundreds of volunteers from Evanston and Skokie to visit households, determine whether voters were favorable, and turn out the vote on Election Day. Nearly the entire black community—including those uncertain about Coffin but committed to his philosophy and innovative programs, and those unhappy with the Caucus system designed to assure uncontested elections for board members—donated time. The organization counted among its supporters school superintendents from Philadelphia; Winchester, Massachusetts; Mountain View, California; and Port Washington, New York. Alice Kreiman chaired the issues committee, known as the Turtles. Her responsibilities included writing *Turtle Talk*. Kreiman filled the newsletter with "snappy" inspirational sayings to build morale, such as "Now is the hour for turtle power." Asked why Citizens didn't retain a public relations firm, Kreiman stated, "Truth sells itself; we don't have a product or a lie to sell."[53] The pro-Coffin group was

governed by a steering committee of delegates from thirty-six neighborhood and civic organizations, fourteen of which were predominantly black. Bennett Johnson, Robin Moran, John Ingram, Roosevelt
Alexander, B. J. Chandler, Thomas Fuller, Shel Newberger, Betty Papangelis, Helen Cooper, and Lorraine Morton were among the delegates.
Minutes from an early steering-committee meeting documented Johnson's determination to win. "This is an army, we are at war," he told his
comrades.

Citizens for 65 operated out of donated space in the Unitarian Church until a permanent headquarters could be found. When
Reverend Jacob Blake gave Citizens the use of the house next to his
church, it packed and moved. Handwritten signs reading "We really
Need Each Other Friends" and the group's motto, "Live and Learn Together," helped break up the decidedly bland interior—beige paneled
walls, carpeting, and curtains. Volunteers used Scotch tape to hang
maps of Evanston's wards, memos, and to-do lists. Donated furniture
filled the basement workspace. Paper coffee cups and ashtrays soon lit-
tered tabletops. Typewriters and rotary phones sat on desks. The office buzzed with organizers, volunteers, and on occasion the candidates
themselves. Committed workers put in twelve hours a day, seven days
a week. They distributed "Keep Coffin" buttons, bumper stickers, car
tops, and posters that one group of innovative kids turned into sandwich boards for protesters to wear. One poster read: "Behold the turtle /
he makes progress only when his neck is out."[54] Staff members continu-
ously added names to the more than ten thousand signatures on a petition calling for Coffin's reinstatement.

Most importantly, Citizens for 65 assumed responsibility for printing and distributing the superintendent's long-awaited response to the
majority report. The board denied him public funds or school distribution, though these had allowed it to circulate its charges against him.
Five thousand copies of the forty-page response document were available at Citizens' headquarters beginning on February 9, 1970. Coffin
prepared the statement on his own time with the help of volunteers.
For the cover Citizens for 65 chose a photo of Coffin looking over the
shoulders of two school-aged children, one black and one white. The
document described major actions taken and educational programs
advanced since July 1966, the start of his administration. Coffin responded to each of the board's charges. He quoted from the State Office of Public Instruction report, issued five months before the majority
report, which commended the board of education for the integration
plan. Teacher attrition rates were normal, he said; some had left for

marriage or maternity. To replace them, the district received a "veritable flood" of applicants who wanted to work in an integrated school system. There had been 2,507 applicants for 140 staff openings in September 1967. Coffin asked the Department of Health, Education and Welfare (HEW) to audit the district's financial records when the charges were first launched against him in August. In the February response he cited the department's early findings that the district's money was indeed used for the specific purpose of forwarding its integration plan. HEW stated that money was administrated in a genuinely satisfactory manner and in accordance with the stated objectives of federal programs. There was no evidence of misuse of federal funds.[55]

It may have been too late. By February the battle lines were drawn. It would be nearly impossible to overcome the privileged status of the General Caucus of Community Consolidated School District 65 (Caucus). It selected and endorsed persons to serve on the school board. The extralegal body had endorsed unopposed candidates for forty years. To this point Caucus endorsement had been tantamount to election; no more than five hundred voters ever cast ballots. The elite group was made up of delegates from fifty-four civic organizations, including twenty-four Parent Teacher Associations and thirty associations such as the Rotary and Kiwanis Clubs, the Chamber of Commerce, and the North Shore Board of Realtors. The organizations represented were primarily nonpolitical, nonsectarian, and local in character. But the Caucus suffered from a credibility gap. Generally it had served the interests of the established white community and did not represent large segments of Evanston including blacks, nonjoiners, and low-income groups. Exercising its privilege, the Caucus defied the HRC when it endorsed candidates for the April election. With backing from CEC, it nominated a single slate committed to upholding the board's decision to terminate Coffin.

Longtime residents, the three Caucus candidates were parents of children who had attended Evanston schools. The only black candidate, Norma Eason, was a homemaker and involved parent. Praised for favoring neighborhood schools and voting against busing black children, she was nominated by Helen Nixon of the Evanston–North Shore Board of Realtors. Mrs. Whiting from the Northwest Evanston Homeowners' Association seconded the motion. Sumner G. Rahr was a fundraising executive at the Adlai Stevenson Institute of International Affairs. In the weeks leading up to the election, the *Examiner* reported that Rahr and his wife had signed a petition in 1966 opposing the CACI integration plan. In fact, 278 people had signed the petition, claiming boundary changes and compulsory busing would destroy Evanston's "neighborhood school" concept. When confronted, Rahr said he had no memory of signing it. The *Examiner* called his reply a convenient "memory lapse." Because the petition was a matter of public record, Rahr was eventually forced to admit that he did sign it. Later he justified his signature by claiming he had objected to boundary changes, not to integration.[56] The third candidate, Martha Baumberger, was less controversial than the other two. She was president of the Illinois Women's Civil Defense Council. All three candidates claimed to be for integrated education of the highest quality, but they lacked endorsement from black groups. If they won, they would undoubtedly uphold the current majority's decision to oust Coffin.

The community was divided, but the era of uncontested school board elections arranged by a select caucus of leading white citizens was over. A series of nominating meetings yielded three candidates for Citizens for 65. A weighted vote ensured that black and white delegates had the same number of votes. Fondly referred to as Bennett, Betty, and Bob, these three winners were also longtime Evanston residents with children who had attended the city's public schools. They differed from the others in that they saw integration not as an act but as a process. Witty and popular, Bennett Johnson was a publishing executive and business leader. Betty Papangelis was an executive at a major private child-welfare agency. Papangelis had dark gray hair and wore red lipstick with conservative but stylish dresses. A serious proponent of racial integration at a time when women weren't taken seriously in the political arena, she always put on her glasses for speeches. Robert Marks was a former state legislator and CACI member. Some said he had the voice of a politician before microphones were used, often beginning a series of comments with "Let's get things straight." Marks doubled as the attorney for Citizens. If members of this slate were victorious, they would join forces with other pro-Coffin members, overturn the board's decision, and reinstate Coffin.

The two slates campaigned hard through the late winter and early spring, providing Evanston with its first fully contested school board race in nearly forty years. A series of "great debates" took place in venues across town. Evanston's first synagogue, Beth Emet, sponsored one. Elementary school PTAs held several at the middle schools. The Evanston Young Republicans hosted a debate at the North Shore Hotel. The format was uniform: between opening and closing statements, the candidates responded to questions for an hour. Voters were urged to attend and become familiar with candidates by hearing them discuss the issues. The stakes were high: the winners would shape the future. Every effort was made to get information out to the public. For those who couldn't attend live sessions, WFLD broadcast a debate at 11:30 p.m. on April 4. Candidates were also introduced to the public at neighborhood coffees in private homes.

Effectively backing the superintendent, the *Review* endorsed two of the three candidates supporting Coffin. Every black organization endorsed Johnson. The *Review* endorsed Eason, the black candidate on the opposite side. Donald Lawson was furious. No one knew better than Eason how the black community felt. Lawson believed that the endorsement should make Eason realize how CEC, "under the guise of representing the Black community," was using her. It was reprehensible and dishonest, he thought. The night before the election, Lawson spoke before a predominantly black audience, reminding them that if they voted the next day the election could be won. If the black community turned out at the polls, they would send a clear message demanding to share power in the city. If not, the clock would be turned back. Hoping to inspire voters, he ended with a rallying cry: "Let's celebrate a VICTORY tomorrow night!"[57]

As was to be expected, the *Examiner* also supported Coffin by endorsing the three who would reinstate him. In the days leading up to the election, the newspaper published letters of support. Darlene Schmalzried titled hers "I knew Dr. Coffin in Darien." In high school she had taken part in Coffin's exchange program with Harlem schools. Darlene was paired with a girl named Rosena. She was both nervous and excited to host Rosena at her home in Connecticut for the weekend. "Our experiment with civil rights was very effective," she wrote. "We learned that Darien was unique—and so was Harlem." The girls also learned that despite their differences they had a lot in common. They acted like typical teenagers, gossiping and partying. Rosena thought Darlene's boyfriend was cute and that he looked like Paul McCartney. They attended a party on Saturday with "guitars and cokes and curiosity." The teenagers sang songs including "Blowin' in the Wind" and "We Shall Overcome" and engaged in frank discussions about the civil rights movement. It was a positive experience for everyone involved. The friendship didn't end with the program. "Rosena still sends me Christmas cards."[58]

Recalling the exchange program that he initiated, Coffin explained, "Nancy and I began to see that our four kids were learning that black people were made only to be maids," a reference to commuters who came from New York to the all-white city for domestic work. His six-point program to introduce civil rights in to the curriculum, including the student exchange that Schmalzried spoke of, had been an effort to reeducate them. The civil rights pioneer had also recruited nonwhite personnel, arranged for a three-week teacher exchange program, invited Negro speakers to schools, developed materials on the Negro in America, and initiated student volunteer programs in neighboring cities.[59] In addition to his parents, Coffin credited two people for helping him "wake up": a Negro teacher in Darien and his cousin Reverend William Sloan Coffin, a civil rights activist and Yale University chaplain.

Civil rights organizations watched closely as local events unfolded. A white Jewish woman, June Shagaloff, was the NAACP's first special assistant for education.[60] NAACP branches across the country petitioned school boards, staged boycotts, and mounted protests. Deeply committed to ending school segregation in all its guises, Shagaloff was the chief investigator of systems outside the South. She knew the fight in Evanston was critical. Her piece "What's at Stake in Evanston," published in the *Examiner*, said as much. Before coming to Evanston, Coffin had had a reputation for being an "innovative, hard-driving administrator," she began. He "raised eyebrows (and tempers) by initiating the nation's first city-to-suburb busing program (in 1965)," which consisted of a teacher exchange and busing of Harlem students to Darien schools. His innovations made him the "kind of man that a progressive, cosmopolitan community like Evanston could be expected to choose." Recounting the historical facts, she wrote that initially the school board was behind the program and that Coffin took charge "quickly and decisively." Shagaloff continued, "Evanston's star, it seemed, had never been higher. But then, a not-so-funny thing happened on the way to true integration. The community—or a sizable element of it—got off the bandwagon." Next came rumblings of heavy-handedness and a refusal to renew Coffin's contract. Support fell on the short end of the 4-3 majority. And then there was an incredible surge of support, and the board was besieged at its meetings. In defense it issued a report, damning and highly questionable. The issues would be dropped until the next board election, when "the public would decide Coffin's fate and, many felt, the fate of integration in Evanston, at the ballot box." The hard-hitting NAACP director continued:

The real problem in Evanston, many blacks feel, is that Coffin and the black community, much to the chagrin of the white establishment, are not content to ease up on integration, now that the first state-body-mixing has been reached. They intend to pursue true integration to its logical course in terms of curriculum, personnel, school community relation . . . and, most disturbing to many white, distribution of power.

Shagaloff ended her letter on an ominous note: "If Gregory Coffin is run out of progressive, enlightened Evanston, where can he survive?"[61]

The editors of *School Management* magazine, the leading journal in the field, also believed that a wish to "ease up" on integration was behind the firing and endorsed Coffin.[62] The magazine quoted Shagaloff: "If the truth of the matter is that our society will not support the kind of dynamic local school leadership the times require, Evanston will be a landmark on our way to a long sharp slide into two societies hopelessly divided—and real public school leadership permanently divided."[63]

Shagaloff understood that separate and unequal go hand in hand. She must have been devastated when Coffin lost his position less than two years after implementing Evanston's desegregation plan. "There is a world of difference between desegregation and integration. The former describes a physical condition; the latter, a state of mind." Coffin grasped the difference and paid the price.[64]

Let's Put a Hurtin' on Them

A symbol of integration in Evanston, Illinois, Dr. Gregory C. Coffin, was rejected. While the Nixon administration debated civil rights at the national level, Evanston was back-pedaling at the local level. The school board election was effectively a referendum on Coffin's tenure. The opposition was defeated, and the controversial superintendent lost his job. A record-breaking twenty-six thousand voters turned out in early April 1970. With a 51 percent margin, CEC claimed victory at 2:00 a.m. on Sunday April 12 at its Ridgeville Hotel headquarters. The last precinct to report was the King Laboratory School, in the heart of the black community, but in the end its votes were not needed. The anti-Coffin majority was reaffirmed—and enlarged by one more vote to stand at 5–2. A happy and tearful Richard Alexander, chairman of the Northwest Evanston Homeowners' Association, declared victory, saying over and over again, "Isn't it wonderful?"

It was 3:00 a.m. before Coffin delivered his concession speech at the Elks Club. Faithful volunteers filled the room. A reporter described the scene: "Turtles were everywhere, the symbol Dr. Coffin uses when he sticks his neck out for something he believes in. A yellow turtle bank, turtle drawings, a turtle pillow, a turtle pin on Mrs. Lyon's collar." Coffin read from a prepared statement—one of several prepared to address the possible outcomes—"I won't say the better people won this election, I don't believe they did." He was "abrasive to the end," snipped the *Review*.[65]

The newly constituted board removed Coffin on April 17. He was retained in a reduced capacity as an educational adviser until his contract ended on June 30. Hill was temporarily promoted until a new superintendent could be selected.

Coffin had been hired to redesign the public school system. He had aggressively implemented district-wide programs, including the experimental program at Foster, teacher training, integrated faculty and staff, and integrated extracurricular activities for students. Coffin was one of the few white superintendents in the country to have the full backing of the black community, and the movement to retain him was integrated. Blacks and whites worked together. He fell victim to a national trend: resisting integration by calling for educators to educate, not integrate. He was a scapegoat. A Coffin supporter mourned that he was "too sad to laugh and too old to cry."[66] Another supporter remembered later: "We lost the fight. That was the year they brought out the old people's homes. Literally, wheeled people in to vote."[67] Indeed the CEC had gone to great lengths, driving the aged and infirm to and from polling places, bringing out what some refer to as the "deathbed vote." Unfortunately, the black community had not turned out as it needed to: an estimated 35 percent did not vote.[68] They would have made a difference. But they had been excluded from the political process in the past, and the cultural norms had not yet changed. When the votes were tallied, it was clear that the race had been close—13,565 to 12,823. Bennett Johnson shook his head: "The time to cry is tomorrow when we are at each other's throats."[69]

"Bitter Aftermath!" read the *Examiner*'s headline. The Citizens' executive committee gathered to draft a response. They shed tears before finding solace in the small margin of loss, hoping it was a sign that integration would not slow down. The group pledged to continue as a permanent organization in the community and be involved in the search for a new superintendent. More immediately, they committed resources to an ad hoc Committee of Concerned Black Parents. Boiling over with frustration, Delores Holmes released a statement calling the loss the "beginning of the end of the Coffin-generated progress towards racial understanding."[70] Neighbors at Work (NAW) chairman Tom Fuller saw an opportunity in defeat and offered full support. He let Holmes set up operations at NAW, a federally funded Office of Economic Opportunity center dedicated to assisting people through lo-

FIGURE 3.4 Concerned Black Parents cochair Delores Holmes makes urgent calls from the group's headquarters. Holmes reflects the mood of the black community. *North Shore Examiner*, April 25–May 15, 1970.

cally controlled community programs. For Fuller, education was just one of several areas that needed attention. He urged the community to build on the momentum and address problems of housing and employment as well.[71] Banding together, Concerned Black Parents organized a massive school boycott in three short days. "Let's Put a Hurtin' on Them," a flyer exhorted.

The boycott was set for Thursday and Friday. Some women kept their children home on Wednesday too. Before long, instructions reached parents across the district. On the morning of April 16, 1970, students assembled at two central locations. Those who lived north of Church Street reported to Foster Community Center. Those who lived south of Church gathered at the Unitarian Church. Bused children were picked up at their stops fifteen minutes later than usual. Others requiring transportation waited at corners along the bus route. Mothers sent sack lunches. From the central locations children were taken to one of five Freedom Schools. Modeled after their southern counterparts, the schools were housed in basements and other donated spaces at the Masonic Temple, NAW's Ebony House, Mt. Zion Church, Sherman Methodist Church, and Garrett Theological Seminary. In keeping with sixties terminology, the group called for "parent power." A full 40 percent of the district's teachers and students heeded the call.

Following in the footsteps of civil rights and Black Power groups, Concerned Black Parents also organized an economic boycott of white businesses deemed exploitative in the black community. Voting against Coffin, whites had demonstrated in the polls that they were not interested in quality education for black children. In retaliation the group called for no black-owned dollars to be spent in any white-owned business. Attached to the announcement calling for the boycott was a list of black-owned businesses that they hoped the community would support instead. To dramatize her determination, Holmes said the economic boycott would continue for an undetermined length of time.

Coffin's loss buried black Evanston's dreams of a shared democracy. The newly elected black board member Norma Eason was denounced for "siding with the racists and bigots who elected you." She did not

FIGURE 3.5 Children sing civil rights songs at one of five Freedom Schools organized to protest the termination of Coffin's contract. *North Shore Examiner*, April 25–May 15, 1970.

receive support from the black community, who felt that her victory afforded them no representation. A candidate of questionable qualifications, she had been selected over Johnson, a college graduate who had had experience as a high school teacher.

Self-determined black parents demanded a voice at the level of policy making. With banners and signs, they marched down Emerson Street to attend a rally at Foster Community Center. Two keynote speakers from Chicago, Charles Hurst, head of the Malcolm X Community Center, and Al Raby, a civil rights leader, addressed the crowd. Like his predecessors, Raby accused the school board of bringing "Dr. Coffin here to talk about integration, not to act." Carl Davis, president of the Evanston NAACP, also spoke to the crowd. Steve Frazier's Soul Experience provided musical accompaniment.[72] Their efforts paid off. The new board agreed to give Concerned Black Parents and Citizens of 65 a direct voice during the search for and screening of candidates to replace Coffin[73]

Unlike black members of the photograph who were bused, most whites only have vague memories of these events. Those I interviewed were amazed to find out that we had been part of the first generation to integrate Evanston's schools: "No way," "Oh my goodness," "I had no clue," "It's amazing to me that was the first year." Shocked but not surprised, they recognized that "Evanston was a little bit forward." Most were convinced that their parents were Coffin supporters. "My parents were pretty outspoken about stuff like that; they were pretty militant in a way for things that they believed in, so they would have been for the integration," Candy told me. She remembers going to school in a church basement but not the reasons why.

Only Ronny had a concrete memory of his parents' involvement. Like many activists at the time, his mother wore a "Keep Coffin" button. He remembers her saying, "Oh, he's so right on and he's so ahead of his time." The rest of us must have been too young, or maybe our parents were on the wrong side of history. Ronny explained, "I don't think the kids were that—tuned into it. Kids have different concerns; of course you're seven or six going 'Who's this guy?' You're worried about polishing your new bike." It's true that in comparison to the South, Evanston's integration was rather quiet. "You think of Birmingham . . . and people throwing rocks at the bus, and . . . that wasn't going on in Evanston as far as I can remember," Ronny said.

While we may not remember Coffin or the controversy surrounding him, we certainly benefited from his efforts. His initiatives would have a profound effect on our middle school experience.

FOUR

Free to Roam

We were pretty much carefree back then; everybody was getting along, having a good time. It wasn't about color or race—it didn't have nothing to do with none of that. JESSE

Neighborhood-based school boundaries channeled friendship patterns and separated would-be friends. Before desegregation most young people didn't leave their local environs for an educational setting that would bring them in contact with those from other neighborhoods until high school. Corrective measures were taken in 1967, when boundaries were changed in order to "distribute the Negro population in the schools as evenly as possible."[1] Desegregating the elementary schools required busing students from the west side to all-white institutions in the east. Socializing was confined to school hours and made interracial friendships difficult to sustain. The district took an important further step toward integration when it decided to use elementary schools as feeders into the middle schools, keeping students together as long as possible and at least through eighth grade.[2] The transition from elementary to middle school was a serious one. Not only was there a different and more demanding curriculum, but there was also greater diversity in the student body. By the 1973–74 academic year, the junior highs were reorganized into three-year institutions.

Our group met at Nichols Middle School, one of four in Evanston. My photograph captures those days along with our brief friendship. Middle school provided more opportunities for relationships to form between students from different racial and class backgrounds. Students arranged their own transport to and from school. While authorities recognized that "the distance to the junior high schools for many children would be greater than that to their elementary school," they believed that because students were older and more responsible, they were capable of a longer walk.[3] During interviews my friends drew maps of their old neighborhoods, explaining their routes to Nichols. Black friends lived next door or across the street. Whites walked from as far away as the lake or came from the other direction, near the high school, or just beyond black homes. Middle schools were built with lunchrooms, so we stayed on the premises to eat. Because of district-sponsored activities, we also lingered in the neighborhood after classes ended. Larger than elementary schools but much smaller than the high school, the middle school with its homeroom model kept students at different academic levels together in the same classroom for part of the school day. Interpersonal relationships developed between homeroom teachers and students.

Negro Children

Candy remembers that Nichols was located in a "much rougher neighborhood." The brick building was "kind of like this big box, and it had a playground all around it, and it was kind of an ugly school because it had these kind of barbed-wire fences around it—maybe not barbed wire but just wire fence." Across the street in every direction were black homes, and beyond them railroad tracks, car dealerships, and other commercial enterprises.

Inside, Nichols was one of the most architecturally and artistically rich schools in Evanston. Embodying the multicultural interests of its namesake, Superintendent Frederick Nichols, Spanish- and Cambodian-themed paintings, murals, Italian tiles, and stained-glass windows adorned the building. The late superintendent's progressive views shone when he commissioned a black artist, Archibald Motley Jr. Motley had trained at the Art Institute in Chicago and was hired during the Depression by the Illinois WPA. An underlying goal of the New Deal initiative was to increase public interest and accessibility. Artwork reflected the WPA's spirit of democratic populism. It hung in public buildings. Southern lynchings and northern riots gave the agency a second goal: to improve race relations.

In 1936 Motley painted three murals for the second-floor music room at Nichols. While the murals no longer exist, we know from Motley's other work that he consistently painted blacks in a positive manner and that in accordance with WPA stipulations he used themes of inter-racial harmony and childhood innocence. Likely an easel study for a mural at Doolittle School in Chicago, *Playground,* for example, shows black and white children embracing during recess. *Band Playing, Dance Scene,* and *Negro Children* were painted for Nichols. *Negro Children,* 2×19 feet, would have wrapped around one entire side of the music room.[4] The wall painting probably reflected more than Nichols's attitude to-ward race. An astute observer, Motley always made numerous site visits to take extensive measurements and to choose appropriate iconogra-phy based on the area where his work would be placed.[5] He wanted to record the world as completely and honestly as he could. During his visits to Evanston he must have seen black children living nearby and attending classes at Nichols. With integration their number increased, giving Nichols one of the highest black-to-white ratios in the district, 22 percent black and 78 percent white.

Reversing the norm, white students traveled in order to integrate Nichols, worrying some parents whose children would be walk-ing through unfamiliar territory for the first time. Concerns about maintaining order were frequently voiced during CACI hearings— "discipline will go to hell, standards will go to hell"—and aided in the polarization of blacks and whites.[6] Some school board members fought to include discipline training in the Teachers' Summer Institute. Once the integration plan was implemented, these same people may have welcomed trouble as proof that integration was not working. On Sep-tember 23, 1968, Ann Pollak was invited to testify at a board meeting to validate their beliefs. Pollak read from a prepared statement: "My son, aged 11, was returning home from Nichols Junior High School last Tuesday, September 10, when he was tripped, held at knife point and robbed by a gang of his fellow students." Pollak understood that the word *discipline* had racist connotations, and so she chose her words carefully. Her plea was based on the simple tenet of human rights but was overshadowed by the example she gave of juvenile misbehavior off school grounds. She was asking for "more parental participation in the schools, and curriculum to teach rights and responsibilities."[7] Some board members seized the opportunity and insisted that a for-mal committee be appointed to restore the community's confidence in integration. Coffin saw through the facade and refused to take part. "Discipline was not only a matter of what to do about unruly children in school; it became more than that. It became a battleground for dif-fering viewpoints about desegregation and its effect on the behavior of children. It also enabled those originally opposed to desegregation to air their views about the manner in which the Negro children behaved in formerly all-white schools."[8] Despite Coffin's refusal, a Rights and Responsibilities Committee was formed in March 1969 to address supposed widespread discipline problems.

Pollak was asked to serve on the committee. Like other concerned parents, she hoped members would be sensitive to the needs of black children. Busing was taking them away from their own communities to new ones that were sometimes unwelcoming and often not understanding of their background. She resisted a rigid disciplinary policy while children were still adjusting to integration. Pollak envisioned the new group as a successor to CACI, ensuring and preserving human rights.

Within the year she would ask the committee to disband. To her dismay, its members were spending most of their time working to write a disciplinary code for the schools. "Rights and responsibilities," it seemed, was a euphemism for "law and order," or more specifically, "how can we clamp down on the black children?" In her statement Pollak said she was "acutely aware of the implications of the term 'discipline' and its possible hazards within a newly heterogeneous society. 'Discipline' without the human understanding and a genuine attempt to get to the nitty-gritty of the individual problem, can cause suffering on the side of the disciplined and a deterioration of societal responsibility on the other."[9] Pollak's colleague Alice Kreiman supported the motion to disband by resigning immediately. Over the course of several months Kreiman had become increasingly aware that the basic concern of the board was "discipline per se, rather than rights & responsibilities." Not a single principal interviewed by the committee expressed a need for a code of discipline. Kreiman had a sinking feeling that the committee had been created as a tool of the board to undermine integration in general and Coffin in particular. Rather than "cracking down," she believed it was important to seek reasons for misbehavior. "There is no need to 'spank' a busy, eager, challenged, interested, understood and loved child," she wrote.[10] Both women understood that good discipline cannot be legislated but good behavior can be nurtured.

One of the committee's first actions was to institute special classes for students with severe behavioral problems in each of the four junior highs. Tales of breakdowns of discipline, of racial hostilities and intimidation, persisted into the 1970s, when our group entered Nichols Middle School. Authorities disrupted Chip's studies for a second time when they insisted that he transfer from Haven to Nichols, following a district policy of removing children who were bad influences on each other. Chip was separated from his friend Stevie and transferred to Nichols for seventh grade. A so-called troublemaker from Nichols was moved to Haven. Chip did not receive a warm welcome at his new school. His homeroom teacher, Miss Davis, was "not happy with me," he told me in an interview. "She sent me home the first day of school to take out my earring and to take off a tank top and to put on a real shirt. She really couldn't stand the way I dressed." Chip was used to the Haven style: "You know, coming from the west side, it was about getting on the 'L' every other weekend and going down to Flagg Brothers and getting clothes."

White children were allegedly nervous in the presence of groups of blacks. They were afraid to go to the bathroom for fear of being beaten up. Blacks who suddenly found themselves surrounded by whites banded together. Individuals aimed their mutual fear and hostility toward members of the other group. Candy recalled, "It was a hard place to live—you had to be strong." Black girls bullied and picked on Candy. "They'd take stick pins and tape 'em to their finger and stick you on the stairwell with a stick pin." It was not unusual for fights to erupt during gym class. Candy remembers a dispute over whose turn it was on the trampoline. Later in the locker room, a black girl came up behind Candy, and "she took my head and slammed it against the locker, and I turned around and we fought." When Candy was older, she appreciated her youth. "I was really glad that I'd had the experience in Evanston, 'cause I knew that I knew more about people than a lot of the other gals my age."

The institution itself was a target for vandalism and burglary. Prince's brothers and their friends broke into Nichols and took speakers and stereo equipment from the auditorium. Some of the goods were taken to Prince's house, where his mother demanded an explanation: "Where did this stuff come from?" Dissatisfied with the answer, she called the police, who came to the house to retrieve the stolen property. Prince's mother had integrity and was an important role model for her children.

When a teacher inappropriately disciplined Prince, his mother sued him. Prince was at Nichols playing basketball one night when a white supervisor told him to "get off the floor." "There was games going on, and the kids go down to one side of the floor—you sneak out there and get a shot," he explained. When Prince refused to move, the supervisor kicked him and yelled, "Keep your black ass off the floor." Prince left the gym and ran home crying. His mother took him to Community

Hospital to see a doctor before they went to court. His mother's message to school authorities was clear: "Don't ever put your hand on my son." She raised her son's self-esteem by acting against the institution that was trying to knock him down.

Carla's mischievousness was easily dismissed. She had a reputation as a troublemaker and was known as the class clown. When she played a prank on the science teacher, she was reprimanded by her homeroom teacher but didn't get in any serious trouble for it. Her parents were never called in for a conference. An end-of-term note sufficed. "I have some of my old report cards, and it's 'I need to be more serious and I was out to get the laugh,'" she told me.

There were double standards for black and white students. Black students were disciplined more often and more harshly. Racial tensions were a result of structural forces, not individual actions. That didn't stop middle-school students from becoming friends.

The Color Line

When W. E. B. DuBois wrote that the problem of the twentieth century was the problem of the color line, he was referring to hard-and-fast boundaries of racial segregation. Children didn't necessarily recognize or abide by them.

Evanston was visibly organized on a grid with natural and manmade landmarks. It was an easy place to maneuver and infuse with meaning. My friends formed strong attachments to the city.[11] Carla told me that she felt "fortunate" to have grown up in an "integrated environment" where her friends "comprised all different races." The city shaped her and made her who she is today: "I'm half black inside. I swear it's a very real thing; it's my humor and the way I dance, French-braiding people's hair."

Other members of the group agreed. Thinking back, Jennifer said, "It just seemed like everyone got along so well. Maybe it was the time—I don't know? And then to also live with middle-class mostly black people, I think is unusual."

Other descriptions concealed racial demographics but suggested them nonetheless. Regina's family had moved to Evanston because it had a reputation for being "artsy" and "liberal." Candy described growing up in Evanston as an "enriching" and "educational" experience. Although Barbara lived on the street that separated her own white neighborhood from a black residential area, she seemed unaware that racial

boundaries existed within Evanston. She believed that the "divider between black and white" was McCormick Avenue, the street that separated Evanston from Skokie, an all-white predominantly Jewish suburb
to the west.

Blacks spoke of Evanston in similar terms. They never used words
like *diverse* or *racially mixed*; they also never described the city as segregated. Bernie did not think of his neighborhood as being representa-
tionally black. He insisted that "the black side was on the west side of
town." Like many northerners, he understood de facto segregation as a
fact or coincidence. "It was just spotty here," he said, referring to the
streets near Nichols; "it just so happened that it was all black over here
at the time, but over here I think there was white people."

Jesse told me that he still "cherishes those years," recalling that "we
were pretty much carefree back then. Everybody was getting along having a good time. It wasn't about color or race—it didn't have nothing
to do with none of that." These memories differ from city government
maps depicting entrenched residential segregation.

Age was an overarching factor. We were less aware of racial norms
than were our parents, who did not have close interracial relationships.
This finding is corroborated in a *Wall Street Journal* article marking the
twentieth anniversary of the Supreme Court's decision in *Brown v. Board
of Education* published in 1974, the same year my photo was taken. The
piece focuses on a six-block area in Southwest Evanston where blacks
made up 20 percent of the population. Beginning in 1962, the area
was integrated gradually, which apparently "didn't result from any concerted effort." Like our parents, adults who were interviewed for this
article said that they had made the choice to relocate because of their
children. They believed, like other postwar open-housing advocates,
that interracial contact would change their children's consciousness
and socialize them for an increasingly multicultural world. A black
resident was quoted as saying, "I think it's good to live in a mixed section for the sake of the kids, but the housing was the main thing."
White residents had similar goals: "My wife and I wanted our children
to get to know all kinds of people." Another white neighbor echoed
this sentiment: "People used to be scared of blacks, but I don't think
that's true any more. The kids sure aren't; Scott [her son] has lots of
black friends." Residential integration, however, was not accompanied
by much "conspicuous chumminess" between black and white adults.
A source revealed that social contact between grown-ups was "pretty
much limited to saying hello on the street." Most of the interracial
friendships that did develop involved children.[12] They befriended each

other without paying too much attention to where one neighborhood ended and another began.

To help me reconcile the contradiction of integration in a segregated city, I used a method pioneered by urban planner Kevin Lynch. Lynch first developed sketch mapping as a method for understanding the meaning people place on the city form.[13] Subsequently, this method has been used to geographically record individual memories of and perspectives on a particular place. I decided to add a map exercise to the interview schedule.

While my friends' maps depicted racially divided neighborhoods, they also revealed that individuals were not merely passive recipients. Rather, they were active agents who used and manipulated public space, engaging with and directing their social environment. Members of our group circumvented the structural environment intended to drive them apart. Before discussing subversive elements, I want to elaborate the extent to which social class and wealth are portrayed in the drawings.

I supplied everyone with a large sketchpad and pencil. I instructed them to mark places of importance; including their homes, where their friends lived, and where they socialized. Additionally, I asked them to mark areas that they perceived as dangerous or any place where they felt unwelcome. Finally, I asked everyone to specify important destinations and the routes or pathways that they took to get to these places. Pictures served as mnemonic devices, allowing my friends to remember important details about their lives while they were drawing. Since illustrations are highly subjective, there were no right or wrong maps, and while the quality of sketch maps is dependent on the graphic skills of those who make them, legibility was not what I was looking for. Assuming that the task was fairly easy, I was surprised when my subjects worried about accuracy and artistic talent.

Everyone needed reassurance and prompting, but no one more than Jesse. By the time it was his turn, I had grown accustomed to this response and was not surprised by his reluctance. I knew about the varying life opportunities of the members of the group. Still, I was caught off guard when I realized that Jesse was afraid to draw the map because he had never learned to spell. I was equally unnerved when Chip's failing health and deteriorating motor skills prevented him from completing the task.

The others drew maps that were visual representations of the neighborhoods where they lived during our middle-school years. The maps themselves were not precise miniaturized models of reality, as purposive simplifications; they were made by reducing, eliminating, or even adding elements.[14] Maps consisted of childhood homes, schools, and routes—all of which were symbols of Evanston and the collective memory of its inhabitants. For most, individual homes provided a baseline and maps branched out from these points. The home was usually the centerpiece. Overall, total structure was distinguished in two ways: either hierarchical—a gradation from superior to subordinate—or dynamic, parts being interconnected by a sequence over time, with images related to the actual experience of moving through neighborhoods.[15] I found both aspects of the maps intriguing.

The diagrams called into question nostalgic versions of our hometown. Place, race, and social class were salient in the hand-drawn maps. They revealed racially segregated communities, class disparities, and power differentiations between blacks and whites. Varying degrees of importance and meaning were given to spaces (white areas were exaggerated, while there was a profound desizing of black space). In both cases the *other* group was rendered invisible: blacks did not include white neighborhoods in their diagrams, and vice versa. This invisibility is made clear by the literal absence of the homes and names of individuals in the *other* group, and is countered by the inclusion of the homes and names of friends from the participant's racialized group.

Barbara, who lived on what was quite literally the boundary between a white and mixed neighborhood, did not include the black community directly adjacent to her childhood home (to the bottom of her map—see fig. 4.1). Her drawing ends abruptly where the black community begins. In some cases, when my friends did incorporate the *other* neighborhood in their drawings, they used landmarks such as a school or train tracks as markers. These examples demonstrate an underlying unfamiliarity that group members had with racialized neighborhoods different from their own.

Mapmaking also revealed themes of socioeconomic disparity, which were supported by pictorial renditions. This became evident when I considered the scale, size, and form of the houses. By comparing the drawings from both groups, I realized how much larger whites' homes were than blacks'.

When Carla's father accepted a tenured position at Northwestern in 1969, the family relocated to Evanston. They purchased a house near the campus and across the street from Lake Michigan. Their home, which cost fifty-four thousand dollars at the time, was one of many ancestral mansions for which Evanston was famous. Among my friends' maps, illustrations of houses owned by whites were often

145

FIGURE 4.1 Barbara's map.

decorated with elaborate detail, exemplified by Carla's drawing of her home, which is pictured on the lower right-hand corner of her map (see fig. 4.2). While maps elucidate the visual dimension of socioeconomic status, her interview also attested to her family's wealth:

It was stucco with big gables, these big points on the top; it was three stories besides the basement. My oldest brother, Gene, got to live in the whole third floor; it was like an apartment, it was huge. And I had a cool big bedroom with two doors, so I could leave it two different ways. And it had one of those electric chairs that would go up the stairs, and there was a button where you could send the chair up alone, so if you asked me to bring something up to you, I could just stick it on there, press the button, and it would go up. Huge big front porch looking out on the lake and that ran the length of the house and wasn't glassed in or screened in, so you could sit there and look at the lake. It was a great house.

By contrast, Earl lived across from Nichols, the large, noisy public middle school that we attended. His family rented the top floor of a two-flat while his aunt and cousins, including one of Carla's elemen-

tary school friends, Dorothy, lived below in the first-floor apartment.
Their household was strict, happy, chaotic, and religious. The family
regularly attended services at Springfield Baptist Church. While the
view from Carla's home looked out over one of the nation's five Great
Lakes, train tracks for two commuter railways ran behind Earl's building. Either to drown out the noise or to add to it, Earl and his siblings
played the guitar and sang. They called themselves the Hutchinson
Family Singers and performed at churches around Chicago. Earl's home
is pictured to the far right on Prince's map (fig. 4.3).

Prince drew his house and those of his black neighbors in the shape
of boxes—small, uniform, and plain. Some of the contrast with Carla's
drawing might be attributable to gender differences; overall, the wom-
en's maps were more intricate than the men's. It is also true that whites
lived in expensive and architecturally distinctive homes that their parents owned, while Prince's and Earl's families rented. When the rent man
came to collect his check, he'd give Prince five dollars to clean the yard.

Candy and Jesse also lived in homes that reflected their class background. Candy grew up in a large Victorian home built in 1885. There

FIGURE 4.2 Carla's map.

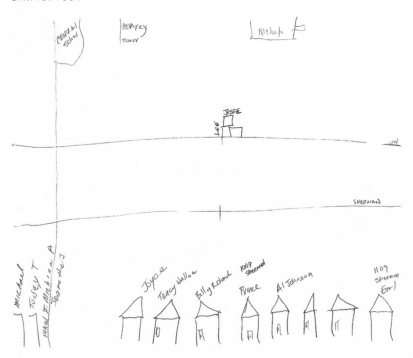

FIGURE 4.3 Prince's map.

were fourteen rooms, including seven bedrooms and three and a half bathrooms. Her parents slept in the master bedroom, and each of the four children also had his or her own room. A private apartment on the third floor provided extra income. In the backyard there was a garage and a tennis court, which the family flooded to make an ice-skating rink in the winter. A wrought-iron gate from the 1893 Chicago World's Fair was set in the fence surrounding the yard.

While Candy's family had more than enough room, Jesse's did not. After moving north from South Carolina, the Floyds shared a four-bedroom apartment with his mother's sisters' families. A total of five adults and fifteen children shared the tight space. A back porch was converted into a sleeping area, and family members slept on pullout couches and rollaway beds, which were stored in closets during the day. Jesse's family had moved frequently, staying no more than a year or two in any given place. The instability was stressful on his parents, and as a young child he was aware of these pressures. By the time Jesse reached sixth grade, his family had enough money to rent their own small apartment adjacent to the Nichols baseball field. More than once a ball broke one of their windows.

Not restricted by racial and gender taboos, Ronny had more access to our black friends' homes than we did. He was struck by the impoverished conditions some of them lived in. Tyrone's house was "really funky." It was "run down. It was really run down. Like, you know, towels on the window instead of curtains, and no money—basically just no money." At another friend's house there were "doors coming off the hinges, nothing painted, floorboards coming up, linoleum coming up, broken dishwasher, broken sink handles, no curtains, furniture way old, no light coverings, bare light bulbs." The landlord wasn't maintaining the building, and the tenant couldn't afford to.

Ronny's family was far better off. He quickly learned his place in the hierarchy of rich and poor. He was expected to give away the items he didn't want anymore. "I would give Tyrone my sneakers after wearing 'em. I sort of became this caretaker for all these kids." Blacks were cast as dependent and recipients of aid. He admits to harboring some resentment: "It's sort of like I was the last in line in my own mind." Prince's envy of the children who appropriated his mother's attention was another example of the emotional response young children had to social inequalities and part of the process that ultimately divided our interracial friendship group.

Buying a house is the largest single investment that most Americans will make. Appreciation of the property's value can lead to economic security, especially in old age. Depreciation can lead to economic ruin. According to interview data, all but one of the white youth in the photograph lived in a home that was owned by their family. The proportion was reversed for black families, who mostly rented. Noted sociologist Dalton Conley has written that in order to understand a family's well-being and the life chances of its children we not only must consider education and occupation, but must take into account accumulated wealth, that is property and assets. A history of discrimination means that blacks have had few opportunities to accumulate wealth and to pass it on to their descendants. According to Conley, in 1865 blacks owned 0.5 percent of the total worth of the United States—not surprising given their status as slaves; however, by 1990 their ownership had increased only to 1 percent.[16]

I came across a mention of my childhood home in a 1974 pamphlet published by the Evanston Planning Department. "Evanston Architecture: A Sample of Self-Guided Tours" directed enthusiasts through

Evanston's neighborhoods—on foot, car or bike—to view significant homes and churches. My house was a stop on the second tour. Myron Hunt designed close to forty homes in Evanston, including the one I grew up in. Commissioned by Harvey Hurd, an ardent abolitionist whose claim to fame came when he escorted Lincoln by train to Evanston on April 4, 1860, my house was built in 1899. Hunt was a student of the Prairie School, the earliest native American architectural style, "born and nurtured" in the Midwest. It was popular between 1895 and 1918. "The horizontal lines favored by architects of the Prairie School were seen as echoing the spirit of the flat prairies of the Middle West, which to them embodied the essence of democracy."[17] A discourse of "democracy" runs throughout descriptions of Evanston from the mid-nineteenth century forward. Early boosters compared the city with the cradle of democracy by giving it the nickname "Athens of the Midwest." But my house was as far west as any of the three tours went. Excluding black neighborhoods seemed antithetical to the democratic values espoused by Evanston. Our group came together under these constraints.

At first glance, it seemed as if the maps contradicted accounts of a racially integrated past, but in the end they supported these memories. Maps were also a way to understand my friends as active agents who used and manipulated public space. By crossing the color line and walking through neighborhoods that were not our own, our group shaped the social environment. In a period when teenagers moved freely through city streets, we developed interracial relationships within divisive segregating structures, befriending each other on our journey to and from school and continuing to build friendships in the afternoon after the schoolday was over. Outdoors we found freedom that was not available in lunchrooms and classrooms, where we were under the watchful eye of authorities. For us streets provided a life outside the private realm of the home that had nothing to do with parents and allowed us to develop interracial relationships.

French philosopher Michel de Certeau claims that individuals "do not obey the law of the place for they are not defined or identified by it"; rather they "use, manipulate and divert spaces" through everyday practices, or tactics.[18] His landmark text was a turning point in cultural studies, away from the producer (city planner) and the product (city street) to the consumer (pedestrian). After, quite literally, drawing the color line, my subjects spoke of the ways in which they crossed it.

Evanston was a safe place to live and raise kids. We enjoyed a certain freedom of mobility due, in part, to a pervasive lack of strict after-school supervision. Some of us had working mothers and came home to empty houses. Most of us never locked the front door of our home. It wasn't unusual to come home from school and find friends waiting in the living room, having let themselves in because no one had locked the doors. During interviews I asked everyone if there were places in Evanston where their parents didn't allow them to go; they told me that they could go anywhere anytime, that there were virtually no restrictions. Bernie summed it up best when he said that we were "free to roam."

Arguably the biggest factor in building interracial friendships and overcoming segregation and racial discrimination was the district policy not to bus to middle schools. Walking to school was an inadvertent mechanism for racial interaction. It facilitated burgeoning relationships. Differences among neighbors seemed to disappear, and interaction took place between equals. Sidewalks allow strangers to dwell in peace together, writes urban activist Jane Jacobs.[19]

The burden of travel was placed on the more privileged of the two groups. To get to Nichols each day whites made their way on foot or

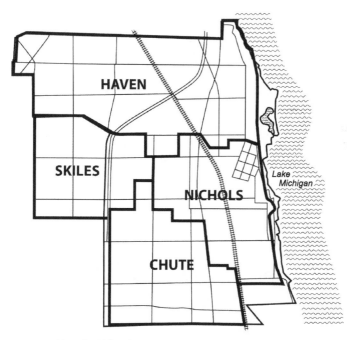

FIGURE 4.4 Map of middle school attendance areas, including a section of Skokie that lies within the Evanston school district. Ron Crawford.

bike, eventually traversing the neighborhood surrounding the school, where many of our black classmates lived. Walking exposed us to a new part of town, allowing us to interact with kids whom we had never met before. Ronny, the only white male subject in this book, lived near Nichols, but he told me that he did not know black neighbors living only blocks away until he had to walk past their houses on his way to and from school. New friendships developed. Ronny's sister Jennifer recalls, "All my friends were black in Nichols." She couldn't say that about any other time in her life.

Earl was a natural protector. He'd carry his niece on his shoulders after it rained—the sidewalks were crawling with worms, and she didn't want to step on them. One day he saw Regina walking home. She looked upset. He lived catty-corner from the school, and she lived to the east, closer to the lake. Earl was a year older than Regina; the two might not have met if her route hadn't taken her by his house. "I was going home crying one day from school, and Earl started following me," she recalled. "Talk to me, talk to me," he insisted as he rode next to her on his bicycle. Regina tried to tell him to "go away." He refused to back off until he knew she was okay. He was "relentless." "Then like every day after school he would follow me home, so we started talking, and then we eventually started dating."

It wasn't a typical teenage romance. The popular black boy and the popular white girl were as close to junior high royalty as you could get.[20] Earl and Regina were together for more than seven years. Adults may have feared interracial intimacy, but children saw each other as human first. Unlike private homes, sidewalks were unregulated public spaces that neutralized racial norms.

Distance was significant. Because in some cases white children lived far away, there may have been an impetus to stay around school before walking back home. Candy and I had to travel the farthest of the group to reach Nichols. Neither of us can believe how far we walked each day. "At least twelve city blocks," Candy remembers. She joked about the need to stop and "refuel for the journey." Everyone went to Bernstein Brothers, a corner store located just blocks from Nichols, across from Barbara's house. We'd fill our coat pockets with Hostess snack cakes and walk out of the store without paying. The store was both a destination and a gathering spot. The days were seamless. Friendships that formed at school continued after it was over.

I don't know exactly how Candy and Jesse met, but it was while they were students at Nichols. Candy loved Jesse—of that I can be certain. She made it clear one day with her colored magic markers and drawing

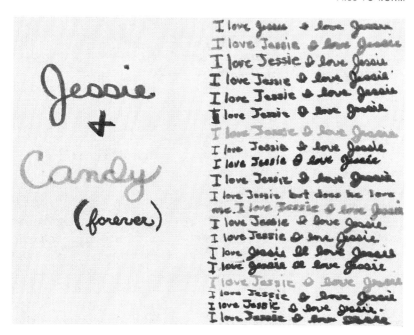

FIGURE 4.5 Candy's doodle confirms her love for Jesse. Courtesy of Jennifer Crawford.

pad. More than likely this wasn't the first time she had copied a phrase in the belief that the writing act itself would either alter her behavior or impact the future. That's why when Candy carefully printed "I love Jessie" and then emphasized the phrase again repeatedly in cursive writing: a part of her believed that because she did so, their relationship might last forever. As a young girl she could not have understood how unlikely it was that she would be with him for the rest of her life— not because they were both only thirteen years old but because she was white and he was black. Despite their close relationship and pronounced love for one another, Candy never went to Jesse's house. Following historical taboos against interracial sexuality, she told me that it was not done. "Quite honestly, I don't even know where he actually lived, where he physically lived. I never met his family." She never knew how close he was. His family lived next to Nichols.

Strolling through the neighborhood did not necessarily mean stopping in black homes. Interracial friendships were common, but afterschool visits almost always meant black children visiting white homes. And private space was more restricted for girls than for boys. White girls did not visit black boys' homes; in fact, girls didn't go to boys' homes, period. Such norms did not apply to Jennifer's brother Ronny, who regularly went over to Perkey's house to "hang out." "We were always building something in his garage," Ronny remembers. Perkey was into cars, engines, and minibikes, "anything that would go." For additional income his mother rented the garage out to a neighbor, whose dragster impressed the boys. Ronny's memories of the period echoed the sentiments of others: "The way everyone hung out was so beautiful; it just felt so much freer, so much fun, just hanging out and laughing."

Not everyone did hang out. Black girls and white boys are absent from my photo. The commodity value of both groups prevented them from socializing with the rest of us on a regular basis. Parents either needed their children to perform labor for the communal good or saw their potential as future breadwinners and regulated their lives accordingly. My black friends' sisters often did not participate in leisurely activities like their brothers because they were required to do domestic chores and maintain the family home. Prince's mother relied on her daughters to help with the household work for her family of seven. They cleaned the house, cooked dinner, and washed dishes. Prince said that on weekends "they spent the bulk of their time either at the Laundromat or grocery shopping. but never just sitting back and hanging out like we did as guys." He continued, "Especially on a Saturday I remember them getting up at 6:00 in the morning and loading the cars and the clothes into the car and going to the Laundromat . . . I never remember them just going out at that age and saying, 'We're going to hang out here or going to hang out there.' But at nighttime I remember the black girls coming out, and seeing them at parties."

Jesse's home life was also illustrative of the domestic responsibilities delegated to young black girls. Because both of his parents worked two jobs, his older sister "was really the one that watched after us." She would "keep an eye on us at night, in between aunts that just had a day job." Jesse's sister would heat up precooked food. "My mom would cook a big meal on Sunday, enough for us to eat it again for two days. . . . And then she'd cook again on Wednesday, enough for two days. And that's how we ate: she'd make a big pot of spaghetti and that would hold us for two days." His sister also helped him with his homework, "'cause my parents didn't have much of an education." Most of the time the children had to "fend for ourselves," as his mother did not get home until ten or eleven at night.

Class structure limited the lives of black girls in our hometown. They had to grow up fast and take on adult responsibilities. At the same time it offered what seemed like limitless opportunities to white girls. It's no wonder that there was antagonism between the two groups. White girls demanded their brothers' time and interest. White girls said they weren't interested in white boys; they were "square" or not as socially or sexually mature. White boys were more often busy with organized activities, such as sports and clubs. Headed to college, they were also more likely to spend their afternoons studying and doing homework. Ronny was the exception.

Adolescence has changed since the postwar period. Children do not walk to school anymore, and their time is much more structured than it used to be. Statistics from the National Household Travel Survey demonstrate this change. In 1969, 41 percent of American children either walked or biked to school; by 2001 that percentage had dropped to 13.[21] Sociologist Annette Lareau's childhood studies explain the change. For much of US history, children played an important economic role in the family. Their contributions declined, however, as child labor laws were put into place after 1920.[22] For a relatively brief period after World War II, children were granted long stretches of unstructured time. They were permitted to play for hours on end with other neighborhood children, after school, during evenings, and on weekends. More recently new social forces, especially the impact of increasing "rationalization," have restricted children's movement and play and have required them to lead more scheduled and regimented lives.[23] Changing perceptions of children's free time, reliance on the automobile, and a culture of fear have relegated walking to school to the past.[24] Today children are not visible on city streets, especially on their own without accompanying adults. If they are outside, they're seen as a threat or nuisance to social order and in need of adult supervision.

Jane Jacobs writes that roaming the streets is infinitely more interesting and less boring to youth than specialized and supervised games. Gyms and playgrounds require expensive equipment, supervision, and a formal plan that can be stifling. Convenience and spontaneity excite kids. Part of the charm is the "sense of freedom to roam up and down the sidewalks."[25] Incidental play gives children a chance to explore and use their imaginations. They run up and down and splash in puddles, finding all manners of ways to amuse themselves. Propinquity, Jacobs argues, is vital because a great part of outdoor play must be sandwiched in after school, before dinner, and in between homework. As children get older, outdoor activity becomes less physically active and entails more loitering, flirting, and talking.[26]

Bernie jumped at the chance to hang out with his older brother Perkey and befriended Ronny in the process. The threesome never worried much about going inside, or even around the corner to the YMCA.

There was never a plan. They did everything on the spur of the moment. They always found things to do outside, using what the environment had to offer as inspiration. When the boys spotted a row of brick buildings on Sherman between Dempster and Greenwood, they saw a perfect opportunity. They climbed to the top on one end and then leaped across from roof to roof to the other end. The buildings were close enough to each other that it wasn't too dangerous. Weather was never a deterrent. The boys wanted to play in the rain: they would ride their Stingray bikes until they were soaking wet, then stop and buy hot chocolate from a vending machine at the cop shop in the lobby of the police station. They rode their bikes so often that they formed their own club. Ronny's father designed T-shirts that read "Schwinn Gang."

Organized sports also gave kids something to do. Jesse and Ray played Little League baseball. A gifted athlete, Jesse would go on to play ball in high school. Some of his early friendships with white boys transcended Little League and continued with high school sports teams. However, it was Ray that he celebrated with after a big championship game between Kiwanis- and Burger King–sponsored teams. "I was pitching that game, and I was throwing all smoke, 'cause I had my fast ball in Little League. I could throw it real hard and real fast, and Ray hit it all the way on the railroad tracks. Ray was just so excited that it was a grand slam he hit off of me." The two boys celebrated at their favorite hot dog stand near Howard Street after the game. Jesse tried to remember the name of the place: "It's real famous; they'd have lines of people all the way out the door, and everybody that you could think of went to this place—grandmothers, mothers, kids. Everybody loved this place."

Structured activities were an increasingly important phenomenon in a developing teenage culture, but we liked hanging out at Jennifer's house better. Her parents, like many other local whites, chose to raise their kids in Evanston so as to expose them to a racially diverse social body—and they practiced what they preached. We nestled in beanbag chairs listening to music and cracking sunflower seed shells open with our teeth. Candy "felt comfortable and welcome there." She doodled Jesse's name with her colored markers; Jennifer scribbled Perkey's. Kids came and went as they pleased, but Perkey "always rang the bell." He'd come over with an album, asking, "Have you heard these guys yet?" He was the first to know about the "coolest songs and groups." He gave Jennifer a ring.

"We weren't really doing anything, but it was fun," Regina remembered. Out of her parents' sight, it was the perfect place to meet Earl.

Bernie's friend Darrin teased him: "Going over that white boy's house again?" Bernie would nod. Barbara went to see Jennifer but knew that Ronny would be there too. It was on the way to the YMCA, so Prince and Ray would stop to see Ronny before basketball. Carla listened to "Build Me Up Buttercup" and laughed at Chip staring at himself in the mirror. I hoped Chip would notice me, and eventually he did.

Jesse looked up to Jennifer's father, Ron. "I admired the relationship he had with his kids, and his family. That's the way I seen things, how they should be, and how I wanted mine to be, by their family. I liked how their family was, and they were always positive. It never seemed like nothing ever bothered them, they just was always upbeat." We gathered outside on the porch and posed for a photo. Ronny took it.

The house sat near the corner of Elmwood and Lake Streets, named for Evanston's natural assets. Inspired by a trip to San Francisco in the early sixties, Jennifer's parents painted it in the psychedelic fashion of the Haight-Asbury hippies. The home reflected a Victorian sense of style, a custom multicolored paint job, stained glass, and carved moldings, with a coach house in back. A flag with an ecology sign flew in the front yard. The combination of quaint, chic, and contemporary made a statement about the residents who lived inside. The house's style was part of the communication of class culture and political identification. Everyone was welcome. While some of our parents wondered what was going on inside, we thought it was the "coolest fucking house in the world."

That house left a mark. Jennifer's father drew it. Candy framed his drawing and put it on the wall of the study in her home in France. She showed it to me when I visited. At the time of the interview, Candy was forty-five years old. She had left Evanston when she was still in high school. When she moved away she lost touch with almost everyone in my photo. Nevertheless, the time and place symbolized by the house remained important and formative. Just as telling, Jennifer and Ronny's house was Chip's first stop when he came home from Germany after leaving the military. When he turned onto Elmwood and pulled up in front, he saw that it had been painted a dingy gray. He surmised that the Crawfords were gone, but he rang the bell anyway. A woman answered to confirm what he already knew.

Lighted Schoolhouse

The district's largest endorsement of interracial friendships was the Lighted Schoolhouse. The program's genius was to utilize schools as neighborhood recreation and education centers. As the name suggests, the lights would go up after the regular school hours were over. The multipurpose school building was considered by many educators to be the coming trend in school and civic planning. Both after-school and evening programs were scheduled to begin with desegregation in the fall of 1967. Five sessions were held during the first year: fall, winter, spring, spring extension, and summer. The district made Nichols Middle School facilities available at no cost, and the recreation department provided responsible leadership or supervision. Herbert H. Henderson, who had experience working for the Office of Economic Opportunity, as a community development officer, and at the Chicago Park District as a supervisor, was named director. An eighteen-person team oversaw the program, which would begin at the close of school each day and continue into the evening hours five nights a week. Evening programs included a drop-in center for high school students three times a week in the school cafeteria and a Y-Teen Club for junior high school girls, which was open Monday–Friday. A Saturday-morning sports program was also planned.

The first session was a huge success. New programs and classes were added to the second session to keep up with the demand. By the end of the first year, a total of 2,161 Evanstonians had enrolled in regular sessions, and 537 were involved in various summer activities. In a progress report submitted to the board of education, Coffin recommended that the Lighted School Center be continued the next year and that the Evanston Parks and Recreation Board expand the program to a second school.[27] Due to the program's popularity, it was renewed. William W. Bushnell won the logo design contest and was awarded a twenty-five-dollar savings bond and a free course for his efforts. He designed a silhouette of a country schoolhouse with a belfry on a round yellow field; the words "Evanston Lighted School Center" surrounded the drawing (see fig. 4.6).[28] The logo was used on brochures, letterheads, and promotional materials.

The program's success was predicated upon inclusion. There was a concerted effort to involve the entire community. First, Lighted Schoolhouse was sponsored by District 65, the Parks and Recreation department, *and* various civic and neighborhood organizations. An eight-member coordinating council was set up to give the community representation, and the Nichols PTA was also encouraged to get involved. The center held "gripe sessions" for teachers whose classrooms were being used at night by other groups, so that complaints could be handled quickly, and to inform teachers about the center.[29] Second, facilities

FIGURE 4.6   The winning logo for the Evanston Lighted School Center. *Evanston Review,* August 1, 1968.

were made available for neighborhood group meetings. Third, registration was convenient for all residents served by District 65. A mobile unit was dispatched on three separate Saturdays to different locations around Evanston: downtown and both black and white residential areas. At each site, recreation leaders were available to discuss the program and distribute literature. Applications were also accepted by mail or in person at Nichols. Finally, registration fees were nominal. No fees were charged for general activities, except to cover the cost of materials or when instructor salaries were high.[30]

Courses and programs targeted a wide range of groups. Classes were offered for all ages, from grade-school students to adults. The center reached out to historically marginalized groups. Art and recreation classes were conducted for "physically and mentally exceptional" children deemed "trainable and educable." The *Review* praised these efforts: "Too often, the care of exceptional children is left to schools and private institutions. By not overlooking these youngsters, the Evanston Parks and Recreation Department demonstrates that it is responsive to the needs of the few as well as the many. The department is to be commended for its efforts in developing the Lighted School and extending its programs to more and more individuals."[31]

A full-page advertisement in the paper listed the seventeen spring term classes, including art, baton, photography, dance, and French. Two courses targeted black Evanstonians. In a course titled Black Is Beautiful, middle schoolers learned techniques of modeling, poise, and grooming as taught by a black model. The course met on Thursdays and cost two dollars. There was a slightly higher fee for Afro-American History, which was offered on Tuesdays for three dollars. The course description read: "Gain racial understanding through knowledge." Thirty-eight adult evening classes were also listed. Hard work paid off: both enrollment and the number of courses offered doubled in the second year.[32]

Lighted Schoolhouse programs provided a friendly and safe atmosphere for children to play together. They also persuaded children to stay in the neighborhood after school hours. Regina remembers watching Earl and his friends play basketball at Nichols. Open Gym was a favorite for the boys. "Everybody went there," Bernie told me. Friends asked, "You going to Open Gym tonight?" Everyone always answered, "Yeah, I'll be there." The gym was open for three hours, from 6:30 until 9:30 p.m. Bernie described the scene: "They had a couple courts where you just shot around, and then the older guys would come in and play full-court basketball." If you didn't feel like playing sports, you could go to the teen drop-in center. "Downstairs they had Ping-Pong tables, card games, or games you could play down there, Candy Land." Bernie recognized the importance of programs like Lighted Schoolhouse: "people stayed out of trouble."

Some teachers at Nichols worked for the Lighted Schoolhouse program after their regular day ended. On Saturday mornings Mr. Crane would "open up the gym for us for three hours," remembers Prince, who lived across the street. Prince noticed the difference. On the weekends children stayed in their own neighborhoods. When school was not in session, "it seemed like the only kids, the only ones that came, was ones that lived right in the neighborhood." Prince thought Mr. Crane's silver Porsche was an "ugly car" until his friends corrected him: "That's a Porsche, man, that's a Porsche." Like other teachers and staff throughout the district, Mr. Crane was kind and caring. When it was time for social dancing, he played his own LPs. We'd wait for our cue to change partners. Halfway through "Me and Mr. Jones," he'd lift the needle, yell "Snowball!" and we'd switch.

Role Models

Girls knew Mr. Crane through gymnastics. Regina remembers that at a time when she felt out of place after she moved from Oak Park, he "always stood up for me and he just kind of took me under his wing." Candy was touched by his "generosity and love for us." One weekend he invited Candy and two of her friends to go skiing. Candy ran home to ask and couldn't believe it when her parents said yes. The girls piled into that "little Porsche car" and took off for the weekend. "He taught us how to ski—for two full days we skied together." When the group, "two Japanese girls, this white, and then this guy with this great big afro, this big black guy," would eat in restaurants. "they got lots of strange looks." Mr. Crane would tease the girls by saying, "Aren't we just a happy family?" Candy and her friends "thought the world of him, and we had the most amazing weekend."

While middle school was a more advanced unit in the educational system, like elementary institutions, it maintained a homeroom organization. The difference was that homerooms were not organized by grade; this allowed for a smoother transition to high school and prepared students for independent work in the module system. Mixed-grade classes also allowed students to work at their own pace with no stigma attached. It was okay to be a sixth-grader working ahead or an eighth-grader who had fallen behind. Students changed rooms throughout the day for various classes and activities but began and ended each day with the same teacher and group of children. Academic ability did not dictate friendships or interaction with other students. From a student's perspective, the homeroom model provided stability. Thinking back, Candy explained the importance of this structural component: "You just kind of felt like you belonged and there was somebody looking out for you." Teachers and students were able to develop interpersonal relationships based on trust and respect. Jesse established a rapport with Miss Anderson, his homeroom teacher. She gave him positive reinforcement that made him feel good. She would tell him that he had a special quality: "charisma, that make people just wanta cling to you and make 'em wanna go that extra mile for you."

Prince remembers "pretty much every teacher I had at Central," his elementary school two blocks away from Nichols. His third-grade teacher, Mrs. Levy, made quite an impression. She was "nice; she never yelled at me—I don't remember getting in any trouble in her class-room." She was also "easy to talk to." She made him feel important by choosing him first and calling on him frequently. After school he'd go to Nichols to be tutored by the reading teacher, Mrs. Pate; "she would work with me with words or reading books. I would go there after school, and I just remember her paying a lot of attention to me." She tried to prepare him for middle school: "'You gonna be here next year, this is the type of stuff you're gonna look at.' . . . So it was kind of funny, when I end up going over to Nichols School, I had her for homeroom." Mrs. Pate also worked with Jesse, and he remembers her teaching him to speed-read.

Teachers took a personal interest in students, helping them with remedial work and taking them places after school. Jesse's academic struggles were becoming more apparent in middle school. "I had to go to speech classes because I was from the country, and that country ac-cent I had, and they wanted to teach me to talk proper." Writing and spelling were also challenging. "That kind of hampered me. . . . When I got like in seventh and eighth grade, that's when it really started to get hard for me; they was giving you so much homework, and I just couldn't keep up." Teachers offered incentives, trips to McDonald's and to carnivals. "Our parents were working and we just didn't have the money, or we didn't have nobody that would take us," Jesse told me. Ray was close to the science teacher, Miss Johnson. She hired some of the boys to paint her house and do other small chores for her. In return she gave them money to buy "school clothes and school supplies." These gestures of kindness made a marked difference in children's lives.

Perhaps Stanley, the school janitor, had higher hopes for Bernie than he was able to muster for himself. Bernie: "At night he used to sweep the halls; he would let me help him every once in a while. He used to have a room in the basement of Nichols, it was like his storage room, it had a table down there, and I remember he used to make coffee down there; then we'd go sweep the hallways. I think he'd give me a dollar or two just for helping him. But I just wanted to help; I didn't care about getting paid. We'd sit in the basement, and he would tell me how stuff worked in the school. He had this little hook key to turn on the lights, 'cause you didn't have a light switch; he gave me one of those little keys." Bernie remembers long conversations about "what he did at the school and then what I was doing with school." Stanley would always ask, "You staying out of trouble?" Bernie answered, "Yeah, I'm staying out of trouble." Stanley would reply, "Okay, 'cause you get in trouble, you can't sweep with me no more."

Arriving from elementary schools across the city, the group had come together. Friendships and teenage romances blossomed as social forces created opportunities for students from different neighborhoods to get to know one another: a school policy that required integrated student bodies but did not depend on busing; a school building with a cafeteria and after-school programming; mixed grade and ability class-rooms; and caring teachers who created a supportive atmosphere. But at the end of the day, children returned to segregated neighborhoods.

Busing black children into white communities proved to be a flawed solution to the dilemma. Restricted housing made it hard to recruit qualified and capable black teachers, as they could not be promised an adequate place to live. School board members were hesitant to endorse a fair housing ordinance, because doing so might alienate the public and thus undermine their agenda to integrate schools.

Without open housing, school integration was destined to fail. Northern-style school segregation began with northern-style housing segregation. It was not a natural happenstance process. Unlike schools, which were public facilities supported by tax revenue, homes were private property and represented the financial accumulation of the individual. Property owners bitterly contested government intervention in this area. Residents were more open to integrating schools than to integrating their neighborhoods.

FIVE

Bringing the
Movement Home

We must respect the dignity of each man as a person; otherwise, whether we live in Birmingham or in Evanston, we will find ourselves in a dark and desolate situation, not knowing where we are going.

MARTIN LUTHER KING JR., MAY 1963[1]

Housing discrimination in Evanston was flagrant. The borders demarcating black and white residential areas were well understood. Even though the black community was burgeoning on the west side of town, there were limits to its geographical growth. Blacks were excluded from renting or purchasing homes in white residential areas. Early developers had included racial and ethnic clauses in deeds restricting property to white Christians. Homeowners banded together to form neighborhood associations and racial covenants to regulate sales and rentals. In the sixties the city reinforced zoning laws prohibiting the construction of apartment buildings and low-income housing. Inspectors condemned black-owned buildings located in white areas. Discriminatory practices and a lack of affordable housing crowded blacks into the west side where the demand was greater than the supply, enabling landlords to neglect housing stock and raise rents. Public policy and private action had created a visibly segregated city.

Although whites clearly held the upper hand, there were limits to their power. Civil rights activists pressured the city to pass a fair housing ordinance. In 1965 the North Shore Summer Project (NSSP) surveyed white homeowners about their willingness to participate in an open market. Inspired by the Mississippi Summer Freedom Movement, student volunteers registered homeowners instead of voters. They thought they could convince real-estate agents by mandate to sell on a nondiscriminatory basis. But calls for justice were met with organized resistance. Whites were not unified, so institutions stepped in when private decisions failed. Real-estate agents used scare tactics, suggesting that the presence of blacks and Jews would lower property values, increase criminal behavior, or cause a decline in the quality of schools. The mayor and eighteen aldermen who made up the city council refused to pass a fair housing ordinance.

Later, under pressure after the death of Martin Luther King Jr., an ordinance was finally approved, but loopholes and weak enforcement procedures left much unchanged. A pervasive lack of affordable housing perpetuated a racialized east-west divide. So the federally funded Neighbors at Work and grassroots organizations such as the Black Caucus forced the city to address its housing crisis.

The Black Triangle

An article published in the *Review* in 1967 boasted about the city's large black population and, by extension, racial integration: "The City of Evanston has made steady progress toward integrating its neighborhoods in the last 20 years. The Negro population has increased from 9½ percent in 1950 to about 13 percent today, and Negroes now live in all but the 6th ward."[2] By 1970, the black population had grown to 12,861 out of a total of 80,113, or 16 percent.[3] For the most part, however, Evanston's version of integration was one that did not disrupt racial exclusivity. City maps from the time reveal the starkness of Evanston's segregated residential areas. Black and white neighbors were as likely to be separated by train tracks and car dealerships as by commercial districts. There was nothing fixed, permanent, or natural about these boundaries, but both racial groups abided by them.

Keen to hold on to its reputation as a "city of homes," Evanston deployed zoning regulations. Owner occupancy was an index of stability and civic pride. Evanston was the largest suburb in the area, yet its zoning policies were remarkably compatible with those of bucolic suburbs farther north. The high-rise apartment building was noticeably absent from the entire North Shore—a means of squeezing out renters who generally had lower incomes. Apartment buildings and other multifamily dwellings were restricted to land along major arteries, reducing the impact of traffic congestion and other characteristics of multiples that North Shore planners considered unsightly and detrimental to single-family areas. The city was willing to make exceptions for powerful institutions like Northwestern University. There was a concentration of "multiples" in its central business area, primarily to serve Northwestern. In 1969 city authorities capitulated to business interests by allowing for the erection of two tall buildings downtown, the fourteen-floor Holiday Inn and the twenty-one-story State National Bank.

The Planning and Conservation Commission had been established in July 1964 to further block affordable housing. Under the direction of Robert Wheeler, the commission led the city to limit the number of persons who were allowed to live on a property—a policy that threatened to put 80 percent of rooming houses out of business. The commission considered revising lot-area requirements and establishing both minimum building heights and yard dimensions. The long-term plan called for "high-density, high-cost development in the central areas and predominantly single-family homes in all the areas now heavily populated by Negroes" by 1980.[4] The commission was known to enforce zoning laws unfairly. According to one white homeowner, city inspectors were "positively deferential" when inspecting property inhabited by whites, but when they inspected black homes the first thing they did was to "count the toothbrushes to check on the number of people living there."[5] Black residents had to comply with high standards in building, zoning, and housing, but no compensatory effort was made to ensure that they would have equal opportunities in housing and financing of housing.

Housing costs were generally higher in black neighborhoods because of a "color tax," attributable to inflated values in a restricted market. The monthly rent per room in the predominantly black Fifth Ward averaged $25, while it averaged $22.44 in the all-white Fourth. Segregation ensured that black poverty was not only likely but also self-perpetuating and permanent.[6] Because North Shore communities, including Evanston, refused to utilize public funds to build low- and medium-income housing, poor blacks were forced to settle for inadequate accommodations at inflated rates. The problem was compounded by the continued use of restrictive housing clauses. There was plenty of available housing, but it was not available to blacks. Figures from the 1960 census indicate that nearly fifteen hundred local families were living below the federal poverty level, with annual incomes of four thousand dollars or less. Census data also indicate that Evanston had 350 dilapidated and 1,000 deteriorating dwelling units, making up 6 percent of the city's housing units. The majority of these buildings were located on the west side. The west side also had the largest amount of overcrowded housing, defined as more than one person to a room. The problem was so acute that Wheeler directed his department to stop inspecting housing for welfare relief recipients, because most low-cost housing did not conform to the city's codes. Sixty percent of these units had substandard conditions.

Hardest hit were the oldest and youngest members of the community. An advocate for the poor Reverend L. M. Geter of Springfield Baptist Church worried about the lack of services for his congregation. Evanston had no old-age homes for elderly blacks and only one low-cost daycare center for black children. Black-owned Robinson's Day Care had opened in 1964 to provide care for forty children, but tuition was out of reach for many. Lucky children who did attend learned their ABCs and how to write their names. They remember how good the lunches Mrs. Robinson prepared were. Less expensive facilities in the Church of God were inadequate and seriously overcrowded. Accordingly, most working mothers receiving Aid to Dependent Children (ADC) had no choice but to leave their children with neighbors during the day. A concerned Geter explained, "They leave their small children with a neighbor they know by first name only" and thus the children had no "bringing up."[7]

While it would have been cheaper to move to Chicago, many low-income blacks preferred to live in Evanston. A consultant for the Northern District Cook County Department of Public Aid recounted the stories of two women receiving ADC who wanted to stay in the suburb. The first woman had seven children and was living in a two-room basement apartment with a shared kitchen and a bath: "There's no place else for them to go. No one wants to rent to a family of that size. But the mother doesn't want to move to Chicago, where rents are lower. She likes Evanston schools and doesn't want her kids roaming the streets of Chicago. She likes a small community, and she's afraid of the 'jungle' of the city." The second woman relied on the "big vegetable garden" in her backyard to help feed her six children. If she had been forced to relocate to Chicago, she would have had to forgo the garden. Furthermore, Evanston's black community was stable and supportive. "Most of these people have lived in Evanston a long time. That's where they grew up, and they're reluctant to leave." Data from the 1960 census confirmed these claims: 80 percent of the black community had lived in Evanston for five or more years, compared to only 65 percent of whites.[8]

Existing low-cost housing was in danger of being demolished. In April 1964 the city council voted to raze a housing project built to temporarily house returning World War II veterans. The city had plans to convert the land, located on the sanitary canal bank, into a park. Ten families with a total of forty children were given three months to move off of the premises.

Veteran and long-term resident Leon Price had been looking for housing for five years. "It's the usual problem. The more kids you have, the higher the rent. We've looked at places for twice as much money that aren't nearly as nice as this." He added, "Many of the duties performed in a city this size are low-salary jobs. But the city doesn't accept the responsibility of providing housing for these people who do the menial labor." Price himself earned $475 a month as a maintenance man at the Foster Field House: "A lot of people look around and ask why so many Negroes are driving fancy cars. I'll tell you why. Because after saving twenty-five hundred dollars for a home, they found that wasn't enough for a down payment. So they did the next best thing."

Some neighbors, complaining of noise and litter, supported demolition. They also thought it was unfair that blacks were given cheaper housing, and somehow missed the part that they were also paid less. Other people thought the buildings made an important statement: "As long as it is habitable, let it stand as a reminder of this city's need for decent housing for those who work in Evanston's factories, shops, and homes."[9]

Moral suasion doesn't often produce change. Privileged people need to feel that their health and welfare are at risk before they'll act to do the right thing. Evanston's growing social and economic problems were directly related to an increasing density of the black population in restricted sections of the city. Intense pressure on the west side was causing overcrowding, violations of zoning and building codes, and high crime rates. Northwestern law professor Howard Sacks foreshadowed the Kerner Report when he cautioned, Evanston must "do something to release pressure of the Negro housing demand or face real trouble in the near future."[10]

From 1950 to 1960, the demand for nonwhite housing had been absorbed in vacant space. Those areas were now long gone, but the demand for such housing and the ability to pay for it were greater. Property values in white residential areas came to be at risk because nonwhite housing was so confined. This could affect the "stability of currently integrated areas and could cause a spilling over into white areas," or what Sacks called "creeping ghettoism," resulting in panic selling.[11] Other cities struggled to maintain peace by letting their communities become *more* racially segregated. According to Sacks, this was the wrong approach.

North Shore Summer Project

Like the nation at large, Evanston considered property rights to be in the realm of the individual, not the social. Legal protection from housing discrimination was not included in either the 1964 Civil Rights Act or the 1965 Voting Rights Act. In fact, "among all areas of civil rights taken up during the 1960s, neighborhood segregation proved to be the most emotional and resistant to change."[12] The failure of federal legislators to come up with a strong fair housing bill spurred a series of local campaigns in the urban North. Activists in dozens of northern cities took to the streets during the mid-1960s to pressure state legislatures and city councils to pass open housing laws. The most visible and violent campaign took place in Chicago in 1965 and 1966, when Martin Luther King Jr. and his Southern Christian Leadership Conference (SCLC) led a number of nonviolent marches through white working-class neighborhoods. King's Chicago Movement had two goals: better conditions in black neighborhoods and unfettered access to housing in white neighborhoods.[13] SCLC sponsored its largest march on August 5, 1966, in Marquette Park. Four thousand hostile whites threw rocks and shouted racial epithets at demonstrators. King was hit in the head with a rock the size of a fist. Evanstonians may not have resorted to violence, but that didn't mean they were willing to open their neighborhoods.

The NAACP led the crusade against discrimination in private housing because it was primarily a middle-class issue. In May 1964 Evanston branches of both the NAACP and Congress for Racial Equality (CORE), a civil rights group founded by students in Chicago, cosponsored a Truth March protesting the city's restrictive housing policies. A spokesperson for the coalition was unapologetic: "We have been negotiating for racial equality in housing since 1958, and we're sick and tired of being put off."[14] Whites were not unified against open housing; many actively fought for it. A protester explained his position: "The whites in the Truth Walk were striving to obtain for themselves the right to have as neighbors Negroes and other 'minority' Americans who share

169

FIGURE 5.1 Truth marchers carry signs demanding that the city pass a housing ordinance. A protester's sign reads: "Dogs in Birmingham, Realtors in Evanston." Another sign reads: "Help Realtors See Reality." Photo by Charles H. Johnson. Shorefront Legacy Center.

their educational and economic backgrounds."[15] He concluded, "I do not want my right to live in a free housing market infringed by an oligarchy of realtors who choose to select my neighbors for me. Let the market work as it will."[16] Liberal whites also banded together in north Evanston, a notoriously racist part of town. They formed the North Evanston Neighbors Association to facilitate the sale and rental of property to all qualified buyers and renters.

Two months later, in July 1964, the Community Relations Commission (CRC), a subcommittee of the city council, began to explore the possibility of open housing in Evanston. The first step was to acknowledge the problem. Results from surveys indicated that whites and blacks had different perspectives. More than half of white respondents preferred to live in a neighborhood that was 100 percent white. In contrast, 72 percent of blacks preferred to live in a neighborhood that had equal numbers of blacks and whites. Brokers were refusing listings of homeowners that wanted to sell on a nondiscriminatory basis and declined to service Negro home seekers. The Evanston–North Shore Board of Realtors listed over two thousand homes for sale in 1964, yet only five black families moved to the North Shore that year. The CRC documented cases of discrimination and took statements from victims.

It published the study's results in an eighteen-page report titled "Inventory '64" in September 1964. The commission concluded that the city's healthiest areas were "those of recreation and public accommodation," while housing was the most "troublesome area."[17] No sooner had CRC drafted a fair housing ordinance than the opposition organized against it.

The debate over open housing legislation juxtaposed one basic right to another—private property versus freedom of residence. Some property owners believed that black rights came at the expense of white rights by placing limitations on the seller's prerogative. As one homeowner put it, "Shall we now accept that ownership entails less rights than non-ownership?"[18] Local groups took their cue from the National Association of Real Estate Brokers' official statement on minority housing: "The right of property owners to determine with whom they will deal is a right fundamental to the American tradition."[19] They believed wholeheartedly that civil rights bills "meddle or interfere with constitutional freedoms."[20] Underlying these accusations was the belief that property values and educational standards would drop if open housing was instituted. Some concealed their racism by declaring a sense of obligation to their neighbors. Editors at the *Review* took sides: "No serious civil rights legislation attempts to change any freedom except the unconstitutional freedom to deny freedom to others."[21]

To serve the interests of their clients and match people with neighborhoods, brokers relied on First Amendment guarantees that protected the right to free speech. The ability to speak candidly allowed an agent to fulfill the "normal function of informing, discussing and advising his client."[22] Impending legislation was an ill-disguised attempt to deprive citizens and businessmen in the community of their rights. A representative of the Northwest Evanston Homeowners' Association (NEHA) released a statement: "This [CRC's draft ordinance] is a patent attempt to curb free speech which the city council is trying to put over on the people of Evanston. Nothing so vicious has been perpetuated since the Alien and Sedition acts."[23] Referring to new legislation as "forced housing," NEHA said that it threatened the rights and freedoms of all Americans.[24] Established to protect real-estate agents' professional freedoms, the Evanston Real Estate Brokers' Council (EREBC) was the "first militant organization of real estate brokers and property owners."[25] The organization launched vigorous counterattacks to defeat the proposed ordinance. Realtors minced no words when it came to associating blacks with declining property values. They created a culture of fear and distrust by insinuating that fair housing would accelerate a shift of neighborhoods from all-white to all-black, causing home values to plummet. The real-estate industry was a tool of segregation, perpetuating and encouraging it. Paradoxically, the professional organization supported state or national housing legislation. Its leaders rationalized that real-estate agents needed legal protection because in following owners' wishes they bore the brunt of discrimination accusations.

Maintaining their innocence, Evanston real-estate agents projected blame on "vociferous minorities and paid and imported agitators and sit-ins" for exaggerating discrimination and painting a "false image of Evanston."[26] They claimed that integration was best accomplished "calmly." Emphasizing voluntary action, they wanted solutions that appealed to people's minds and hearts. They did not believe that the community was ready, so government should not dictate where people lived. Brokers could not dictate in matters of conscience: "We don't understand the harassment of the real estate man. He cannot bring brotherly love if the majority of the people don't want it."[27]

An important city hall advocate, Alderman Quaife M. Ward, pointed to progress in race relations made in the schools. He said, "These developments are not chance occurrences; they came about by people, Negro and white, who willed and worked to make them so."[28] He downplayed the necessity for legal intervention by suggesting that newly established neighborhood associations, improved recreation facilities, and programs to maintain streets and alleys would enable "families to become acquainted naturally and on equal terms."[29] It would take a mandate from the people to change stubborn minds.

The North Shore Summer Project (NSSP) was the region's largest effort to combat housing discrimination. The group targeted Chicago's lily-white suburbs from Evanston north to Highland Park. With the exception of a clearly defined area in Evanston and a small enclave in Glencoe, the North Shore was whites only. Real-estate ads made it clear that it was in the designated areas only that blacks could purchase homes. Jews were confined to areas in Skokie, Glencoe, and Highland Park, and along the Edens Expressway, an area sometimes referred to as the Gaza Strip.

Through education and nonviolent persuasion, NSSP planned to correct a condition stemming largely from misunderstanding and only in part from prejudice and bigotry. Bringing diversity through open housing required an uncompromising agenda: (1) publicly dramatize the housing problem; (2) register whites willing to sell or rent on a nondiscriminatory basis; And (3) assist Negro renters and buyers. By the end of the summer NSSP expected to convince the real-estate industry to adopt nondiscriminatory practices. Active in both southern and northern cities, the civil rights movement was ripe to take on the suburbs.

Inspired by the 1964 Mississippi Summer Project, which utilized student volunteers to register voters, the North Shore project recruited students to register homeowners willing to sell on a nondiscriminatory basis. Students from the Chicago area had witnessed racism firsthand working in Mississippi with the Student Non-violent Coordinating Committee (SNCC), a youth offshoot of SCLC. When the summer was over, SNCC leaders had urged white volunteers to return north and create change in their own communities. It was hypocritical to agitate in the South if they weren't working equally hard to remove barriers of injustice at home. The North Shore Summer Project was patterned after the Mississippi project. The name "summer project" itself was inspired by the southern event. NSSP's mission statement read: "We condemn these closed societies, yet we ourselves live in a closed community. Negroes are prevented by real estate men from buying homes here, just as the registrars prevent them from voting in the south."[30] It's more difficult to confront racism and complicity at home than to go to far-off places like Mississippi. Once they realized this, students could not in "good conscience" leave the North to work in the South."[31] Project organizers had high expectations: "Negro families will have to stand in line outside of North Shore real estate offices waiting to be served just like Negros are standing in line at the court houses in Selma, Greenwood and McComb demanding their rights."[32] The group may have been overly optimistic.

Several months earlier, the disenfranchisement of black voters had inspired a group of Evanston housewives to join marchers in Montgomery, Alabama. "Watching those newsreels on television of the rioting at the bridge was the deciding point," Mrs. Nathaniel Raskin said, referring to Bloody Sunday. They got their first taste of the South when their bus driver abandoned the trip halfway through and had to be replaced. The *Review* reported that the women were a "little rumpled and tousled" after their twenty-hour bus ride, but that was the "only indication they hadn't walked right out of their Evanston kitchens on a Thursday morning into the largest demonstration the south has ever seen." The housewives joined marchers outside of Montgomery for the last leg of the fifty-mile march to the capital to hear King speak.

On the way home, their bus driver warned them about meddling,

FIGURE 5.2 People stand silently at Fountain Square in downtown Evanston. The observance was held in memory of slain civil rights worker Viola Liuzzo. *Chicago Sun Times*, April 4, 1965.

and they may have agreed after learning about the fate of Viola Liuzzo. A white housewife from Michigan, Liuzzo had also seen television footage and gone south to volunteer. The Ku Klux Klan murdered her after the Selma to Montgomery march. Stunned, Evanston housewives sent President Johnson a telegram demanding legislation to make such murders a federal offense. When the bus pulled into "sparkling, snowy-clean Evanston," the "muggy, tense streets of Montgomery were far behind."[33] A few days later a silent vigil for the slain civil rights worker was held in the center of town at Fountain Square.

Many young people embraced the North Shore movement. Recruitment packages were sent to colleges and universities. Applications included an essay question asking why students wanted to participate. A short list of applicants received in-person interviews. Preference was given to (1) students living on the North Shore who had gone away to college and (2) Negro students from Chicago. At the end of a long vetting process, an equal number of white and black college students were recruited for the eight-week campaign.[34] Mundelein College undergraduates JoAnn Ugolani, a white student from Highland Park who had marched in Selma, and June Carter, a black student from Chicago, were among the nearly one hundred volunteers. Both girls were eager to bring the civil rights movement home. On the centennial of Lincoln's Emancipation Proclamation, the volunteers attended a weeklong orientation beginning on June 25. For seven days they were schooled on race and housing on the North Shore. They learned interviewing techniques as well as the history and methods of the nonviolent movement. Everyone was given a ten-dollar weekly stipend. Those from outside the area received room and board from North Shore residents.

Organizers were also veterans of the 1964 Mississippi Freedom Summer. The executive director, William H. Moyer, had spent the summer in Mississippi registering black voters. He was a member of the American Friends Service Committee (AFSC), a Quaker organization dedicated to peace and nonviolence. AFSC sponsored the North Shore movement. Churches and synagogues were also important sources of support. A prominent figure in NSSP, Reverend Buckner Coe, of the First Congregational Church in Wilmette, had marched in Selma. Moyer and Coe worked together at NSSP headquarters in Winnetka, a suburb to the north of Evanston.[35] Reverend Emory G. Davis of Bethel AME Church in Evanston was chairman of the steering committee. He was also co-chair of the Evanston committee, along with Mrs. Edward L. Williams. Davis and Williams ran operations out of a Freedom Center located in the Evanston Council of Churches. Ten centers were placed throughout the North Shore suburbs.

Students arrived by 9:00 each morning to receive lists of families selling homes through the Evanston–North Shore Board of Realtors. So as not to alarm potential respondents, Mrs. L. G. Mitten, student recruitment chair, made sure that canvassers arrived in daylight, had credentials and badges, and were dressed nicely—"no dirty sweatshirts and jeans."[36] She instructed students to be polite, to use friendly persuasion to get answers, and to leave gracefully if faced with resistance. Student canvassers visited home sellers in pairs. They introduced themselves, explained that they were NSSP fieldworkers, and conducted interviews. Residents were asked whether they were willing to show their homes on a nondiscriminatory basis and how they would feel if blacks moved in next door. Those who were opposed projected blame on racist neighbors. If they favored open housing, homeowners were asked to sign pledge cards (eventually shown to brokers and Negro buyers) and petitions.

Students faced a lot of hostility. North Evanston was the most closed area among the North Shore communities because of its "staid old families." During an interview conducted in southeast Evanston, a student volunteer reported that a woman became "very emotional." She stood behind her screen door and scolded him: "Negroes want to live next door so they can 'marry our daughters.'"[37] The group was best received on Evanston's west side, where they conducted door-to-door interviews to discuss closed housing policies. They asked black residents what might be done to further the project's purposes. By 6:00 each evening volunteers returned to the center with the information they'd gathered that day.

While the students were busy collecting data, adults did administrative work and fundraising. A Negro couple tested realty companies. Time and time again they were turned away and told there was nothing available. Beginning on July 9, for an entire month protesters held daily vigils between 10:00 and 2:00 at real-estate offices that didn't adhere to fair housing standards. Vigils had been developed in nonviolent social movements, most notably the American southern civil rights movement. They introduced a spiritual element to protest and were a traditional civil rights tactic. During their watch, the open housing activists reflected deeply. They bore witness to the injustice of the real-estate industry.

Martin Luther King Jr. visited Evanston several times during the last decade of his life. In 1958 he spoke at Beth Emet Synagogue, then spent the night in its basement because no hotel would take his reservation. Donald Frey, executive director of Freedom of Residence (FOR), invited King to speak a second time in October 1962. Founded in Chicago in June 1960, FOR evolved into a national organization concerned with open housing issues. One hundred fifty people attended dinner at the Orrington Hotel before moving to the Unitarian Church on Ridge Avenue to hear King's public address. Various reports claim that somewhere between seven hundred and fifteen hundred people were present to hear him speak. Blacks and whites were evenly distributed, making it one of the largest interracial gatherings in Evanston history. Studs Terkel introduced the Baptist minister and moderated the subsequent discussion. Drawing attention to local issues, King began: "The problem is not limited to the South; it is a national problem." He emphasized the interconnectedness of social problems: "As long as there is discrimination in housing there will be de facto segregation in the schools, the churches and the community facilities." Pressing for federal oversight, he added, "It may be true that morality can't be legislated, but behavior can be regulated. In the south, we say that the law may not be able to make a man love me, but it can keep him from lynching me."[38] King ended by asking the crowd to join him in a letter-writing campaign urging President Kennedy to sign an executive order barring discrimination in federally assisted housing. His efforts paid off. One month later Kennedy signed Executive Order 11063, prohibiting discrimination in sale or rental of property owned or operated by the federal government.

King was invited to Evanston again in May 1963 to speak at First Methodist Church, the same church that had welcomed W. E. B. DuBois many years earlier. Reverend Dow Kirkpatrick knew King from Atlanta, where he had served as a pastor before coming to Evanston. King delivered one of his favorite sermons, "Three Dimensions of a Complete Life," and retold the parable of the good Samaritan, relating it to racial justice issues of the day.

When King was invited to give the keynote address at a rally sponsored by NSSP one year later, he drew a record-breaking crowd. He was the fourth speaker in a series that included notable civil rights leaders such as Reverend C. T. Vivian, John Hope Franklin, and Lerone Bennett Jr. Ten thousand people, three-fourths of them white, turned out to hear the Nobel Peace Prize winner, and president of SCLC, speak on the village green in Winnetka. The crowd gathered early with blankets, folding chairs, and picnic baskets. Folk singers entertained eager listeners with freedom songs that likely included the North Shore Project

Song, "You sent your food and books to Mississippi, / You even traveled to Montgomery; Which one of you will be the first on your block / To integrate your own community?" Student volunteer June Carter sang before King spoke.

The speech climaxed a day of talks given by King, who arrived an hour late with fellow SCLC leader Ralph D. Abernathy. Reverend Davis welcomed the crowd. "Civil Rights has come to the North shore," he announced. "Yesterday's white liberal must become today's white activist that will show and sell [his home] to any qualified buyer."[39] He continued, "We believe that those forces which stand in opposition to integrated, equal, quality education in Chicago, living out here in these plush suburbs, are the same forces that stand in support of maintaining the closed society that bars Negroes and Jews" from certain North Shore areas.

Martin Bickham of Wilmette introduced King, who was greeted with a full minute of applause. He began, "History has presented us with a cosmic challenge. We must learn to live together as brothers or we will perish together as fools." The crowd was mesmerized. King charged that America was suffering from "a schizophrenic personality," believing in principle in equality but practicing discrimination. To make the American dream a reality, he said, "we must affirm the essential immorality and evilness of racial segregation, whether in educational institutions, housing, recreational facilities or churches. . . . We must reject segregation not merely because it is sociologically untenable and politically unsound but because it is morally wrong and sinful." King ended with a reference to the summer project: "Racism in housing will not be removed until there is an assault on the structures of power that profit from it. What may be profitable to a realtor is not profitable to a city."[40]

King's words inspired volunteers in the last days of their campaign. When the city tried to deny NSSP a permit for its final event, a march followed by a rally, a spokesman for the group drew parallels between the city's denial and Governor George Wallace's attempt to ban the Selma-Montgomery March down south.

To stir trouble and incite fear, one Evanstonian claimed that the event threatened public safety: "It was the arrest of one drunken driver, which set off riots causing scores of deaths and tremendous damage in Los Angeles. The realtors have not worried about the project's vigils this summer, because we have ignored them. But we must worry about what a mass meeting such as this could degenerate into."[41]

A store owner whose business was located on the proposed route of the march agreed: "With all due respect to our little police force, there is no way you can control 1,000 rioting people without the National Guard."[42] Others were concerned about the privacy rights of citizens who lived along the route, particularly because the march would disrupt a Sunday afternoon.

Outraged by connections that were being drawn between the proposed march and Los Angeles and Chicago uprisings, Reverend Coe defended the summer project: "We have abided by legal and peaceful limits during the entire summer and were quite surprised to find we are now considered insurrectionists."[43] Project coordinators threatened to take legal action: "The right of free assembly is constitutionally guaranteed. We find it hard to believe that Evanston would attempt to deny such rights and require us to seek remedial steps."[44] Reluctantly, the city granted a permit. Governor Wallace also lost his bid.

On August 29, 1965, five hundred people walked down Green Bay Road for four miles from Kenilworth to Evanston. It was a beautiful Sunday afternoon for the first civil rights march through the North Shore villages. When they reached Evanston, they turned west on Central. After pausing for silent prayer in front of the Evanston–North Shore Board of Realtors' offices, the crowd descended on Bent Park to celebrate three months of fair housing advocacy work. National civil rights leaders were invited, as well as Vice President Hubert Humphrey, who could not attend but sent word that he would be with activists in spirit.

Reverend Davis addressed the crowd: "The North Shore Summer Project ends. But the civil rights movement is on the North Shore to stay. We've proved we can march at home as well as in Selma."

John Lewis, president of SNCC, was also a featured speaker at the rally. There is nothing wrong with being an agitator, he said, "if you're agitating for the right thing."[45] He continued, "It's like a washing machine shaking dirt out of the clothes."

The crowd chanted and sang several civil rights songs. "Black and White Together" called for people to unite behind a common cause: "Together we can build a nation / of love and integration." The lyrics resonated with the multiracial group that had worked tirelessly to end racial segregation.

The day's activities reverberated. The media reported no disturbances. About an hour after the rally ended, "six or eight children, all white, were swinging at the playground and singing 'Black and White Together,' one of several civil rights songs sung at the rally."[46]

During the rally, project leaders presented a summary of its findings.

More details were given at a news conference held immediately after the event. A report containing facts, figures, and conclusions was distributed to the media. William Moyer spoke to reporters: "Our surveys and interviews have shown the segregated housing patterns here on the north shore do not correspond to the feelings of the homesellers, the neighbors or the community at large."[47] He called on real-estate agents to take positive steps to change their policy of discrimination and open the doors of closed communities on the North Shore. While organizers spoke with the media, volunteers began an all-night vigil in front of the Evanston–North Shore Board of Realtors headquarters two blocks east. The next day NSSP shared its findings with major realty agencies that still refused to serve Negros.

After months of research, the civil rights group concluded that segregation on the North Shore reflected the wishes of only a small percentage of residents. NSSP's findings were summarized in a ten-page report: "The realtor has obviously conducted his business according to his own fears and prejudices—not according to the unknown wishes of the seller." Conclusions were based on interviews with 462 homeowners with property for sale. 73 percent of whom said they were willing to show their homes on a nondiscriminatory basis. Fifty-seven percent said they had never discussed the issue with their agent, because they did not place restrictions themselves and they assumed that their home was being shown to all potential buyers. Of the respondents, 322 said they were not influenced by the racial or religious composition of a prospective neighborhood. There were 209 homeowners who had refused to be interviewed; however, even if they had responded negatively, that meant 50 percent of homeowners were in favor of nondiscriminatory selling. Additionally, of the 1,560 property owners who were interviewed and did not have homes for sale, 1,277 said that "if a Negro moved next door to them they would not move, not agitate for removal, nor 'do anything.'" Of owners who were not moving, 82 percent said they would accept Negros as neighbors, corresponding to the nationwide figure of 80 percent obtained by a recent Gallup poll. Further, 12,059 North Shore residents signed a petition endorsing fair housing. Reverend Davis personally presented the report to Louis A. Pfaff, president of the Evanston–North Shore Board of Realtors, on Monday morning.

A spokesperson for the Evanston–North Shore Board of Realtors refrained from commenting before the facts were analyzed from the industry's point of view. "Before this summer, listings were never marked open occupancy because there was no market for this. Now, because of all the hullabaloo, there's supposed to be a market for these homes. It has to be searched out." He noted, "*One* Negro family was served by a member realtor and bought in Northfield last month."[48] Several years later Mrs. Edward Williams, cochair of the Evanston committee, was asked to reflect on the project. She felt the project's appeal had failed: having asked real estate agents to "open their doors," she found that "they refused to acknowledge our request."[49]

Fair Housing Ordinance

An open housing ordinance that had been under consideration for close to two years underwent twenty-eight amendments in the weeks leading up to a June 1966 vote. Although the council had to consult legal experts to fashion an airtight definition of "real estate agent," the final version regulated and licensed brokers. Before the vote, Alderman Nott asked fellow members to "consider what, if anything, the ordinance might accomplish," since "most discrimination has been by property owners and not the real estate brokers." He claimed that the "ordinance did not hit squarely on the issue of prejudice which only would be solved through education and association."

Problems were class based, according to Alderman Mayme Spencer, who indicated that she would favor an even stronger ordinance. She voted for it but also recognized its futility, for it would not "alter the number of Negroes or their location. It is the cold, hard, green dollar that dictates who will live where."

But the efforts to derail it failed. The housing ordinance was approved by a narrow margin of 10–8. All that was needed was Mayor Emory's signature. Explaining that he was not against integration but against taking away individual rights, the mayor vetoed the ordinance. When the council failed to override his decision, the ordinance did not become law.[50]

It is difficult to see what was to be gained by this early iteration, as it was no more than an anti-panic-peddling law that would have regulated brokers. Blockbusting was not practiced in Evanston, where neighborhoods did not undergo rapid change because property was too expensive for it to be a real possibility. Rapid block-by-block change and neighborhood transition happened in relatively low-income areas around the country. Additionally, while blacks were locked into the west side, the North Shore was not adjacent to a large Negro settlement. For once realtors were right when they declared: "We have been watching with growing concern the efforts of certain elements to stir up tensions in the city and to magnify and exaggerate the problems that exist. Take for example the various proposals to stop block busting, stop panic peddling. These simply do not exist. There is not a single shred of evidence that any Realtor has engaged in these practices. Our board would be the first to interfere and prevent such conduct."[51]

Blockbusting was not a problem in Evanston. Perhaps that was the point behind the virtually meaningless ordinance. Maybe it was a stall tactic. It would be over a year and a half before the council revisited the issue of housing discrimination.

In October 1967 two hundred spectators jammed into city council chambers to witness the passage of a stronger housing ordinance. Aldermen voted 11–7 in favor of a refinement of the vetoed law. Mayor Emory did not attend the meeting. Instead, Alderman McCourt served as mayor pro tempore and signed the ordinance with Emory's consent. The new law had broader coverage than its predecessor. It prohibited brokers from discriminating or accepting discriminatory listings. The ordinance did not, however, cover every type of seller. Property owners, financial institutions, and real-estate agencies were exempt. The ordinance also dissipated enforcement powers, placing them in the hands of a five-man board. Reactions were varied. Local real-estate agents said they were not prepared to comment.

The ordinance had been in effect for less than four months when on April 4, 1968, Martin Luther King Jr. was assassinated in Memphis, Tennessee. Shocked that the nation's leading advocate of nonviolence had been brutally slain, Congress passed the 1968 Civil Rights Act. On April 11, one week after King's assassination, Johnson signed it. The bill featured a strong housing measure. Title VIII, often referred to as the Fair Housing Act, expanded existing laws by prohibiting discrimination in the sale, rental, and financing of housing. The bill's fundamental weakness was its reliance on individual efforts to combat a social problem that was systemic and institutional in nature. It would not, in the end, have much of an effect because recourse was time consuming and expensive. The act was "intentionally designed so that it would not and could not work."[52] It would be easier for plaintiffs to seek recourse under local laws. But Evanston's power brokers wouldn't budge.

At the civil rights leader's memorial service in Evanston, Waldo Graton, the executive director of the CRC, echoed the hope of many Evanstonians when he suggested that King's assassination be used to press for stronger local housing legislation: "Respect for the dead means nothing without respect for the living. Let us now also bury the

FIGURE 5.3 A crowd gathers for King's memorial service at Raymond Park in Evanston. *Chicago Sun Times*, April 7, 1968.

prejudices and excuses which have prevailed for over 100 years."[53] It had been four years since CRC published Inventory '64, and fair housing advocates were still waiting for something to be done. Graton challenged city leaders to follow the lead of national legislation.

The day after King was killed two angry black youth stormed in to the mayor's office demanding a memorial march through the city for their hero. When they got the runaround, they left and went to see Reverend Jacob Blake of Ebenezer AME.

In the wake of King's death, a spasm of racial violence ripped through dozens of American cities. Fires burned on Chicago's west side, where nine people were killed and many more injured. The mayor contacted the Evanston Council of Churches to ask for help with a memorial march. Reverend Charles Eddis of the Unitarian Church and Reverend Blake agreed, with one condition: Blake demanded the "immediate" passage of an effective and comprehensive housing law.[54] Maybe it was because King had spoken at his church years earlier. An emboldened Eddis put the demand in no uncertain terms: "We'll lead your march, but you need to pass that open housing law."[55]

Church leaders called a meeting to plan a memorial. A strategy committee formed and was given the name NOW, a loose coalition of organizations and citizens dedicated to improving human rights in

FIGURE 5.4 Marching in pairs, Evanstonians protest the city's discriminatory housing policies. Photo by Arnold Kapp.

Evanston. Blake and Eddis were named convener and co-convener respectively. Three thousand people attended a memorial at Raymond Park. At the conclusion of the ceremony, the mayor was presented with a resolution calling for a meaningful open occupancy ordinance.

The crowd agreed to march repeatedly until the council adopted a stronger ordinance. Day and night they marched. Reverends Blake and Eddis, a black Methodist from Chicago and a white Unitarian from Canada, led the way, locked arm and arm. Every evening for a week approximately eight hundred people—church members and other open housing advocates—walked two abreast. They would begin at a black church and end at a white church, or vice versa. They sang freedom songs and marched through white neighborhoods, stopping in front of the mayor's house or other city council members' homes. Terrified, the mayor reportedly peered from his window with a shotgun in hand. On Easter Sunday the marchers numbered five thousand. Every Monday night thereafter they filled city council chambers.

Black Power groups joined forces with Blake and Eddis. Translating anger into action, they escalated their tactics. They passed out handbills that parodied Smokey the Bear posters, picturing a black farmer in overalls, holding a hoe upright, with the slogan "Remember Uncle Tom says, 'Only You Can Prevent Ghetto Fires.'" They distributed literature that read, "Violence is necessary; it is as American as cherry pie." A "Statement of Intent" stated "emphatically and unequivocally that if [an] ordinance was not passed on or before April 29, 1968," the movement would move from "non-violent protest to non-violent resistance" by boycotting businesses and transportation systems.[56] Carl Ledford, one of NOW's leaders, warned Mayor Emory that he could not control "militant Negroes" after the council meeting scheduled for August 29, 1968. He said, "I've got a lot of [Molotov] cocktails on my hands, and I can't hold them past then."

Residents opposed to open housing legislation may have privately welcomed militant threats as an excuse for not taking a moral stand against segregated housing: "The gravest problem we all must face is whether we believe in government by reason—through fair discussion and ultimate trust in our elected officials to do what is best for the greatest good of the greatest number of citizens, both white and Negro—or whether we are to return to pre-civilization days (3000 BC) and have government by threat, intimidation, and blackmail."[57]

Editors at the *Review* concurred. Proponents of gradualism, they advised, "The city council should not legislate because it has a gun trained at its head."[58] The earlier housing ordinance had been in effect only since January 1, they argued, and it was too soon to see results. Federal legislation, which still preserved the rights of individuals selling or renting without a broker, was not scheduled to take effect until December 31, 1969.[59] The proposed Evanston ordinance was actually stronger: it would ban discrimination by private individuals. No wonder the white establishment wanted to stall.

On April 29, 1968, after nearly four years of debate, blacks and whites filled the gallery and balcony of council chambers at city hall. An overflowing mass waited outside. Because the ordinance under consideration would be more comprehensive than the older version, it required at least ten votes to pass. In the end, the city council voted 15–1 in favor of the new housing measure. It prohibited housing discrimination by real-estate brokers, property management agents, financial institutions, individual homeowners, bankers, and persons who showed property for out-of-town owners. It also covered all types of real-estate transactions, including renting, leasing, and transfers. The cornerstone of the new ordinance was the establishment of the Fair Housing Review Board (FHRB) to investigate cases of discrimination.

But it was not politically sensible for white council members or the mayor to support open housing when popular opposition among powerful whites ran high. The city attorney Jack Siegel claimed that a

FIGURE 5.5 Wishing they lived closer to one another, two friends with the same name attend an open housing march and rally. *Chicago Sun Times,* April 21, 1968.

local ordinance intruded on the jurisdiction of the state and that the city had no legal authority to pass it. He advised Mayor Emory against signing it. Both Siegel and Emory said they hoped that laws would be enacted at state and federal levels instead. The mayor's continued insistence on a nationwide law gave cover to open housing opponents.[60] The state of Illinois had not passed an open housing law, and Congress had only recently approved the 1968 Civil Rights Act.[61] The mayor released the following statement: "I hold with you the same hope for achieving full equality and freedom for every American. I differ with you only in my conclusion that a higher level of government has the responsibility for enacting any necessary open occupancy legislation. Therefore, the ordinance becomes effective without my signature."[62]

If the mayor sincerely believed that the bill was illegal, why did he choose this occasion to allow it to pass after vetoing a previous bill on the same ground? Protesters may have scared him enough to do it. The ordinance went into effect on May 19, 1968, without his signature.

Backed into a corner, the Evanston–North Shore Board of Realtors changed its tune and reprioritized economics. The organization assured the public that "after Negro families move into all-white blocks, property values continue to rise just as much as property values elsewhere." It cited evidence that "Negro families moving into good neighborhoods tend to maintain and improve property the same way as their neighbors" and claimed that blacks were generally "educated, articulate, and acceptable as neighbors by any objective criteria other than the color of skin." Conceding that neighborhoods with new black residents might suffer a small exodus of white residents, the board tried to stem the flow: "You can run, but you can't hide." It dismissed fears of widespread civil disobedience: "Although possible, it is not likely on the North Shore because of the climate created by churches, schools, and human relations groups." Brokers who were afraid they'd lose business because some individuals would attempt to bypass the ordinance by selling their own homes were reassured that the practice was costly and would be "abandoned when the first fears of open occupancy are forgotten."[63]

Editors at the *Review* praised the board's initiative. The Evanston–North Shore Board of Realtors was the first group in the country, they said, to "face this issue with optimism and forthrightness by issuing a general policy statement." The newspaper gave the public facts about integrated housing: "Negro families that have moved to Evanston and the North Shore have had absolutely no effect on rising property values. . . . Negroes want exactly the same advantages we have been promising and delivering to other newcomers for decades, and they are willing to pay the same price in cash and character." The editors reminded homeowners of the benefits of integration: "Generally speaking, the more customers interested in a property, the higher the price."[64]

Stronger than its predecessor, the new ordinance nevertheless had some basic weaknesses. It did not apply to owner-occupied buildings. Nor did it require an owner to sell or lease to a person who was not negotiating in good faith—a convenient loophole that some property owners seized on. The Fair Housing Review Board drew the most concern. First, members were not professionals in the field of fair housing—the board was composed of a real-estate broker, an attorney, a member of the Human Relations Commission, and two members at large. It was nearly impossible to reach a quorum. For example, the broker never voted to find probable cause of discrimination by property owners or agents. Second, FHRB lacked injunctive powers, which would have allowed it to freeze the sale or rental of property until a case was decided. This was an essential enforcement tool that many municipal fair housing laws lacked.[65] Third, the ordinance suffered from overlapping investigative and judicial roles. By the time a preliminary investigation was complete, members were prejudiced and could not be effective as mediators. Together these weaknesses discouraged the use of the ordinance. As a result, FHRB did not receive many complaints. Whites saw this as an indicator of progress. Blacks knew their complaints wouldn't make much of a difference.

Described by the *Examiner* as "weak and wishy-washy" and in need of "some additional teeth," the ordinance was of no use in a discrimination case involving a young black couple. Andrew and Elenor Devold tried to lease an apartment at 1005 Dewey from Wezel Wabiszewski. When they were denied, the couple bypassed the FHRB, which lacked injunctive powers and was not empowered to seek court orders. They filed suit in US district court. The grievance sought a temporary injunction enjoining Wabiszewski from renting to anyone else pending a hearing. This pressure forced the landlord to quickly settle out of court, and the Devolds signed a one-year lease. If the Devolds had gone to the FHRB first, Wabiszewski would have been able to rent to another party in the meantime, forcing them to look elsewhere for an apartment.[66]

Having become aware of these problems, the city council voted 11–5 to amend the ordinance on June 29, 1969. The board was expanded to seven members who could investigate, seek compliance, hold hearings, issue recommendations, and publish findings. Provisions were made for an administrator who would conduct preliminary investigations prior to the board's judgment. The city's Human Relations Commission could also file complaints. Overall, the amendment enabled the law to apply pressure at the early stages. A tradition of discrimination and prejudice under the guise of freedom and rights had begun to erode. By 1969, then, Evanston had a fair housing ordinance and had established a review board with impressive powers of subpoena and injunction.

Its success, however, was debatable: houses and apartments were still expensive, and brokers and owners made decisions less on the grounds of race than on the pragmatic question of credit. The ordinance had divided the community with several years of campaigns utilizing agitation, demonstrations, and sit-ins, and had pitted blacks, students, and liberals against the town's mostly white homeowners and conservatives. Evanston's natural, manmade, and imagined borders continued to demarcate racially segregated residential neighborhoods. Moreover, injunction was an individual solution to a social problem. It ensured the Devolds' right to rent an apartment, but they were only one black family out of many. Housing discrimination persisted in part because of informal aspects of real-estate practices that made the industry hard to regulate, as well as continuing racial bias by homeowners and in banking.

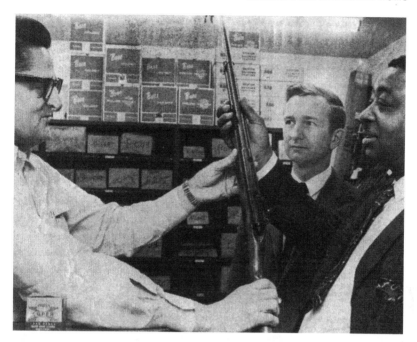

FIGURE 5.6 NOW leaders Reverends Eddis and Blake hand a shotgun over to police as part of a gun turn-in initiative. *Evanston Review,* June, 20, 1968.

NOW continued working toward the betterment of the community, responding to new situations as they occurred. Following the assassination of Senator Robert Kennedy on June 6, 1968, NOW called on citizens to turn in firearms and the city to enact new gun control legislation. Adherents to the nonviolent tradition, it sponsored a gun turn-in.

Affordable Housing

Private lending institutions continued to discriminate against blacks by withholding mortgages and other loans. Black applicants had difficulty securing mortgage financing. A senior counselor for the Evanston office of the Cook County Legal Assistance Foundation explained: "This is especially true if the applicant wants the money to purchase a home in a 'white area.' This blockade is imposed as an obvious deterrent to blacks who consider encroaching onto forbidden grounds."[67]

The banking industry denied these charges. A white banker who declined to be identified "scoffed" at this. "Ridiculous," he said. "These things are based on the collateral and the financial responsibility of the applicant. Skin color has no bearing on this. The trouble these days is that blacks are touchy. They see evidence of discrimination everywhere."[68]

A white real-estate agent also denied charges of discrimination: "These people simply want preferential treatment. They haven't learned that the only way to be accepted and get ahead is to work and save, the way the rest of us had to do. I'm not prejudiced against 'em, Lord knows, but I do think they should show a little more pride and initiative."[69]

Further, the enactment of a fair housing ordinance did not necessarily solve housing shortages. Blacks in Evanston faced a "tight market," defined as excessive demand met by limited supply and inflated rents. In 1960 approximately 8 percent of families living in Evanston had incomes below the federal poverty level of $4,000; 5.6 percent had annual incomes of less than $3,600. Moreover, during the decade of the 1960s, seven hundred housing units were eliminated by code enforcements and demolition for redevelopment. The Cook County Legal Aid Foundation estimated that two hundred families were being evicted from Evanston housing units annually. Anguished black families were being forced out of Evanston and into Chicago, where rents were 10 percent lower. Some residents, refusing to leave, moved into basements.[70]

In testimony before the Evanston Planning Commission in March 1968, Clyde Brooks, the new director of Neighbors at Work (NAW), elaborated on the problem of high rent and substandard housing for low-income residents. Two to three hundred low-income, mostly black, residents lived in "roach-infested dwellings with sub-standard plumbing, heating and other facilities," he said. "These problems are not caused by the tenants but are the result of landlords failing to maintain their property."[71] High rents caused many to spend 50 percent of their income on housing.

Property owners routinely failed to bring their buildings up to code. Northwestern's practices were especially egregious. The university's growth and expansion contributed to the housing shortage by displacing residents when housing was razed to make room for new construction. In one such case, ninety families were evicted when Northwestern began construction on a graduate housing center.[72] The university was collecting income from vast property holdings throughout the city but was exempt from municipal, state, and federal taxes, not giving back to the community from which it was gaining. In a black neighborhood on the west side of Maple Avenue, university-owned property consisted of "dilapidated, slummy-looking structures which the university has neglected to keep in good repair." The apartments could only be described as "social blight as evidenced by two recent fires."[73]

Unrepaired fire damage was common on the west side. In August 1969 the *Chicago Sun Times* ran a story about a townhouse on Fowler Street where a fire had done extensive damage to the second floor two months earlier. The owners still had not made repairs by August. The Black Caucus stepped in to help the tenant, Mrs. Calhoun, an employee of North Shore Uniform Service. The caucus called for a rent boycott unless the city took action against the owner, who didn't seem worried about consequences. Until then Mrs. Calhoun's eight children would be playing in a burned-out room.

The city's policy of demolishing low-cost housing for the poor in order to build parks and playgrounds for the middle class came to a fore in November 1969. Evanston had seventy-four parks, an impressive 262 acres including undeveloped areas. The city was considering building a golf course on undeveloped land bordering the sanitary canal. NAW thought the land could be put to better use as a site for low-cost housing. Low-income blacks were paying the price for city parks. NAW pointed to a 1944 report titled "Evanston Housing—Some Facts, Some Problems" as evidence that the city had historically made a conscious effort to segregate. Published by the committee on postwar planning, the report revealed the motivation behind park acquisitions: "In considering the matter of parks, the committee has had in mind not only the use of park areas as recreational facilities, but also their use as 'buffers' or 'green' areas." The report elaborated on the committees' true intentions: "Areas might be acquired as buffer strips between different localities, and . . . in certain instances, the acquiring of such buffer strips might be worth many times their cost in the preventing of the spread of blight and other deterioration in certain neighborhoods." This approach was utilized in 1963 when the Evanston Planning Commission acquired additional parklands to "suit specific needs of the areas they serve." The language of the report was purposefully vague, but it was clear that "preventing spread" and "certain neighborhoods" were references to the black community.[74]

Other sections of the report were more explicit. Preserving zoning and code requirements was the "greatest insurance" for maintaining value. Not unlike the 1917 Plan of Evanston, the report called for restricting population growth. The suburban ideal allocated 10 acres per 1,000 people. Evanston already fell short, with only 2.3 acres per 1,000 people. The city was zoned for ninety-six thousand people and could accommodate only twenty-five thousand more. Only 17 percent of land remained vacant. The largest proportion of open land was on the west side. Blacks threatened the status quo, numbering six thousand, or 8.8 percent of the population, a proportion that was equal to that of Chicago and exceeded that of Illinois. According to the report, they did not pay enough taxes to support the services they consumed. "Negroes should maintain their proportion of the population," the committee recommended; "otherwise taxes will go up and whites will move out or taxes will remain as is and services will go down." Ward 5, on the west side, had the highest number of dilapidated homes, percentage of renters, and number of people per room. Low-income blacks and whites were living with no running water, no refrigeration, no cooking facilities, no bathing facilities, and no electricity. Instead of recommending a fair housing law, the report cautioned against it: "One bad apple can spoil a bushel." Substandard housing mattered to wealthy whites not because it was inhumane but because it might harm them: "Our children are in school together. They are exposed to each other's diseases. There is more tuberculosis in poorly housed areas."[75]

In November 1969 the city announced the development of a new park. NAW and the Black Caucus mobilized to organize a march. Activists walked two abreast singing, "You've got a house, they've got a house . . . all the Lord's children got a house." They chanted "Housing, housing, we want housing," punctuated by "Right now!" and "Housing first, parks second."[76] At city hall they jammed into council chambers and held up signs that read "Roofs before Swings."

Some residents were appalled by the conduct of the protesters. Lloyd Hinze expressed this view in a letter published in the *Review*: "They are always looking for something for nothing. Let them get out and work for homes and decent rents like the rest of us. Look at the expensive cars they [the marchers] drive. Maybe if they would live like the rest of us they could live in decent homes of their own."[77] In December the city council passed a resolution 15–1 as a sign of good faith. The council would take a serious look at constructing low-cost housing units, especially for the elderly.[78]

Putting profit before people, however, the city allowed the construction of a giant municipal garage on Sherman Avenue in downtown Evanston. Shoppers appreciated the convenience, and business leaders looked forward to their patronage. Sponsored by the Chamber of Commerce, the garage cost $2.8 million to build. NAW organized a boycott of the garage on the first day that it opened. It called on shoppers to stay out of downtown businesses until something was done about housing. Beginning early in the morning, the group picketed and distributed leaflets at the main entrance. NAW staff member Ross Adams said, "We want to dramatize the hypocrisy of city action, on the one hand spending $2,825,000 to house cars, but at the same time doing nothing to meet the housing needs of low and moderate income people."[79]

———

Residential segregation made it more difficult for friendships among the youth in my photo to continue in high school. Each day when school was over, we headed home in different directions. While Barbara's story is extreme, it's also exemplary. She moved to Skokie after graduating from Nichols. "I went from being in a very integrated community to literally going across McCormick to Jewish white world." It was hard to maintain friendships from junior high because "I couldn't go home with these people anymore; they weren't in my neighborhood anymore." Barbara may have moved, but her reputation followed her: "I remember getting sneers from the white Jewish kids. . . . I had a really big reputation of being a white girl hanging with black people." One day when she was walking home, someone yelled out a window, "You're that nigger lover, go back there!"

It wasn't only her peers. Barbara's parents were pressuring her to embrace her ethnic identity. They sent her to Camp Yehudah to immerse her in Jewish culture. "It was really the first time I was around other Jewish people in a concentrated setting," she told me. Immediately her cultural tastes clashed with those of the other campers. One day she was in her cabin watching *Soul Train*, a black musical variety show. She was singing the lyrics and dancing to the music. Some of the other campers watched in disbelief; they did not understand how she could be familiar with the show's content.

SIX

Friends Disappear

I have spent many days in the school system of this town at Foster, Noyes, Haven and Evanston Township High School. During all of those years, I can remember only one day when I was proud to be Black and it was the day that Paul Robeson sang to the student body at E.T.H.S. and Gaylord Mance and I helped him with his coat. That one day in my school I was fiercely proud to be Black. BENNETT JOHNSON

Pictured together in 1975, Carla and Earl signified racial integration. They were standing on a street corner near Evanston Township High School (ETHS) when a reporter took their picture. It was early December. Carla's favorite jacket protected her from the afternoon chill. For school athletes it was dress-up Friday. A football player and wrestler, Earl was wearing his finest pants, shirt, and sweater vest. They were looking around anxiously, probably watching for security guards who might order them back inside the school building. The two teenagers, one white and the other black, were among the first generation to integrate the city's public schools; they had been friends since their time at Miller. The photograph of their afternoon rendezvous was chosen for the cover of the *Evanston Review*'s special issue commemorating the integration of city schools. The caption, "Integration: does it work?," guided the inquiry inside.

While the photograph suggests success, the image belies the truth. Published in 1975, eight years after the city's elementary schools desegregated, the retrospective drew from interviews with school officials, local politicians, and students who had been on the frontlines of integration. Some

FIGURE 6.1   Carla and Earl stand outside Evanston Township High School. *Evanston Review,* December 4, 1975. Courtesy of Allison Burnett.

believed measures taken to desegregate local schools had been successful. The presence of black bodies in formerly all-white institutions was
victory enough. Others, claiming that the resolution had failed, cited
standardized test results from 1973 showing that Evanston's black high
school students scored significantly worse than their white classmates.[1]
Today skeptics might reach the same conclusion by pointing to Carla's
and Earl's subsequent educational accomplishments, the first a PhD and

the second a high school dropout. Together Carla and Earl illustrate the hope and failure of public education in the United States.

When I interviewed Carla in 2004, she had just completed her dissertation in Latin American history at the University of Illinois at Chicago. I asked her to reflect on the cover shot and its implications. She pointed to the cigarette in her hand in the photo and told me that at the time she was concerned that her mother would find out that she smoked. She also confessed to worrying that Earl's girlfriend, Regina, might become suspicious about their street-corner conversation. She had been fourteen at the time, and her concerns were quite different from the larger issues surrounding her contact with Earl and other black students.

The next time Earl appeared in the media was March 2000. It was 5:00 p.m., and the "L" platform near Wrigley Field was busy with commuters heading home after a long day at work. Earl wanted to take advantage of the remaining daylight and the crowd. Politely he asked people for their paper transfers. An officer told him to leave, and he did. He went down to the alley under the elevated train tracks. The officer followed, approaching him again and telling him to leave the area altogether. Allegedly Earl became "belligerent and confrontational" and lunged at the officer with a knife. The officer fired one shot, hitting Earl in the center of his chest and killing him. The knife turned out to be a fork.

Family and friends rushed to the hospital but were barred from seeing Earl's body. The man they identified later at the morgue was well groomed, his hair and beard newly cut and shaved. When his sister looked down and saw his clean white gym shoes, she knew he hadn't done anything wrong. The paper justified police action, describing Earl as homeless and a "formerly imprisoned thief and armed robber." A police report filed after the incident claimed that he was "panhandling" and that "the handle of the fork—not the tines—protruded from his fist, making it appear Hutchinson was holding a knife."[2]

When he was a teenager, Earl's presence on school grounds had been celebrated as a sign of progress. His death at the age of forty demands that we reconsider Evanston's esteemed educational institutions. The truth is that at all levels integration was undermined, and students were socialized into a racialized hierarchy that valued whites over blacks. The high school finished the job. It seems that education was not, in the end, the pathway to full economic and social parity.[3]

To Be a *Re*union, There Must Have Been a Union

A member of the ETHS class of 1946, Robert Douglas Mead joined approximately four hundred other alumni for a weekend celebration in 1971. With almost two-thirds of the mostly white high school class in attendance, the reunion was heralded a success—a strange pronouncement, given that only two black students attended. In 1942, 10 percent of the school's entering class had been black; by graduation time their percentage had diminished to 6. Of those black alumni who did graduate, nearly half could not be located when it came time to plan the twenty-fifth reunion.[4] Moreover, not one of the seventeen contacted was willing to serve on the reunion committee. Bennett Johnson and his sister were the only two blacks to accept invitations to the gathering itself. Writing later about the reunion, Mead conceded, "The buoyant success had been marred only by the disquieting fact that, except for Bennett himself and his sister, the Negroes in the class had stayed away."[5]

Eager in the beginning, Roy King had quickly changed his mind after the reunion committee's first planning session. Confused white committee members worried that they had patronized King. Some thought he was a Black Panther organizing a boycott. Their hunches were wrong. Mead's interview with King uncovered a much simpler truth. Black alumni felt unwelcome:

I went to the committee meeting for this reunion. I was really looking forward to this. I wondered why we hadn't had a reunion. . . . I set there and there was something wrong and I couldn't put my finger on it. . . . The people were very courteous, all the things that—. But there was something wrong. The next morning I knew what it was and I called some more black classmates. They laughed because none of *them* would go to the committee meeting. . . . They all agreed: "Well look, man, we were never a part of any class at high school." And we weren't. We might be in English class together, we might sit in biology together, we might sing in the choir together. When that class broke up we went our separate ways, that was the end of it. I wrote a letter to the committee. Because this is something I had to say. I was not ashamed of what I had to say . . . but I couldn't go, under any circumstances. And as I said, "To be a *re*union, there must have been a union." And we were never together. . . . We kind of melted into the walls when we were at Evanston High School, and this is how we would feel at this reunion.[6]

Recalling white attitudes toward black classmates, King said: "I don't feel that there was hostility. . . . There was indifference, which is worse."[7]

A white classmate corroborated King's observations. Asked about black friends from middle school, he told Mead, "My observation is that they disappeared."[8]

In 1945 principal Francis Bacon had invited famed actor Paul Robeson to perform as part of the high school's "Inspirational Speakers" series. Robeson's performance in Chicago as Othello was earning rave reviews, not just because he was the first Negro to play Othello on an American stage and kiss a white woman before a mixed audience, but also because of his ability to translate Shakespeare into human terms.[9] His visit to Evanston had a profound effect on Bennett Johnson, who was asked to perform with the singer. Decades later, in a scathing speech delivered to the school board regarding Gregory Coffin's termination, Johnson recalled meeting Robeson. He began, "I have spent many days in the school system of this town at Foster, Noyes, Haven and Evanston Township High School." Echoing the sentiments of other black alumni, he continued: "During all of those years, I can remember only one day when I was proud to be Black and it was the day that Paul Robeson sang to the student body at E.T.H.S. and Gaylord Mance and I helped him with his coat. That one day in my school I was fiercely proud to be Black."[10]

Including black cultural events among cocurricular activities was racial progress. Yet Robeson's performance is not recorded in the school yearbook. More telling, the four yearbooks published while Mead, Johnson, and King were students do not include photographs of any black students or staff, aside from the portraits of graduating seniors. Robeson's omission may have been because yearbook staff faced paper and film shortages due to World War II rationing, and apparently the deadline to submit materials for the book was earlier than usual. It's more likely, however, that like that of the black students excited to see their idol, Robeson's presence was not valued or acknowledged.

Mead writes, "What is astonishing about our black contemporaries' perception of the situation is that we, the whites, were totally unaware of it at the time and that we were able to live with the same set of facts and find in them the opposite meaning."[11] Mead's observations resonate with my own. A process of reinforcing inequality begins early but typically becomes more pronounced in high school. Overnight, it seems, our black friends disappeared once we all entered high school, and we didn't notice they were gone until many years later. The high school was integrated, if only because it was the only one in town. But students were resegregated within a desegregated school. Instead of promoting social equality, the school reinforced social hierarchies by indoctrinating children in culturally prescribed ways.[12] The institution created racial difference and promoted segregation through semi-independent schools established to manage large enrollments. Blacks were made historically and socially invisible in the curriculum, and students were divided and sorted by race and class through academic tracking.

Schools within Schools

With all Evanston students attending the same high school, the potential for real integration seemed great. Evanston certainly had the resources it needed to run a well-respected high school, and it was no surprise when *Ladies' Home Journal* ranked it number one in the nation in 1968. Administrators were successfully facing many challenges, including meeting the needs of a student body from diverse socioeconomic backgrounds; "there are children there whose parents are pushing for acceptance at the best colleges, and kids from homes with no indoor plumbing." The school's success was predicated on "freedom and money." Students were given autonomy to design their own studies through innovative scheduling: a total of twenty-one fifteen-minute modules (MODs) per day were allocated to students empowered to make decisions about their learning experiences. Additionally, the district spent $1,280 a year on each pupil, almost double the national average. Not surprisingly, a full 75 percent of the senior class went on to four-year colleges. Still, Evanston was facing its share of problems. Statistics from 1965 suggest a grim reality. Negro students accounted for 20.7 percent of the school population in District 65, but only 13.7 percent in District 202 (the high school). The nearly one hundred whites entering ETHS every year from parochial schools explained some of the difference. The black dropout rate, however, was responsible for the rest. Only 50 percent of graduating blacks went to college; this was the highest percentage in the nation, but comparison with the college-bound rate among white ETHS graduates still showed evidence of disparity. Clearly the district's fifth superintendent (1968–74), Scott D. Thompson, a PhD from Stanford University, had his work cut out for him.[13]

The high school's central facilities were state of the art: library, television studio, planetarium, home economic rooms, gymnasiums, and offices for the school's award-winning newspaper, the *Evanstonian*. Performance venues included a fifteen-hundred-seat auditorium, two additional theaters, and cable television and radio broadcasting studios. There were fifteen gyms (including a dance studio and fitness center), two swimming pools, a field house with indoor track and tennis courts, an asphalt track, as well as a stadium and baseball and soccer fields. A broad curriculum let students chose among three hundred courses. The school offered everything from "Chinese to computer programming, from service-station management to 'The Negro Heritage.'"

The building was immense, a red brick mass with stone-trimmed Gothic towers and new structures extending in all directions. The campus occupied sixty-five acres on Evanston's west side. The same year that the city's elementary schools desegregated, this newly constructed high school had opened. Rebuilding and adding onto the existing structure ostensibly solidified the district's commitment to integration on all educational levels. There were three miles of corridors and three million square feet of floor space. The administrative heart of the school was at the core, both the superintendent's and the main office. Instead of constructing a new school, as other suburban school districts did when enrollment increased, ETHS had added four smaller high schools, self-contained but connected, onto the earlier edifice. Administrators did not have a choice, as there was no available land left in Evanston to build a second high school. The goal was to divide the large student body of nearly five thousand students into more manageable groups.

Four high school divisions—named for the district's first four superintendents—Boltwood (west), Beardsley (north), Bacon (south), and Michael (east)—were housed in one building. Each wing was a semi-independent school with its own principal, teachers, and guidance counselors. Each school or hall had its own courtyard, resource center, classrooms, laboratories, cafeteria, student lounge, health center, study hall, and vivarium. Classmates spent only about 40 percent of their time with students from other schools, usually in classes using special or expensive equipment such as driver's education, fine arts, or industrial arts.

Students were assigned to halls based on an alphabetical list of eighth-grade graduates. At a joint school board meeting, Coffin criticized this pattern of assignment because it broke up friendships developed in the lower grades. "The result could be gravitation back toward members of the students' own race in seeking new friends in high school," he warned. Committed to integration, Coffin suggested that the four middle schools be used as feeders into the hall system. He reasoned, "Although all Evanston public schools are now fully integrated physically, this move might help in social and psychological integration. . . . We face a decade or more of psychological integration. It is most essential that we demonstrate our commitment to a long-term plan to relieve cumulative frustrations."

High school board members were not convinced; Frederic D. Lake worried that "students from different areas would never meet."[14] Lake based his comment on placement patterns at the junior highs, which generally assigned students to schools by region: Haven (north), Nichols (southeast), Chute (southwest), and Skiles (west).

Movement at ETHS was highly regulated. Students were required to carry an identification card printed with photo and school name at all times. If they were in the hallways during any time other than the five-minute passing period between MODs, they were required to carry passes. "Hall wanderers," or students without passes, were given corridor-warning notices, much like traffic tickets. Inside the school, security guards and teachers acted as hall monitors. Outside, a guard patrolled the school grounds in a Cushman cruiser. Students were unhappy with hall arrangements; two female pupils went to the superintendent to tell him that they thought "he was running a prison because they were not allowed to visit friends in other wings." Instead of causing concern, their complaints contributed to the school's high ranking: "the fact that they had the nerve to bring their grievance to the superintendent tells a great deal about the atmosphere at Evanston," a reporter for the *Ladies' Home Journal* wrote.[15]

Student activism was at the fore. White students applauded Superintendent Thompson's efforts to drop the dress code, which prohibited girls from wearing slacks and boots and boys from having long hair. Almost simultaneously, black students embraced an Africana style, including dashikis and natural hair, and launched their own set of protests. Black student activism increased as civil rights and Black Power movements spread into the suburbs. Racial tensions at high schools around the country were mounting. For these students, the two ideological themes, integration and racial identity, merged into a cultural awakening with a political agenda.

Black Student Activism

In October 1967 a disturbance after a football game with Proviso East High School and accusations of police misconduct incited a small uprising near Evanston's campus. Storefront windows were broken on the corner of Church and Dodge Streets, where a cluster of small businesses sat adjacent to the school. (The area was a business mecca that reached its peak during the 1960s. There was a grocery store, beauty and bar-ber shops, record and book stores. The SCLC had a branch office there. Students frequented burger joints and a pool hall.) Police arrived in riot gear to quell the crowd. The disturbance caught the attention of authorities and the public. Black students recognized a window of op-portunity and quickly drew up a list of seven demands, which they presented to Superintendent Thompson. Most urgently, they called for Negro history and literature course additions to the curriculum.[16]

Evanston's black community presented a united front against racism, putting its support behind the young activists. Most adults in the com-munity had attended ETHS themselves, and they knew what a hostile place it could be. Some were present at a public meeting sponsored by the Federation of Citizens for an Unsegregated Society (FOCUS), an um-brella group for several antiracist organizations, held at Mt. Zion Bap-tist Church in early 1968. School District 202 board members listened as parents expressed concerns at the meeting. Inspired by the students, FOCUS issued its own set of demands. Chief among the group's worries was academic tracking, a practice of sorting students into classes based on presumed academic abilities. Tracking, FOCUS maintained, "fosters educational discrimination and injustice by reducing the challenge and motivation for educational excellence." As a solution it called for mixed-ability classrooms: "Many Negroes from disadvantaged families are in slow-learning classes. Their parents are demanding that they be placed with brighter children." The group was also critical of a US his-tory course for omitting the "historical role of the Negro." They called for integration of the black experience: "The tardy device of a special and separate course in Negro history falsely implies that American and Afro-American history were separate developments."[17] FOCUS spon-sored peaceful protests. On at least one occasion members picketed in front of the school. They promised to continue until their demands were met.

The black student experience encompassed every level of education. Across town, Northwestern University students were also fighting for representation and inclusion. Although enrollments in US colleges in-creased 85 percent between 1964 and 1968, blacks were still only 6 per-cent of the US student population.[18] Northwestern black alumni say they could not have made it without the support of Evanston's black community, who welcomed them with open arms. Arriving from the

South, many young black students had assumed that conditions would improve not only because they were going north but also because of Northwestern's proximity to Chicago's black metropolis. Many were surprised that the campus and the community were as segregated as the hometowns they came from. Some of these students left before the first semester ended. Those willing to tough it out received support from black residents in the form of housing (they could not live in residential halls through the 1940s), employment, and religious and social activities.

Charles "Doc" Glass and his wife Helen personified this benevolence. Doc was a recruiter for university sports teams and successfully drafted scores of black athletes to Northwestern. There were no facilities where these students could socialize once they arrived. To fill the breach, the couple opened up their home on Brown Avenue. Parents rested easier knowing that their children were safe. During the week students came over to do homework and use the kitchen. On weekends they watched TV, played cards, and made out to Marvin Gaye.

Glamour magazine's first black cover girl, Daphne Maxwell, commanded the boys' attention after she became a Northwestern student. The girls were equally smitten. When she was featured in *Seventeen*, they convinced her to run for homecoming queen. In 1967 she won. Because she was the school's first black homecoming queen, *Jet* put her on its November cover. Years later, in an interview for the same magazine, she recounted what happened after her name was called at the homecoming ceremony: "I walked up and the [university] president put a crown of roses on my head and looked at me in total shock. No one said anything to me. No one congratulated me. It was like I had the plague."[19]

Black students at Northwestern had endured discrimination and insults for years without coordinated protests in response. That changed when Martin Luther King Jr. was assassinated on April 4, 1968. Giving up on moral suasion as a means for social change, Maxwell put her modeling career on hold and joined a student-led takeover of the university's administrative offices.

Reflecting the radicalization that the civil rights movement underwent in the mid-sixties, two student groups, For Members Only (FMO) and the Afro-American Student Union (AASU), descended on the bursar's office on May 3, 1968. The takeover of the administrative heart of the university was carefully organized down to every detail. The bursar's office was chosen because it was a small, self-contained building and easy to take control of. Most important, it was the nerve center of the university. New computers controlled payroll and records for both the undergraduate college in Evanston and the professional schools located in downtown Chicago. The students understood that by taking over the building they would have an upper hand when negotiating with the university. Everyone was given a task.

Town-and-gown tensions may have existed between Evanston residents and Northwestern, but there was no such gap between black students and black university employees. A black security guard looked the other way when students arrived and started filing through the entrance early on the morning of May 3. Black students from the high school also played a key role in the takeover. After Northwestern students had secured themselves inside, a truck filled with a week's worth of groceries pulled up in an alley next to the building. Wayne Watson, a student at Northwestern and a wrestling coach at ETHS, had recruited athletes to help with the peaceful protest. On cue they unloaded the truck, handing groceries through an open window to college students inside. According to Watson, they emptied the truck in just five minutes and then fled before the police arrived.

Caught off-guard, the university faced a public relations disaster. Wanting to avoid police action, officials were forced to consider student demands. By the second day they had agreed to most requests: Northwestern would recruit black students and faculty and would take a strong stand for open housing in Evanston. The university also agreed to diversify the curriculum by adding courses on the African American experience and to provide an activity space for black students, eventually known as the Black House. Most impressive, the administration agreed, albeit reluctantly, to begin its response with the following phrase "Northwestern admits that for most of its history it has been a racist institution."

But overall the compromise was not much of an adjustment, according to one administrator: the recruitment and admittance of more black students actually fit into a larger admissions goal, an effort to move away from Northwestern's current narrow, provincial profile. Within this framework more black students were admitted and the curriculum was broadened. A faculty committee relied on student recommendations to recruit both Lerone Bennett Jr. and C. L. R. James. Bennett, a journalist who worked for *Jet* and *Ebony*, was offered a one-year visiting professorship in history beginning in the fall of 1968. Several years later, in 1972, he became the first chair of the new Afro-American Studies Department. James taught some of the first black studies courses at Northwestern during the spring semester 1969. His survey course titled

"Race and Radicalism" covered a lot of ground. The syllabus started with the Bible and ended with Black Power. Poet Margaret Walker Alexander was hired to teach African American literature.[20]

Black student activism at Northwestern was closely tied to actions at the high school. Teenagers also wanted courses relevant to the black experience in Africa and the Americas. They wanted to correct the history that ignored their contribution to the past and made them invisible in the present. That university students were waging successful battles inspired them to take a stand in the fall of 1968. Just as it had the year before, Evanston's football team was set to play Proviso East for homecoming. Black students staged a boycott when a black band hired to play the regular homecoming dance was paid three hundred dollars less than the budgeted five hundred. They had already been arranging a separate dance and had even reserved a hall at First Presbyterian Church in September. Thompson was not happy and called the students' actions "militant and separatist." Defending the difference in pay, he explained that it was because a student group, rather than a union band, had been hired.[21]

Black teens were associated with deviant behavior. Black student activism may have reinforced this racial stereotype. A massive fallout of rumors circulated the city when a number of incidents at the high school occurred within a two-week period. The facts became so distorted that Thompson was compelled to set up a hotline and write a letter to parents to clarify the situation. He labeled as false three popular rumors: gangs of uncontrolled black students were roaming the halls, a student had been stabbed, and faculty cars had been overturned. It was true that there had been a rash of "physical assault and of petty extortion surrounded by an atmosphere of racial tension"; it was also true that assaults were "primarily, but not entirely, by black students against white."[22] The district took comfort in the fact that the incidents involved a small minority, and the superintendent was quick to point out that Negro students as a group were not to be blamed: of 750 black students, only 40 were involved. The majority of black students were magnificent, he said. Thompson hoped to contain the situation with a warning. If students were caught with drugs or found guilty of any crime, they would be suspended from day school and placed in either a special extension program or night school.

The reality was that drug use was comparable across racial categories, and extortion existed in varying degrees in all groups. But whites were more likely to get away with these things than blacks.

To address tracking issues first raised by FOCUS, the school announced plans to put students at different academic levels in the same English classes beginning in September 1969. School administrators were trying to avoid a repeat of the Northwestern takeover. By approving a "Black Culture" workshop for the spring semester 1969, they hoped to placate students. Proposed by William E. Cross Jr., director of the West Side Services Center, a community gathering spot for black youth, the seminar would emphasize ideas and attitudes as opposed to specific academic skills. It would include instruction on black heritage, history, and art and be team taught by invited lecturers. Administrators expected that the workshop would put students' "energy to a positive purpose."[23] It was a new approach for dealing with problems and seeking alternatives to violence as expressions of black power—an attempt to instill pride in students. Coffin watched with interest, intending to apply the model to the junior highs if it was successful. School officials wanted to change the attitudes of "angry Negro students" and to cut attrition rates.

But the proposal proved to be too little, too late. A newly formed student group, Black Organization for Youth (BOY), presented Thompson with a list of ten demands, an extension of the seven-point program from the preceding year. BOY was an estimated one hundred members strong. They were organized, businesslike, and more sophisticated than other groups in the past. Dorothy Magett, the new human relations coordinator at ETHS, and William Cross were present when BOY presented its demands. Cross was so impressed that he withdrew his request for the workshop and instead put his support behind the student platform. BOY asked for curricular changes, the hiring of black teachers and staff, and economic support for black businesses.

In his position as a lecturer at Northwestern, Lerone Bennett Jr. helped the group draw up new course proposals: an Afro-American history class exploring Africa, the slave trade, the civil rights movement, and the development of Black Power; an Afro-American literature course; and a survey of the contemporary racial scene in America. Bennett's book *Before the Mayflower: A History of the Negro in America* (1969), developed from a series of articles originally written for *Ebony* magazine, made him an expert consultant. "The time has come," Bennett said, "for black people to become aware of their past—from the gloriousness of Africa to the legacy of slavery to the lies and distortions which we have so faithfully believed."[24] While new courses were intended to educate both black and white students, BOY felt that black teachers could relate best to the subject matter and to black students. They asked the school board to hire more black teachers, administrators, coaches, and counselors. They also requested that black recruiters from both integrated and historically black colleges and universities be invited to visit the high school. Finally, the group asked administrators to purchase at minimum 20 percent of supplies needed to operate the school from black-owned businesses.

Within two days Thompson responded. The school board reviewed his recommendations and approved all but one of the demands. To avoid giving the false impression that black history was somehow separate from American history, the board agreed to change the title "Negro Heritage" to "Afro-American History." It also agreed to recruit black teachers to teach the course. Thirty additional black professionals, including teachers, administrators, counselors, and coaches, would be hired, increasing the total number of black employees from twelve to forty-two. While the board voted to create a twenty-member black student advisory educational committee on curriculum, it declined to give the group decision-making powers. The board, not students, would invite job candidates and hire them, and if need be make decisions about firing faculty.[25] Until the school could hire counselors for each of the four halls, black graduate students from Northwestern were invited to hold mentoring sessions. Recruiters from black colleges were invited to visit. Lastly, authorities contacted black business firms about purchasing products for the school. Melvin D. Pettit, operations director for ETHS, commented on one such product: "Diamond Sparkle Industrial 125 Wax now being tested will be judged by the school's new head custodian—a Negro."[26] Authorities also negotiated prices and volume with Joe Louis Milk Company for the 1969–70 school year milk contract. An African American boxer and hero, Louis was also a successful entrepreneur.

In January 1969 Thompson faced his first protest when three hundred students challenged a school policy requiring a parent's note to excuse absences. The students attended memorial services on Martin Luther King Jr.'s birthday without permission. Utilizing tactics from the civil rights and Black Power movements, they then staged a sit-in at the superintendent's office and raised their fists in salute. More protests occurred in March of that year after twenty-five black seniors were suspended over a dispute with white students in the Michael (East) Hall senior lounge. A mural of a black couple with the inscription "Black is Beautiful" was painted on the lounge's window. White students decided to remove it without consulting their black classmates. Reportedly they cheered and made derogatory statements as it came down. Thompson was quick to explain that for anyone to be suspended there

FIGURE 6.2 Two hundred ETHS students stage a sit-in outside the superintendent's office, protesting the administration's refusal to excuse absences on King's birthday one year after the civil rights hero's assassination. The demonstration was organized by the Black Organization for Youth (BOY). *Evanstonian*, January 21, 1969. Courtesy of Hecky Powell.

had to be an eyewitness, and authority figures had not seen any white students break rules. In response, black students staged a walkout.

That the small incident snowballed into a much larger crisis was indicative of underlying racial tensions. Thompson believed that the entire incident was a "symptom of a generally high level of apprehension and suspicion in the community."[27] With regard to the failure to impose any suspensions, he criticized black students for turning all discipline cases into racial incidents. Thompson believed that current problems in the schools were a reflection of relations in the community, and he said it was impossible for the high school to absorb all of Evanston's dissatisfaction and discontent. "After all, the school is the only place where many blacks and whites meet together, and the angers, fears and frustrations they face here are simply an extension of tensions which exist in the community."[28]

Mary Zavett, a senior counselor for Michael Hall, wasn't so ready to rationalize failure. "We have spent a lot of time taking pride and calling ourselves number one. We're number one for all the white college-bound kids who gather educational laurels for us. Not for blacks. That's what the black community is saying."[29]

An article published in the *Review* titled "Schools: Arena of Racial Crises" documented black student frustration. Sheldon Nahmod, an attorney for the Evanston office of the Cook County Legal Assistance Foundation, charged that school officials had "adopted practices deliberately intended to force black students out of school." Black students were either being expelled outright or forced to enroll in night classes.

Carl Hickman, a spokesman for BOY, concurred: "Teachers talk down to us, as though we were little children—as though we didn't have good sense." [30]

Dorothy Magett, human relations coordinator, was more optimistic. "We still have a long, long way to go, but we've made tremendous progress the past year." She noted that all but one of the demands made by BOY had been implemented.[31]

The overwhelming consensus among school counselors was that meddling parents exacerbated racial tensions more often than their "more liberal children." The low participation rates of black students in extracurricular activities such as drama, speech, and dance could in part be blamed on their parents. Negro alumni were "burdening their children with old beliefs and prejudices" based on their own negative experiences as students at ETHS. Convincing black parents that conditions were improving would be an uphill battle, according to Emory Williams, a vocational education counselor. He had a hard time persuading Negro parents to get involved in their children's schooling. More frustrating, black students resisted his advice, telling Williams that "my mother or my aunt told me not to do anything you tell me to do."[32]

White parents were also getting in the way. Jane Koten, a counselor for West Hall, confided, "Some white children tell me you just wouldn't believe how prejudiced my parents are." When Mrs. Merle, a member of the Citizens Advisory Committee on Intercultural Relations, hosted a meeting at her home to discuss racial tensions, seventy students attended. Of that total, only twenty were Negro. White students in attendance had had to either lie to their parents or not tell them where they were going.[33]

The increasing impatience of blacks in the face of progress would seem to give credence to white critics who thought they were unreasonable in demanding instant solutions. On the one hand, conservatives pointed out that Evanston had been one of the first cities in the nation to "achieve genuine, thoroughgoing integration of its school system" under the leadership of Thompson and Coffin; "equity would seem to be approaching with commendable dispatch." On the other hand, Joseph Hill, assistant superintendent to Coffin, compared the district's progress to the first quarter of a football game:

We have introduced the players, the band has played, and we've just kicked off, but victory will depend on several factors, including these: First, the commitment of the total community to the goal of true integration—not just desegregation. Housing and job opportunities are important, for the child must be considered in the context of the community. Second, a continuing effort to help teachers and others on staff to understand racial interaction, and third, we must seek greater involvement of parents—both black and white—in a frank and honest interaction leading to mutual respect for each other.[34]

To a large extent, educational backgrounds determined life opportunities and chances. The black community had waited long enough.

Tracking

The young people in my photograph had progressed as a body through several elementary schools and one middle school and nervously looked forward to the immense high school with its unfamiliar names and faces. Prince gave voice to our concerns when he declared, "I did not want to go to Evanston Township!" He would listen nervously when Mr. Daloney, his science teacher at Nichols, cautioned misbehaving students, "You not going to be able to do that when you get over to the high school."

Every time Prince heard the warning he wondered to himself, "What is going on at the high school?" His older brothers were already there and at risk of failing.

When the time came, his worried mother enrolled Prince in a small private school, which he attended for about a week before he begged her to let him "go to Evanston." Scared that her youngest son would drop out, she gave him an ultimatum: "If you go over to that high school and you don't get good grades, I'm telling you now, you're coming back here."

Barbara doesn't remember seeing her black friends again once high school began. "I don't know what happened, I just never saw 'em again, that was it. The end. It was over. I don't even remember running into 'em in the halls."

Jennifer's relationship with Perkey seemed to end abruptly. "Well I think he went for awhile and he might've dropped out." Jennifer blamed the sheer size of the school. "Well, there was *thousands* of students there," she explained.

I asked Candy if she remembered seeing Jesse after eighth grade. "Nope, I don't remember seeing him in high school. I'm sure I must have; he must have gone to ETHS. Where else would he have gone? Everybody went to ETHS, but then again we were four thousand students."

When I asked Ronny if his friendships with Perkey and Fred had endured, he said, "It all faded. There was no decision like 'we're not friends anymore.' Right, it just sort of faded."

Hall assignments were partly responsible for severing friendships between black and white students. Ignoring Coffin's warnings that friendships developed in the lower grades would end as students gravitated toward members of their own race to seek new friends, high school administrators did not use middle schools as feeders. In 1974 the kids in the photograph were dispersed by the hall system.[35]

An overarching fear seemed to prevent students from interacting across racial lines at ETHS. Barbara remembers that the crowd got "tougher." Halls and attendant school wings were racialized. North and East were white; South and West were "associated with black people" and intimidating to whites. Black students would stand at the side of the corridor, and "sometimes you felt scared as a white person walking down certain areas of the school."

Jesse had other reasons to be afraid. Assigned to special education classes and having his intellectual abilities labeled in a public way, he knew that others were defining him in these terms. He worried about what people thought and deliberately avoided old friends because he did not want them to know. "It was embarrassing because you don't want your friends to know you going to special ed, so you sneak into the hallways; you coming to class two or three minutes late because everybody else is in their class."

With their old friends gone, members of our group joined cliques and made new friends. Growing apart was a "natural evolution of finding new friends," according to Ronny. Jennifer made sense of it in much the same way: "we were older" and "not as innocent anymore."

Girls preoccupied Bernie. He started dating Sharon Robinson, and his friendships suffered as a result. Sharon's family was part of Evanston's black elite and had money. When they went out, Sharon would drive; "she had a big Cadillac." Bernie reminded me that "*that* was the bus company family."

Peer approval and acceptance became more important, accelerating the process of separation. Barbara was one of the "burnouts" until she joined the "Jewish crowd." "I think it's just normal for people to separate out. I think it's just a natural process that people will gravitate to what they're comfortable with," she rationalized.

For Jesse, change came when he was introduced to a "whole group of people that I ain't never seen before from the west side." His perception was that the white friends in the photo had changed: "They started hanging with more white folks than black folks. It seemed like the blinds were pulled down. . . . As far as my loyalty to my friends, I was still a friend, . . . but I didn't hang out with them that much because they didn't hang out with me. It's like everybody found a different clique of people to hang with." Jesse wanted me to know that this was not the way he had wanted it to be. "When I seen someone that I knew, I never act like I didn't know 'em. . . . I don't know what they said, but I will always be their friend. I would see Jennifer from time to time, and we would speak."

While the hall system began the process of separating students by race and class, academic tracking ensured it. Elementary and middle school students were not divided into distinct academic or vocational categories; everyone more or less followed the same program. Some students were pulled out of homeroom or placed into small groups within classrooms for extra help, but they were never separated for the entire day. Classrooms contained students from different backgrounds and academic strengths, and they were given the opportunity to get to know each other. In high school, however, students entered a rigid tracking system. Like the hall system, tracking was a means for managing a large and diverse student body, the implications of which were racially divisive. For the most part, whites were enrolled in programs that prepared them for college or at the very least ensured their graduation, while blacks were steered toward remedial and vocational coursework. Those of us in the photo generally followed this pattern and had markedly different learning experiences as a result. Even whites who disengaged from school did not suffer the same consequences as blacks.

Tracking is a process whereby students are divided into ability categories and take classes that best address their presumed academic capabilities. At the high end, students are prepared for college. At the low end, they're prepared for jobs. Sociologist Jeanne Oakes's research demonstrates how subjective the process is. Rather than alleviate problems, tracking contributes to them. Assignments are based on teachers' subjective recommendations; test scores, which are a small indicator of future success; and parent or student choice, which is not a neutral process. Academic tracking is the primary source of unequal educational opportunities and outcomes. Virtually every study finds that affluent whites are found in upper tracks while poor and minority students are disproportionately represented in bottom groups.[36]

There is a correspondence between educational institutions and the economy, according to economists Samuel Bowles and Herbert Gintis. Schools teach students at the top the behaviors most appropriate for professional and leadership roles, and students on the other end, at the bottom of the educational hierarchy, are taught behaviors that will prepare them to fit in at the lowest levels of the economy.[37] Put bluntly, schools teach kids at the top how to get ahead and kids at the bottom how to stay there.[38] Schools create difference; they don't reflect it.

Academically, Ronny "skimmed by." He does not know exactly how he managed, but he attributes his passing grades to his lenient parents and his own popularity. He had considerably more opportunities to exercise his "choices" than his black friends did. His parents had "whatever, don't worry about it" attitudes, and he was well liked by both students and teachers. Ronny described his biology class to me: "I had this lab table, it was just all girls and me, and . . . we were always laughing." His teacher was indifferent, "kind of like 'whatever, you're a good kid.'" For his final project, Ronny brought in two photos that his father had of "a hippie girl at some concert" with six toes. The photos sufficed: "I passed like with a D minus." He explained, "You know everyone clearly likes you, and . . . you're not doing any work." Ronny also received preferential treatment in an upper-level math class: "I was just in way over my head," but Mr. Benson, the teacher, was "really cool 'cause he knew I had come up from the other class." Ronny may not have been applying himself in school, but he was also not in danger of dropping out.

White middle-class parents lobbied schools and gained their children's admission to specialized programs more than other parents did. Ronny's mother had time and knowledge to search out an alternative to ensure his graduation. Senior Seminar was a unique yearlong experimental program for privileged students who could afford to be creative with their schooling. The curriculum resonated with Ronny's home life; "it was definitely like a free school environment, . . . 'no boundaries.' . . . It was almost like kindergarten . . . in high school." An emphasis was placed on active learning exercises. Students learned to be independent when they spent three weeks on a farm. They conducted original research by visiting Chicago neighborhoods and interviewing residents. They were given expository writing assignments and learned to express ideas in short stories and narrative essays to fulfill their English requirement. There was tremendous rapport between the teachers and the students. The students cooperated with and trusted their peers. The emphasis was on learning by doing and problem solving rather than rote memorization. From Ronny's perspective, it was "more like a life class." Many of these skills would come in handy if he decided to go to college.

Routinely bringing home Cs and Ds, Carla did not apply herself scholastically. She exercised her "choice" when she took the easy way out. "I checked myself into alternative school," she told me. Carla's decision was partly motivated by vanity, a concern she could afford to have. She told me she was "very self-conscious about putting on the gym uniform; I loved alternative school gym 'cause you just wore your street clothes." But Carla stood out from her classmates, struggling youth who didn't have the same choices. Teacher-student relations were strained. Peers argued and fought with each other. Teachers spent less time on instruction and more time getting kids to behave. They would distribute textbooks, and inevitably some student would "throw the book back." The work was "less rigorous; I can't even remember if we had homework." Lessons were dumbed down. While advanced placement (AP) math classes emphasized complex mathematical ideas, models, and concepts, low track courses focused on basic computational skills and arithmetic facts. Teachers emphasized self-control, manners, and rote memorization. Hoping to relate to his students, the math teacher might begin an arithmetic story problem with "You got an ounce of weed; if you sell, you know, three dime bags . . ." With little effort Carla's grades improved, and she moved back into the mainstream for her junior and senior years. The consequences of Carla's choice to downgrade her educational experience were not detrimental in the long run because of her parents' social position.

There were few safety nets to protect Jesse when his grades faltered. During his sophomore year, the work got so hard that he was put in a special class with "other kids that were having problems." To play sports, he had to maintain a C average. He told me he knew "I had to get my grades up." At the same time he realized, "I can't do the work. I can't keep up with them. I can't write. . . . I couldn't take notes 'cause I couldn't spell that good." Desperate, he'd looked at another student's paper, but "they would think I'm copying." His parents were called to the school for a meeting, and "they put me in a special ed class." But Jesse did not get the attention that he needed. With limited space and resources, the class was overcrowded. He remembers that "there was a lot of kids having problems."

Black employees stepped in when the institution failed. Two security guards, Otis Mopkins and Gene Bell, made sure Jesse finished school. Jesse imagined a conversation between the two men went like this: "Mnm, no way that he is not graduating; this guy has done a lot for this school, he's not a bad kid and he's done everything we asked him to do, and so what if he's a credit short?" They saw to it that Jesse walked with his class, although it took him an extra year to finish. Jesse is thankful. "Man, if I didn't have this degree a lot of jobs wouldn't even be hiring me. . . . You at least need a high school diploma."

Jesse needed more help but got less. Jeannie Oakes writes, "Those children who seem to have the least of everything in the rest of their lives most often get less at school as well."[39]

When compensatory programs are used by elites, they don't address disparities in life chances. Instead they encourage them further. In 1967 ETHS began offering night classes on Monday and Wednesday evenings from 6:30 to 9:30 p.m. to accommodate students with full-time jobs or who needed to be home to care for children. The program filled a void between high school–age students and adult education for persons over twenty-one. To be eligible, students had to be juniors or seniors and recent dropouts who wanted to return to earn their diploma. The pilot program had fifty-six students its first year, and it continued to grow. The stakes were high for at-risk youth. If they didn't graduate, their life chances were considerably reduced over time.

Like many other normal teenagers, Jennifer and Regina didn't like school. Enrolling in night classes made it bearable. Jennifer recalled her decision to leave day school: "We were looking for alternative places for me to go to. I got lost in the shuffle, I was frustrated. I ended up going to night school because I don't think I would have finished if I hadn't." I asked her whether she thought the work was equivalent. "I found it a little bit easier—I ended up getting all As, whereas I couldn't even get through at all in the daytime," she said.

Regina heard about the program through Jennifer and decided, "Oh, I'll go to night school too." Both girls took on jobs during the day to earn extra spending money. Jennifer answered phones at National Towel Service, where Jesse's mother did laundry. Regina worked as a dental assistant. Like other white participants, the girls did not suffer negative consequences when they decided against college-preparatory coursework. A compensatory program for students with limited resources, it was misappropriated by privileged teens.

Night school did not carry the same stigma for whites that it did for blacks. "Somehow you were always made to feel like you fucked up, like you failed," Jennifer said, but she would not endure that label for long. When I asked Bernie and Prince if they had considered night school as an option, however, they were adamant—it was out of the question. They associated night school with suspension or expulsion. It had been the last chance for some of their relatives.

Auto-mechanic courses taught Barbara how to take better care of the "gorgeous" 1968 Camaro that her father purchased for her. He may have been motivated to buy it so that his daughter could drive into Evanston for school and just as quickly return home to Skokie after it was over. Barbara told me that it was "a really cool class 'cause it taught me how to change my oil and take care under the hood, and I really liked auto mechanics." Other than that, "I don't remember any classes that impressed me. I just took the regular curriculum. I was an average student. I didn't have any aspirations past that, like I didn't say 'Oh, I'm gonna go to college.' . . . I never was in danger of flunking, but I don't remember ever being proud of my report card. I was a average student." School didn't seem to leave much of an impression; her only other vivid recollection was "the break room." Barbara's early indifference did not limit her choices later in life.

Offered through the Vocational Education (VE) curriculum, auto mechanics served a different purpose for students from working-class backgrounds. By his own account, Bernie "blew" his entire sophomore year "hanging out being cool." When his mother saw Ds, Fs, and incompletes on his report card, she intervened. Bernie was the youngest, and his mother, like Prince's, had watched her older sons struggle and eventually drop out. Determined to keep him in school, she made a bold decision. She took Bernie to truancy court in Skokie. "We caught the bus or something out there," he remembered. They'd spent time together on the bus before when he was younger, when she was trying to ensure his success. She must have felt discouraged riding with him again, but equally determined.

Bernie was assigned a blind judge, who asked him point blank, "What are you doing?"

He replied, "Well, I'm not going to class."

The judge gave him an ultimatum: "If I see you in my courtroom again, you're going to jail."

It was a defining moment for Bernie. "I got me back into school." He found the prospect of not graduating "embarrassing" and did not "want to be the guy that doesn't graduate." Bernie's mother looked to

Emory Williams, a guidance counselor, for advice. Affectionately known as Patches because "he had like patches of hair on his head," Williams knew the Foster family well. He'd helped Bernie's brother Bobby after he dropped out; he had advised their sister Tina when she wanted to transfer into VE. Williams arranged for Bernie to enroll in the same program. Bernie spent half of his day at school and the other half at Leroy's gas station. The program took him off campus for extended periods, distancing him from academics and the regular context of schooling. He learned to pump gas and repair cars. Eventually he would walk with his class, but like Jesse, he had to make up credits before receiving his diploma.

Minorities enrolled earlier and more extensively in training programs for low-status occupations.[40] To increase their economic opportunities by gaining marketable occupational skills, students learned trades in industrial arts and childcare. According to Oakes, the underlying function of VE is more insidious: poor and minority students are segregated into occupational training programs in order to preserve the academic curriculum for mid- to upper-class students. The differentiated curriculum serves to "reinforce the racial and socioeconomic stratification of society."[41] The end result is that large numbers of nonwhite students are channeled into education and training for low-level occupations rather than encouraged to continue in academic programs. They are eased out of the school setting through on-the-job training during the school day. They are likely to leave school early, believing they have been trained in marketable skills, only to find that they cannot translate these skills into occupational advantage.[42] The Job Corps is the most transparent example of this process.

"I loved every class except for social studies," Chip assured me. But things changed in high school and he struggled. "They didn't have things like dyslexia back then, but I knew something was wrong, you know. I knew I was not slow by any means. . . . I could read a whole book and enjoy the book, but if you asked me to write it, everything was scrambled." Chip adapted. He would "open the book and take words out of it." He also relied on the familial component of both hall and tracking systems, all but guaranteeing that he'd have relatives in his classroom. "I had a sister and a cousin in most of my classes," he said. His little sister helped him. "I could dictate to her what I was thinking about. . . . Sometimes she'd write it down for me, because I could tell a damn good story." Chip's struggles with writing partly explain his grades: "C+ average, sometimes a B." He did better in courses that demanded quantitative skills; "math I was pretty sharp in." His talents weren't recognized or encouraged.

When a student was hit in the back with a dart, Chip was one of four boys questioned by security. The principal gave the boys an ultimatum: tattle on their friend or be expelled. Chip was one of the two who refused to say who did it, and he suffered the consequences. "I wasn't supposed to set foot on ETHS's property," he told me. "I mean I couldn't even come to night school. My mom tried to fight that: 'What do you mean? He didn't throw the dart.' Security knew I didn't throw the dart. The principal knew I didn't throw the dart." Chip's mother was willing to challenge authorities only to a point. When she was met with resistance and skepticism, she backed off. If he had been white or had money, he wouldn't have been kicked out. Chip agreed: "Oh no, no, no. My parents would have been there and maybe even brought a lawyer." Instead, school authorities arranged for Chip to transfer to Senn High School on the north side of Chicago. Getting there would have required taking a bus and a train. I asked whether he ever made the trip. "I never once," he replied. Chip "coasted" for a few months before signing up for the Job Corps, a government residential education and job-training program for teens.

Chip was only sixteen years old when he enrolled. He left his family and friends behind in Evanston to spend eight months in Atterbury, Indiana, a rural area where he says he and other black teenagers felt unwelcome. The Ku Klux Klan burned crosses on his teachers' lawns. With a number of trades available to choose from, Chip decided to earn a certificate in Electricity and Electricians. He lived in a dorm and took classes during the day. For recreation he went to Indianapolis on the weekend or stayed on the compound to shoot pool, watch movies, or go to the bowling alley. For extra money he sold pin joints and little bottles of Richards. Close to finishing, he got in more trouble and joined the army to avoid jail. Chip headed south for basic training, then left for Germany, where he eventually earned his GED.

Two months before he left the Job Corps, Ray showed up. Jesse told me how Ray had struggled at the high school: "Ray took a left and I took a right; he just got all into Jimi Hendrix, he started smoking a lot of weed, he really was into the drugs scene. I wasn't into all of that acid and mescaline, because I was a athlete and I wasn't going to put no poisons into my body. I smoked a little weed, but who didn't back then? Ray was weak; you abuse something and eventually it'll begin to abuse you. He became a downward spiral."

Chip recalled that Ray was in and out of the penitentiary. A burglar, he stole cars and broke into houses—"it didn't matter." He had a "bad addiction problem." Chip remembered, "The last time I saw Ray, him and Ikie had went to do something, and Ikie got away and Ray didn't. . . . After that I heard he was sick." Ray had died sometime between 1992 and 1996. Chip had been wary of the rumor. You never know, he told me; "I've been dead twice in Evanston. . . . It's a common occurrence though. If you go back in the hood and you ain't been there in a few years—you know, either you've been in the penitentiary or you're dead." Back in Evanston, Ray's father had confirmed the bad news. It was only then that Chip believed it was true.

When students actively reject school, this suggests an agency absent from the simple correspondence between school and work that funnels poor working-class youth into manual labor.[43] Because they do have agency, students assert a measure of control over school and classroom environments by participating in delinquent acts. Dropping out stems not just from what schools offer students but also from students' response to it. This interaction is the reproductive force.[44] There are far-reaching effects. By rejecting school, they also renounce careers. At some level they accept restricted choices. As a result, they come to see industrial work as desirable and appropriate. These "uncoerced outcomes" can be a blessing in disguise. Acceptance will make life tolerable in the future.[45]

Black youth hanging out on the corner of Church and Dodge Streets were associated with delinquent behavior; white youth engaging in similar behavior were said to be going through a phase. Prince recalled, "Church Street was for people that was on drugs or up to no good." His mother forbade going there: "Don't never let me catch you on Church Street or hear anybody telling me that you're on Church Street," she'd say. Invested in his success, relatives monitored his whereabouts; "everybody watched what I was doing and where I was going as I was coming up." Sometimes he would rebel: "I would sneak over there every now and then, but hanging out there, no, un-uh." Mostly he did not "want to get caught by one of the aunts driving by and seeing you on Church Street." The kids that were hanging out there had a reputation for "breaking in people's places, getting things and selling them, and selling drugs."

Jesse and Ray would ditch school. If they saw Prince they'd say, "Hey man, come on with us, we going over here, we going to do this," but Prince would tell them, "No, I got a class." The boys were headed down different paths. "I guess that's kinda where we fell off," Prince said.

Barbara was smoking on the corner when her stepmother "drove by in a white convertible Cadillac." Later at home, her parents reprimanded her. They gave her no choice but to sever her relationships.

"You need to get with the Jewish white people program," they'd tell her. Barbara was torn between two worlds—black friends from junior high and the Jewish friends her parents were making for her in high school. "I was on the road to start to be bad, and they caught me right before I crossed into being more like a hood," she recalls. "I used to wear like bandannas on my head, and I was very black in my way." Mr. Paneer, a guidance counselor, saw promise in her white skin, pulled her into his office, and said, "You have too much potential, you're hanging out with a bad crowd." He continued, "You are better than this. Get your shit together, get the rag off your head, get yourself directed toward your education, towards people who have a goal, and not just hanging out and dropping out."

Regina recalled Earl's last years in school: "He was on the football team; he was barely making his grades in order to qualify, and then I think, by the time he got through sophomore year, he didn't. He just got into the pot too much. And his whole family fell apart during high school; his parents got divorced." Things started to unravel after the divorce, and "pot was a good escape from reality." The family had to move. Then they started moving a lot, and the little stability Earl had was gone. He quit wrestling and then football. Eventually he dropped out of school altogether. Regina's parents worried about their daughter. "They wanted me to break up with Earl, 'cause they thought he was a bad influence on me. He was already at the high school when I started as a freshman, and my freshman year I didn't do well. I was getting high, I was fucking around." Regina was grounded.

Private schools were an option for families who could afford them. I hated school too, and I loved hanging out on Church Street. We'd go to Butch's, a hot dog stand with a private club in back where the jukebox blared music by the Ohio Players. While my teachers marked me absent, I danced to *Skintight*. I smoked Kool cigarettes and didn't care if the rumor that menthol crystallized lungs was true. Schoolwork was the last thing on my mind. Eventually I got into so much trouble that my parents sent me away to boarding school. Unlike the Northeast, where boarding schools prepare students for placement in the Ivy League, residential schools in the Midwest are frequently associated with juvenile reform; they are for middle- and upper-class students who are messing up in public school. For me, Elgin Academy was a safety net that I did not necessarily deserve. Living at school made it harder to skip class. I studied harder, but when I flunked chemistry, I was given a passing grade anyway. As long as the tuition was paid, my graduation was all but guaranteed.

Photographs in *The Key*, Evanston's yearbook, make clear that inter-racial contact on school premises was not as great as might be expected by enrollments. While phenotype is a less than ideal way to identify racial groups, I used it to get a broader sense of participation than the interviews gave me. Unlike Bennett Johnson's earlier yearbooks, in ours blacks were represented in both staged and candid shots. But members of a given club or sports team were primarily from one racial group or the other. There was an unequal participation of black students in extracurricular activities. Photographs of academic programs show white students in math, art, science, and foreign language, while blacks are featured in photos for vocational programs. A section titled "Student Organizations" juxtaposes a photo of Organization Black (likely a later iteration of BOY) and its black members to one of the all-white Ski Club. White students are pictured in images from theater, dance, and music performances. Sports were also racially segregated. Basketball, football, and track teams, which had both black and white members, were the most integrated of all activities. Blacks, however, were over-represented on football and basketball teams. White youth were more likely to participate in hockey, swimming, baseball, and soccer.

Because friendships often develop through social activities more than in classrooms, the yearbook provided further insight into why our group dissolved once we entered high school. Many of us were not involved in extracurricular activities; we spent our time hanging out and getting high. Barbara felt as if she missed out. "I was not involved in anything. I went to work after school and waitressed, and that was it." Research demonstrates that lower-track students participate less in extracurricular activities at school and are involved more often in de-linquent behavior outside school. They are more alienated from school and have higher dropout rates.[46]

To a certain extent black friends in the photograph defied that trend. Most were involved in sports. But coaches found ways of making them feel inferior. Dress codes were strict; "they didn't want you walking around with braids in your hair. Back then you couldn't wear braids—it was too, too black—and you had to look appropriate, almost yuppie, preppie," Jesse remembered. Playing sports was also contingent on maintaining a certain grade point average. Jesse's potential was jeopardized because of low grades. He was a member of two teams; "I wasn't that good in school, so I knew I had to be good at sports because that was going to be my ticket out. . . . I wouldn't say it was the ghetto, because I think we was raised in a fairly middle-class neighborhood." When he was accused of smoking marijuana in "Pneumonia

Alley," a walkway between school buildings, he was kicked off the base-ball team—"not the type of stuff that they want to send you away to college and you representing ETHS." Jesse did not understand that he could have fought the decision until it was too late. A dean told him, "You should've came to me, because it's kids that played sports that did cocaine, and just because their parents are doctors we was able to overlook it." But Jesse told me, "I didn't know nothing about none of that." Jesse had pinned all his hopes on "going pro." When I asked him what happened, he replied, "Well, I didn't make it." He reconciled his disappointment through his religious beliefs: "I'm not going to ques-tion God, maybe he don't want me to go pro."

Labeled a "high achiever," Candy had substantially higher educa-tional aspirations and a considerably more positive self-concept. At ETHS she was involved in dance and theater. Her family left Evanston before she graduated because her father was offered a job in Nashville. Her experiences in Nashville were much different from the ones she had in Evanston. She spent her senior year at Harpeth Hall, one of the best private schools in the city; "they send a lot of their girls to Ivy League schools." In terms of race and class, the student body was white and well-off. "We all drove sports cars," she told me. In terms of edu-cation, she said, "I don't remember ever being extremely challenged academically until going to the private school." She believes that she learned more academically in one year at Harpeth than she did in three years at ETHS. However, she attributes valuable social lessons to her ex-periences in Evanston.

Prince was headed to college. Unlike Candy, he had to overcome ob-stacles to get there. He felt ostracized by his black peers and didn't fit in with white students. During his junior year his basketball coach made him a role model for the other players: "Prince is on the honor roll, he got all As, what are the rest of you guys doing?" Rather than being impressed, his teammates called him a "teacher's pet" and a "kiss off." That same year Prince excelled in chemistry, and his teacher encour-aged him to take physics the following year. On the first day of physics class, he looked around the room and saw white faces staring back. He decided not to stay in it. "I just did not want to be in the class with just being the only black in that class." He was tired of the way his cousins regularly taunted both him and his sister: "You guys think you're bet-ter than this and better than that." For Prince "that got to be kind of hard sometimes." Teachers supported him. Every day instead of taking a hour-and-a-half lunch, he would "spend thirty or forty-five minutes with Miss Konasky; she really helped me get through those subjects that year."

Most of the members of our group say they never received college counseling. They were not encouraged by either parents or the school to pursue higher education. Black participants who graduated entered the workforce. Jesse hoped to parlay a high school sports career into a college scholarship; when that did not happen, he started working full time. Bernie used the skills that he gained in vocational education courses to work full time at Leroy's garage. Students in low-track classes had the most negative views of themselves, both academically and generally, and the lowest expectations for their educational futures. Earl dropped out and got his own apartment with Regina. Ray and Perkey left school before they finished. Chip dropped out but earned his GED while serving in the military. Prince delayed college for full-time work at a supermarket.

After high school, white group members took classes at art and music institutes and community colleges and entered certification programs. Jennifer enrolled part time at the Art Institute of Chicago. Ronny signed up for music lessons. Regina took classes at DePaul University. Later, she enrolled in a real-estate certification program. Carla never took college admissions tests, because "I never thought I would go." She explained, "I got out of high school. I took a year off and did nothing, went to an art school for two years, took another year off." Barbara vaguely remembers taking the SATs in the school cafeteria. At the time she was more interested in her boyfriend, Mario. Her parents did not like him, although they were "relieved that he wasn't black." Barbara's father told her, "You're going to college," and she told her boyfriend, "I got to go to college, my dad is making me, but don't worry, I'll drop out freshman semester." She was admitted to Illinois State in Bloomington-Normal on probation, which made her happy because it would be easier to leave. She told Mario, "All I have to do is screw up and they'll kick me out, because I'm on probation." I went to the University of Kansas in Lawrence to major in theater; I left after two years. Prince and Candy were the only two of the entire group that took high school academics seriously and had plans to attend college. Prince was the only black member of the group to go to college. He enrolled at Southern Illinois University in Edwardsville. Candy went to Southern Methodist University, a prestigious private school in Dallas.

Blacks in our group do not associate racism with their school experiences. On the contrary, most believe that Evanston's public school system was fully integrated and that students were given the same educational opportunities. Prince told me, "I didn't experience any racism that really opened my eyes that it was there, until I went to college." Jesse blames his failures not on the school system but on his family's vices:

I had problems in school with learning disabilities, and I couldn't catch on as fast as the other kids. My people were down South; they used to drink grain alcohol, and that can have an effect with your fetus, and my mother started smoking when she was ten years old—that's before they knew about the side effects of smoking. And so I look back on all that and I say, well, maybe that's some of the reasons why I had problems in school, 'cause they drunk grain alcohol, which is 150% grain alcohol. I really can't pinpoint why I didn't get as far as educational wise as maybe Prince or maybe some of my white friends; I just couldn't learn like everybody else.

According to Jeannie Oakes, educational failure is not due to families, neighborhoods, genes, culture, or other such factors; rather, it is what happens inside of schools.[47] A lack of interest is not a characteristic trait of students who end up in low tracks; an interaction of student characteristics and school experience or treatment produces a student who is noncompliant and uninterested.[48] It is the social consequences of tracking—sorting students according to preconceptions based on race and social class and providing them with different and unequal access—as much as the organizational or pedagogical details that matter most.[49]

All seven white members of our group graduated from high school, and eventually most of us went to college. Four of seven black members dropped out before receiving their high school diploma, and only one earned a college degree. To some extent our present-day occupations reflect our educational backgrounds. However, with safety nets in place, most white participants were able to overcome poor school performance. Black members of the group, who ostensibly had the same opportunities, were never able to surmount their own educational deficiencies. What our work histories illustrate are structural limitations and the consequences of our choices.

SEVEN

Stuff for the Kids That Are Less Fortunate

North Carolina banks have been hiring Negro employees for years, but I understand this has happened in Evanston only recently.

ROY WILKINS, NAACP PRESIDENT, 1965

With the economy struggling under a national poverty rate of around 25 percent, translating into the destitution of over thirty-five million Americans, the federal government declared war on poverty. Social programs were not a new strategy; in the 1930s and 1940s President Franklin D. Roosevelt's New Deal instituted welfare programs for relief from economic depression. During the 1950s, class-based issues fell off the national agenda due to a surge in the economy resulting from wartime profits. But by the 1960s poverty was once again a key concern.

Only weeks after coming into office in the wake of Kennedy's assassination, President Lyndon B. Johnson laid out the details for his assault on poverty in his first State of the Union address. As part of his larger aim of a Great Society, Johnson sought to expand the government's role in social welfare programs, from education to health care. His speech inspired Congress to pass the Economic Opportunity Act, establishing the Office of Economic Opportunity (OEO), a national headquarters for the war against poverty. The OEO was responsible for administrating many of Johnson's programs, including job training, Head Start, food stamps, and Medicaid.

Federal programs targeting unemployment have been

widely criticized for having prepared people for work that either did not exist or did not pay a living wage. Initially, they presented hope and new possibilities. In a heartfelt speech to Congress, Johnson explained how the bill would train disadvantaged people for meaningful work: "It will give almost half a million underprivileged young Americans the opportunity to develop skills, continue education, and find useful work." Johnson promised to "give high priority to helping young Americans who lack skills, who have not completed their education or who cannot complete it because they are too poor." Among his recommendations were the Job Corps, a Work-Training Program, and a Work Study Program.[1]

As the national economy moved from goods to service production, "what had once been envisioned as a 'Promised Land' for anyone willing to work hard now offered opportunities mainly to educated men and women."[2] Recession and the erosion of central city manufacturing resulted in plant closures and layoffs in the 1970s.[3] There was a demand for workers at both ends of the spectrum, but very little in the middle. Jobs near the bottom didn't pay a living wage. Long-term unemployment, impoverishment, and simmering frustration in metropolitan areas meant deteriorated conditions for poor and working-class people living paycheck to paycheck. This reflected the economic structure of a capitalist society, not a failure of individual effort.[4]

Economic inequality did not generate as much interest in the mainstream media as discrimination in education and housing had. Rather than reporting on the consequences of the city's dual economy, the *Evanston Review* either ignored the problem or covered federal policies and local charities addressing it. By contrast, the black press provided critique and resolution. The *North Shore Examiner* addressed Evanston's class divide by doing its part to revive and stimulate the black economy. Grassroots community action groups made national issues relevant to local matters. Local civil rights and Black Power organizations demanded jobs that paid a living wage. An unequal distribution of resources had created the richest and poorest members of the community. White elites cemented their class advantage by doling out charity and aid. They shirked responsibility by projecting blame for poverty-related problems on individuals.

The jobs eventually held (or sought) by friends in my photograph mirrored those of their parents. Indeed, there was more consistency than intergenerational difference. Education level was not necessarily determinant. Socioeconomic status profoundly affects life experiences and opportunities. It encompasses more than wages or salaries. It also includes abstract advantages like power, influence, and reputation. Black members of the group who struggled in school had a tough time finding employment. Gone were the factory and semiskilled service jobs held by their parents. Whites didn't suffer the same consequences. They overcame poor educational backgrounds and early academic disengagement with inherited wealth, cultural capital, and powerful social networks.

Poverty: Does It Really Exist in Evanston?

Leading the fight against a national epidemic of poverty, the Women's Christian Temperance Union (WCTU) viewed alcohol consumption as the cause, not a symptom. Mrs. Fred J. Tooze, president of the Evanston-based organization, spoke at the WCTU's ninety-first annual convention at the Pick-Congress Hotel in Chicago in 1965. Responding to Johnson's programs, she argued that national sobriety was the "master key to a great society" and that the "federal war on poverty can be defeated by currently increasing alcoholism." She said, "Drink and alcoholism create poverty . . . Many in the country's low-income and no-income groups are among the 7,500,000 alcoholics."[5] Relishing a culture of morality, Evanston enforced both temperance and Sabbatarian codes, prohibiting work and public amusement on Sundays.

Tax revenues provided an incentive to relax these rules, however. Evanston's downtown shopping district had thrived during the 1940s and 50s. But in 1956 the Old Orchard shopping mall opened in nearby Skokie. Restaurants in Evanston began to struggle because they were unable to serve wine with dinner. Before voting to update antiquated laws, the city council's administrative committee asked the chamber of commerce to poll its members. One hundred fifty-four respondents said that they were against changing the liquor ordinance. "This town is in bad enough condition with all this unnecessary licensing without adding neon lighted taverns and liquor stores," wrote one respondent.[6] But a large majority, 224 members, expressed a need for change. Recommendations were class-biased. Most favored the sale of alcohol with meals in "quality restaurants and hotels," as opposed to package stores. One advocate reasoned that drinking establishments located within the city limits would cut drunk driving because people could walk to restaurants and bars.[7] Sabbatarian codes were vigorously defended. Only 63 members favored a repeal, while 272 voted against Sunday retail trade.

The city council voted one year later, in July 1968. Devoted to up-holding Evanston's reputation, they did not pass legislation allowing li-quor sales, Sunday business transactions, and barber poles. A licensing system for a limited number of package stores and restaurants would have broadened the city's tax base. The WCTU opposed any alcohol sales, however, and Evanston remained dry.[8] To increase profit and trade, Wieboldt's Department store lobbied hard to be allowed to open on the four Sundays before Christmas. Its request was also denied. Re-flecting the importance of the automobile to suburban culture, a spe-cial exemption was given to local car dealerships, which were allowed to be open on one Sunday a month. A "little-enforced law against re-volving signs" was receiving national publicity. The law was being used to turn off Evanston's revolving barber poles. It was said that advertis-ing by way of a recognizable symbol wasn't required in a well-educated and literate city. The issue was relegated to a committee for examina-tion.[9] Evanston was wedded to its image and reputation.

Denial and erasure were key strategies. Residential segregation and political disenfranchisement render poverty invisible in the United States. The media also play a role. Elite perspectives dominated Evans-ton's culturally diverse community and were assumed as the norm by some news outlets.[10] An article published in the *Evanston Review* on Sep-tember 9, 1965, illustrates this by its very title: "Poverty: Does It Really Exist in Evanston?" Painting a near-perfect picture of the quintessen-tial suburb, the author begins by setting the scene: "Shady streets, wide lawns with big houses, neat brick apartment buildings with geraniums in the courtyard, a few children cycling by, a cleaning woman walk-ing the dog . . . this is Evanston, a city with a median income is [*sic*] $9,193." The article never makes a connection between the domestic worker and the disproportionately privileged lifestyle of her employer.[11] Or the average income made high because of abundance at the top. If poverty did exist, the city was doing its part by providing plenty of support for those who needed it. Social service officials working in the fields of "public assistance, health, police and employment" were inter-viewed for the piece.

When the mainstream press acknowledged poverty, it was quickly compartmentalized and rendered as a black problem. According to a re-port published in the *Review*, Evanston's predominantly black west side, census tracts 19, 20, and 23, consisting of the entire Fifth ward and parts of the Second, contained a higher rate of poverty than the city as a whole. Close to 20 percent of the families residing in Tract 19 were living below the poverty line, earning an annual income of $3,000 or less, a figure set by the federal government. Portraying these areas as unrepresentative, the *Review* called them "pockets of poverty." The containment and social isolation of Evanston's black population made the problem easy to ignore. Making light of the facts, the paper suggested that poor blacks were better off than their counterparts living elsewhere: "These people are as poor as those in Appalachia or on Chicago's west side, in terms designated in the U.S. poverty program. But they aren't as surrounded by poverty. There aren't as many of them. There are more agencies to help."[12] The fact of the matter was that poverty was a growing concern for the nation at large, Evanston included.

Whites called for patience and gradual change. A resident interviewed by the *Review* was sympathetic to black oppression, but only to a point: "I'm not a racist. It's impossible to deny that there is racial discrimination in Evanston. But this has been going on for a century, and it's just not reasonable to suppose that it's going to be cleared up overnight. . . . Blacks who throw tantrums over the situation are acting like children. They've simply got to show some patience, difficult though it may be."[13] The *Review* concluded, "All told, the testimony on race relations in Evanston is both heartening and alarming"—heartening because it suggests "much progress has been made," alarming because Evanston's blacks don't believe it is "being made fast enough."[14]

The black press struggled to democratize and diversify the media. An important source of information, the *Examiner* advocated black economic development. Job seekers found information about employment opportunities and were inspired by articles featuring successful businessmen. Black-owned businesses increased their clientele through advertisements encouraging consumer loyalty. These stories often made the front page so as not to be missed by readers. The editor, Randolph R. Tomlinson, was committed to bringing more industry to the North Shore in order to provide jobs for blacks. When Neighbors at Work (NAW), a local OEO agency, hosted a job fair, the paper agreed to announce it. Representatives from manufacturing and utility companies and supermarket chains including Jewel Foods met with applicants at NAW's office.[15] When FEP CO, a job-recruiting program dedicated to training and placing blacks in office positions on all levels, was hiring, Tomlinson announced it by way of a headline, "Seek 300 for Jobs," and offered his offices for interview counseling sessions. FEP CO acted as an intermediary between black job seekers and firms that were relocating to the North Shore and dedicated to fair employment practices.[16] The paper also regularly featured articles about the black middle and upper classes. For example, when black businessmen and professionals formed a new association to assist Negro businesses and encourage the growth of the black economy, the *Examiner* offered a detailed account.[17]

Nearby in Cleveland, Ohio, Carl Stokes was struggling to repair the local black economy. Stokes was the first black mayor of a major city. When Bennett Johnson realized that Stokes "couldn't handle it," he left politics to focus on economic development, where he thought he had a better chance of making a difference. Johnson was named president of the newly formed Talent Assistance Program (TAP), which supported black entrepreneurship. After a fire ripped through the VIP Snack Bar, TAP made funds available so that the owners could reopen.[18] When Northshore Community Development received nonprofit status from the state, the paper announced that economic opportunities for Evanston's black community would be available through various enterprises owned, operated, and controlled by blacks.[19] Finally, after Superintendent Coffin lost his job, the paper endorsed a boycott of "exploitive" white businesses and asked instead for the patronage of black-owned businesses.[20]

Black Power

Civil rights organizations did not make as much progress in the economic sphere as they did in education and housing. According to political scientist Ira Katznelson, for blacks working in the secondary labor force, where workplace unionization was rare, the community-based voluntary association or movement organization "provided the only collective vehicle available for the expression of discontent."[21] These organizations responded to the period's demand for community control. While they appeared to empower their constituencies, they absorbed the energies of insurgents, transforming protests and rendering them harmless. "These institutions did so by reconnecting the disaffected to political life and in this way making them part of the regular, legitimate, and predictable political process." [22] Furthermore, local organizations may have played a key role in dissipating the national thrust for civil rights by fragmenting issues into community-sized components, thus separating community from community and one set of concerns from another. The gains activists did make in opening up new channels of political participation and influence proved to be substitutes for structural economic changes and for a basic redistribution of wealth and power among classes and races. Evanston modeled these patterns.

Blacks joined the national fight to curtail poverty through employment. The black community, compared to Evanston as a whole, suffered disproportionately from joblessness. Census Bureau data from 1960 reveal that 1.9 percent of the city's population was unemployed, as compared to 5.5 percent in Tract 19 and 3.4 in Tract 23, both areas in the city's all-black Fifth Ward. Census data also indicated that the number of professionals in these areas was small compared with the city as a whole. Low-wage employment was one strategy for suppressing discontent and cutting criminal activity. Believing that hard work would secure the American dream, blacks joined local chapters of both the National Association for the Advancement of Colored People (NAACP) and Southern Christian Leadership Conference (SCLC).

The membership base was so strong that leaders of these organizations made Evanston a regular stop on their speaking tours and attempted to place the local community in a national context. Roy Wilkins, executive secretary of the NAACP, was the keynote speaker at the Freedom Fund banquet in May 1965. Speaking at the Orrington Hotel, in a ballroom filled to capacity with an audience of six hundred, Wilkins, in "serious jest," congratulated Evanston for "finally catching up with North Carolina in fair employment. North Carolina banks have been hiring Negro employees for years, but I understand this has happened in Evanston only recently." He blamed whites but also urged blacks to stop "putting up with it."

Several months later, Evanston hosted the NAACP Illinois state conference, drawing audiences large enough to require both the Orrington and North Shore Hotels as venues. Theodore M. Berry, director of community action programs for the OEO in Washington, was the featured speaker. The topic of his speech was the Economic Opportunity Act of 1964.[23]

A local arm of the Cook County OEO, Neighbors at Work (NAW) opened its doors on September 19, 1968. Located at 1231 Emerson Street in the heart of Evanston's black west side, the new center offered a variety of services for low-income residents. The city was proud. NAW was featured on the *Review*'s cover a year and a half later.[24] The center's motto, "Building a stronger community," inspired graphic designers. Images were superimposed on building blocks promoting services, including the youth center Ebony House (which served as a freedom school when Coffin lost), employment and housing divisions, and the Head Start program. A portrait of the center's director, Clyde H. Brooks, was also featured on a building block. Prior to his appointment Brooks had mediated a deal with the Evanston Boy Scouts. The organization donated its camp located in Barrington, Illinois, for weekend use by low-income children from Evanston. Brooks believed this exchange could be a model for Evanston's business sector: "This offer by the Boy Scouts is an example of the kind of cooperation agencies ought to have in community programs."[25]

Supermarket chains including A&P, Jewel, and Dominick's performed two functions for Evanston: they cultivated the luxury and convenience that wealthy suburbanites desired, and they provided jobs for low-income minorities. Black civil rights groups grew to rely on these employment opportunities for their constituencies. Companies that failed to produce enough jobs came under fire. The A&P chain was the target of much criticism from SCLC's Operation Breadbasket. SCLC launched a boycott against all the chain's Chicago-area stores, including those at Central and Main Street locations in Evanston.[26] Demonstrators distributed handbills and placards accusing A&P of failing to create 770 jobs for unemployed blacks in the Chicago area and not fulfilling its jobs-for-Negroes covenant. Managers of both Evanston stores reported that the demonstrations were "orderly." In fact, picketing continued for a month with just one incident. A customer and two protesters filed charges against each other. A policeman said, "Each of the three men charged the other with having spat on him."[27] White supremacists regularly spat on civil rights protesters in the South. Trained not to react, most didn't. These activists had reached their limit.

A "dignity of regular work" program may have put the Jewel Food Store chain at the other end of the spectrum in the eyes of black leaders. The company boasted that 170 Chicago-area residents had been hired under the new program. "Many of these people live in ghetto areas. By normal definition, virtually all of them would be considered unemployable." The problem, according to the company, was not that "ghetto-dwellers are unemployable, but that they simply don't respond to traditional recruiting and training programs" because they are "suspicious and fearful." Jewel highlighted its new plan in a twenty-minute color film featuring a young black man staring into the camera. "His voice was mechanical and toneless as he described his new job as a grocery man. Then, his obviously memorized testimonial ended, he added an eloquent, unrehearsed postscript. 'I just wanna say,' he exploded, 'that now I'm married and supporting a wife. I feel like someone, I feel like a man again.' The words came in a torrent—an incoherent, joyful tribute to salvation."

Vice president of personnel development Lee D. Smith reiterated the sentiment: "They simply can't believe that doors are now opening to them." Jewel was recruiting workers and had "taken its message to the

FIGURE 7.1 A Dominick's advertisement reveals who the chain's intended clientele are—affluent and traditional couples or white homemakers and their husbands. *Evanston Review*, November 19, 1964.

ghetto." The company set up "indoctrination centers" to teach potential employees about the nature of their jobs, "what they can expect from the firm, and what the firm expects of them." Once hired, they were put in separate, slower training courses. Managers boasted about the success of the program.[28] Evanston was scheduled to get its own store soon. Until then, residents traveled either south to Chicago or west to Skokie to shop.

To much fanfare Dominick's opened a branch in Evanston in November 1964. The chain's logo made very clear who the store's target demographic was (fig. 7.1). A young couple reinforced a white norm and the importance of the nuclear family to Evanston's "social imagination."

Photographs from the store's opening party reiterate the message. Managers invited potential customers, all of whom were white. The store itself was described as a "one-stop food shopping headquarters. In effect, it is 12 stores in one, including a bakery, delicatessen, meats, groceries, dairy products, frozen foods, poultry and fish, vegetables, fruits, drugs and toiletries, and non-food needs." Dominick Di Matteo Jr., president of the Chicago-area chain, added, "The selective shopper may choose from ready-to-serve-and-eat-foods, table-trimmed meats, more than 72 varieties of imported and domestic cheeses, fresh and fresh-frozen poultry, farm-fresh vegetables, orchard-ripe fruits and oven-fresh bakery goods." He noted, "Extra planning was given to aisle spaciousness, shelf accessibility and item relationship." He was confident that "all homemakers who visit and shop in Dominick's Evanston store will be impressed with the many services and conveniences that have been especially created for them." The president made it clear that workers were there to serve the elite: "Every one of the men and women who works in Dominick's has only one primary mission and that is to give the very best service possible with courtesy and efficiency."[29]

Showing clear signs of rebellion against the subservient role they were assigned, blacks also banded together under the banner of the Black Power movement. The list of grievances was long. Blacks in Evanston were being denied equality in housing, education, and employment. Black Power, as theory and in practice, "understood these issues as aspects of a larger situation, not as isolated matters to be taken up on their own terms at the community level."[30] The holistic worldview of Black Nationalism, according to Katznelson, produced demands that in two respects were radically different from the usual articulation of urban issues. First, it did not respect traditional boundaries between issues; issues were treated together as aspects of a total condition. Second, these policy areas were the objects of demands for a radical redistribution of resources and opportunities.[31]

Following the death of King, local authorities were eager to channel black rage into constructive action. They worked with "responsible" black leaders to create the West Side Service Center (WSSC). The center was charged with creating proactive programs to engage black youth. The executive director, William Cross, steered WSSC away from cooling-off projects and toward a higher state of black consciousness. For him King's death triggered a new appreciation for cultural nationalism. The ideals of the Black Power movement were omnipresent. They inspired Cross to open the House of Blackness, a bookstore across the street from the high school that sold books on black culture as well as African artwork. During Afro-American History Week, the center sponsored a series of talks to promote various career tracks available to black youth.[32] Cross explained that the series was a "prelude to weekly 'rapping sessions,' in which Negroes will meet to discuss issues affecting their lives."[33] Invited speakers included two social activists, a Black Panther Party member, a Northwestern University graduate who had led the revolt at the college, and an Olympic athlete.

Black youth embraced their ethnic heritage, building their self-esteem in the process. The Black Arts movement, referred to as the artistic branch of Black Power, produced works across the country. The Organization of Black American Culture (OBAC) was a local manifestation. Cross attended meetings on Chicago's South Side and at Northwestern to gain new insights on empowerment through artistic expression. After each meeting he would rush back to WSSC to implement what he'd learned. A mural covering an entire wall in the center's lounge area was a likely result. It may have been inspired by OBAC's Wall of Respect, an outdoor mural created in 1967 on the South Side of Chicago. The theme of the mural was "Black Heroes," and it contained portraits of Malcolm X and W. E. B. DuBois, among others. Cross's mural was similarly conceived to instill pride in teens visiting WSSC. The *Review* described it: portraits of a black soldier, musician, craftsman, and doctor "leap out," "commanding instant attention"; the faces are "proud, purposeful, unafraid." There was, however, a dual meaning to the portraits. "For some, the paintings reflect a racial spirit that warms the soul. For others, they reflect a militancy which, if denied, could bring massive disorders to Evanston in the predictable future."[34]

With new hope, Cross watched the transformation of middle-class and upwardly mobile working-class blacks at Northwestern as they embraced their ethnicity. Through Jimmy Reid's unofficial Black Panther organization, Cross saw the difference these ideas made for at-risk youth, who became focused and committed through Black Power philosophies. When the police raided Panther headquarters in Chicago, everyone was convinced the same would happen in Evanston. Panthers surrounded the center on Church Street. They were stationed at windows and on the roof, with guns loaded and drawn to protect the black community. Nothing happened. Months later, the group disbanded and members returned to their old ways. Black Power threatened Evanston's status quo, as well as ideas about gradual progress. Reid was found shot execution style near the train tracks. From that tragedy Cross learned that identity politics must be accompanied by material change, or else individuals fall back into survival mode.[35]

As the decade came to a close, both Brooks and Cross had the foresight to see the consequences of a class divide. In an interview with the *Review*, Brooks predicted an increase in racial tensions: "These conditions are producing a situation where many blacks may die. And maybe some whites will die too." Brooks's words were ominous. A reporter remarked, "The chilling thing about the statement was that it was delivered calmly. The words were as unimpassioned as those of a forecaster predicting rain."

Cross was also fed up: "When it comes to jobs, shelter, and education, we just can't wait. We need these things now!" Black Power "isn't a threat to any white except those who are now exploiting us." Then according to the reporter, Cross paused, weighing his words, "coolly deliberate," and said, "But heed this warning. As I learn of my glorious past and my present potential, I shall have little patience for negotiating my humanity. Either you realize my humanness or I will confront you by whatever means necessary to prove it." In fact, there was a long list of grievances that supported the urgency of these demands.[36] Authorities were charged with managing a conflict that was much more intense and less susceptible to piecemeal solutions than they had been accustomed to.

Managing Poverty

With racial tensions mounting, Evanston expanded its relief-giving efforts, a strategy that sociologists Frances Fox Piven and Richard A. Cloward claim is common among political bodies invested in maintaining the status quo. Charity organizations operate as a stopgap that serves the larger economic and political order. Historical evidence suggests that "relief arrangements are initiated or expanded during the occasional outbreaks of civil disorder produced by mass unemployment, and are then abolished or contracted when political stability is restored."[37] Economic order in the United States is dependent upon cheap labor and racism that confines blacks to low-skilled jobs, low wages, and unsatisfactory employment. To maintain economic order, Evanston had to manage the consequences of capitalism and economic inequality, efforts that had "less to do with substantive problem-solving than with channeling and controlling discontent and potential rebellion."[38] To this end the city's political and cultural institutions were agencies of social control.

Evanston had a history of benevolence and paternalism. These ideologies were easily adaptable to any time period. In the sixties and seventies, the numbers of families eligible for social services from both federal and municipal governments grew. When the *Review* announced, "350 Evanston families are eating better this summer as the result of the Department of Agriculture's food stamp program for low-income families," it sounded like bragging.[39] There were two Evanstons. The braggers usually ignored the substandard side. As liberal welfare moved right, blacks became underclass and dependent. The effect on blacks was deleterious.

Bernie felt ashamed. He was in middle school when he first realized that his mother relied on food stamps to feed the family: "She'd try to send me to the store and I'd go 'nope.' I couldn't. I couldn't do it. I was embarrassed and I couldn't do it. I mean, I know that's the way she had to make it, but I wouldn't—"I'm not going, nope." I'd run out of the house or something, go get lost for a while—couldn't do it." Bernie was desperate to escape the stigma. He didn't want to be associated with dependence and welfare.

Charity served several purposes. On the surface it supported the myth of equality. More deeply, it muted potential conflict, enhanced white feelings of superiority, and reinforced segregation.

Jesse's parents relied on donations to give their children new clothes and supplies for school each year. Jesse remembers that there were "places you could go to and they would help you out, to get you started off in the year right." He wasn't sure exactly where it was, but he remembers a "big place right behind a Catholic church, something to do with the school district." There were long lines. Inside "they will get your foot size, and they give you vouchers to get the gym shoes; you can go through this line, and they'd have baskets of stuff that's been donated from stores. Stuff for the kids that are less fortunate." They also distributed clothing, including "blue jeans you could pick through, not really worn jeans, nice stuff, new stuff, packets of underwear, packets of socks, gym shoes and T-shirts, toothbrushes." Luckily "they gave you coats too, brand-new coats, gloves, hat, 'cause you got to have it in Chicago, you'll freeze out there. . . . You could go in there and get what you need: pencils, pen, colored markers, stuff you need for school. Notebooks, everything. And that's how we would get our school supplies." Jesse's mother wanted him to have everything he needed. She always found a way to buy items for her children that the charities didn't distribute—"a nice book bag or lunch pail, they would go buy it, or a thermos."

To feed and clothe the poor was one thing; subsidizing day care was another. More than any other issue, child care shook Evanston's social imagination. Patriarchal norms governed Evanston's staid old families. Yet subsidized facilities were necessary to ensure a workforce of low-wage domestic laborers. Established in 1944, when women were entering the workforce in large numbers, the Evanston Child Care Center Association (ECCCA) lost support when the war ended. By 1960 more than nine hundred working mothers were seeking supervision for their children. Nine licensed day care centers provided less than one-third of what 1960 census figures indicated was needed.[40] The demand for day care was greater than the supply, according to a report released by ECCCA. The center was performing a valuable social service for preschoolers of low-income working mothers. "Most of the children there are from two-parent homes, where even with both working the total income is very low."[41] Without affordable child-care services, single mothers trying to make ends meet on one income would be further impoverished. To meet growing needs, ECCCA, which served only fifty children, embarked on a fundraising drive for larger facilities. The association hoped to raise $350,000 by the fall of 1969, when the center was scheduled to vacate its location at the First Congregational Church. When residents "vigorously opposed" a special-use permit that would allow the center to build at 1406–08 Main Street, one had to wonder if it was really because they feared an increase in traffic in the area. Everyone agreed that it was best to place the new center in a "neighborhood where it will be warmly received by the neighbors."[42]

Appealing to the public's humanity, Mrs. William Brackett, president of ECCCA, explained that her facility accommodated children between three and five whose parents were unable to pay private nursery fees and whose mothers "must be out of the home because of financial or extraordinary needs."[43] She added that without a center many of those who could not find licensed accommodations would have to rely on "neighbors, frequently under unhealthy or creatively stultifying conditions."[44] Brackett wanted the public to know that ECCCA had a thirty-year record of producing "good citizens," a term resonating with the tenets of Republican Motherhood. The career choices of many alumni supported her point: they had grown up to be "reporters, teachers, doctors and social workers."[45] The center acted to replicate a mother's care. Children received regular hearing tests, dental checkups, and eye examinations, along with food and a nap each day. Through group games and structured activities, children learned teamwork, an important cornerstone of the nation's work ethic.

Under the condition that no more than eighty children be enrolled at any given time, the city council approved use of an old nursing home at 1840 Asbury Avenue. Superintendent Coffin understood the relationship between social issues. He attended the ribbon-cutting ceremonies on July 28, 1969.

Bike riding was a popular pastime for older youth. Evanston's city streets, parks, and lakeshore paths were fun to ride. Bikes allowed children easy access to areas outside their own neighborhood and the ability to trespass strict racialized residential boundaries. But whites expected blacks to enter white neighborhoods as laborers, not for recreational purposes. Black youth were perceived as a threat. Crime statistics validated the stereotype. In 1965, a total of 629 bikes were stolen in Evanston; of this number only 141 were eventually recovered. By the middle of the summer the following year, when it appeared that the total would surpass the previous year's number, the police department announced that the sharp increase would result in new regulations. New policies required bikes to be licensed and registered with the city. Sergeant James Getchtus explained that "a virtually indestructible registration tag" would be applied to the bicycle frame with synthetic cement; "the tag is like that used by the government on missile nose cones, which can defy most efforts at removal or coverage."[46] In 1968 an editorial in the *Review* admonished parents to take advantage of registration efforts. The program helped reduce the number of bike thefts from 773 bike thefts in 1966 to 576 in 1967.[47]

Anecdotal evidence suggests that impoverished black youth were the perpetrators of bike thefts. Stark economic disparities were partly to blame. Stolen bikes redistributed a bit of the city's wealth from rich to poor. Ronny remembers his black friends stealing bikes from North Evanston and taking them home to "chop 'em up." Their rationale, he said, was primarily economic: "Fuck, we don't have any money, I can't buy a bike." Meanwhile his friends who lived in North Evanston "were wealthier; they were sort of the next tier in Evanston . . . and they had three of the same bikes, and they were all perfect and brand new, and tennis rackets, and a garage full of stuff."

Bike theft could also be viewed as a gateway offense to committing more serious crimes. Ray fit this profile. He "had a good heart," but with limited resources and few opportunities, he started stealing bikes as a source of revenue. Jesse watched as his friend spiraled out of control. "It hurted me a lot. I tried to talk to him. I tried to reach him in every way I could. He go steal somebody's bike and go sell it, and get him some liquor, and I'd find him where he always hung out over by the park and you'd find him over there under a tree drunk, young tough, young drunk. . . . Richards, that's what he used to like to drink." Ray's mother would plead with Jesse to find her son: "I don't know where he's at, he's been drinking that Wild Irish Rose."

According to statistics, Evanston crime had increased steadily since 1960. The largest numbers of police calls were coming from the black community. A disproportionate number of juvenile offenders were black.[48] Sergeant Getchius, head of the department's youth section, blamed unemployment. "I hear them say over and over, 'If I could just get a job, things would be better.'"[49]

After-School Jobs

Unlike white members of our group, blacks worked from an early age. If Prince wanted to play basketball at the YMCA, he had to find a job to pay the membership fee. A four-year membership was only twenty-six dollars, but if he asked his mother for it, she would tell him "I don't have it." Scholarships were limited and "very hard to get." When Prince didn't get one, he started working. He was in fourth grade when he got his first paper route. "I would get on my bike and deliver newspapers right after school and on Sunday morning." The Sunday editions of the *Daily News* were "a lot heavier than they were during the week—I remember that, that's for sure!" He also earned money doing yard work for the landlord—"everybody knew him as the rent man." Prince earned five dollars to clean up the properties, "our backyard and the one next to it." Working two jobs, Prince "finally saved up enough money" to pay for his Y membership.

Chip started delivering the afternoon edition in fifth grade. By the time he was at Nichols, he was working the early morning shift. Before sunrise, as early as 3:00 a.m., a truck unloaded newspapers for him to roll. An hour later Chip was throwing them from his bike onto people's front lawns. Usually he finished and was back home by 5:00 a.m. He earned a promotion and began riding on the delivery truck, dropping bundles for other boys to roll. The driver would pull over and Chip would jump off. With this job he finished earlier and was back home in time to get more sleep before school started. He should have been resting for school the next day; instead he was out in the middle of the night working. It must have been hard for him to concentrate in school. His parents' separation led to deeper financial troubles for his mother. Sensitive to her situation, he told me, "You don't want to come to the house every day asking Mom for something that she really doesn't have."

When I asked Jesse about pocket money, he was surprised by my naïveté. "We couldn't get no allowances, we didn't have it!" He also had a paper route but earned money doing maintenance work as well, any odd job he could find after school and on the weekends. He survives on those skills today. His uncles taught him home maintenance and repair and heavy lifting. "We used to have to paint our families' houses, and then we moved people and made money too." During high school Jesse worked outdoors. He helped maintain the yards of wealthy homeowners. "We would go down by the lakefront" cutting lawns during the spring and summer. During the winter months, "when it be bad snow we would shovel snow off the roofs of people's garages for they wouldn't collapse." Servicing the elite, he also cleared snow from drive-ways and sidewalks. When teenagers are working in adult jobs, they often see employment as a viable alternative to schooling.

Bernie was fifteen when he was hired to work at the Shell gas sta-tion near his home. He persevered even when older employees treated him "like garbage 'cause I was a little black kid." The age difference coupled with a sense of racial superiority entitled them to shout things like "Hey, get out there and get that car, boy." Bernie threatened to quit if they continued: "If you say one more thing I'm leaving." After three or four months he had had enough and "just walked out, never came back." He believes "some of it was racial; these were guys in their early twenties, real immature guys." The job didn't last long, but it set him on a path that transcended high school and a Vocational Education program. To fulfill requirements for his auto mechanics class, he took a job with Leroy, who owned a gas station and car repair shop. Bernie learned his trade working at both. "I'd go from the gas station to the shop." At the gas station Leroy "did repairs and sold gas," but the shop was "repairs only." Bernie continued working for Leroy after he gradu-ated. "I was pretty much at the shop; he finally sold the gas station. So, I think, I worked there for a total of seven years or so."

Black participants contributed part of their income to their families. Regina told me that Earl "always worked, and he always gave his fam-ily half of everything he made, which I just couldn't grasp, but they needed the money." He would buy his parents the luxury items that they could not afford or would not spend the money to buy them-selves. Regina recalls one incident in particular. Earl bought his father expensive cologne for Christmas. His father was strong and domineer-ing, and Earl loved him a lot. He was really excited; "it was a big deal for him, and he wrapped it up, and he gave it to his dad, and his dad opened it, and barely said thank you, and then rewrapped it and gave it to somebody else." Earl was so hurt he cried. "He was just trying to please his dad."

Whites in the photo didn't need to work. We had our basic needs met. We spent our weekly allowance any way we wanted. Carla was "one of those people that didn't work through high school." Her mother always took her shopping right before school started each fall. During these excursions she picked out the wardrobe essentials important to young teenage girls. She would choose "a few items," including Con-verse All-Stars Chuck Taylor gym shoes with colored laces—"the whole thing would come to fifteen bucks." As other needs arose, her mother would dip into savings. One year Carla needed a dress for the prom, and her mother "took out some money." Sometimes she was forced to take her brothers' hand-me-downs, including a bike, but she also remembers getting a new one. A ten-dollar-a-week allowance paid for snacks at Bernstein Brothers, like the "eighteen-cent Twinkie." Because of her parents' class position, Carla could afford to be cavalier about part-time work. She took babysitting jobs intermittently and only lasted "a week in the Dannon Yogurt Store."

I Have Grammar Capital

Prince started bagging groceries at Dominick's when he was a sophomore in high school. He had to get the job even though it took time away from sports and homework. To make up for it, he "cut back" on extracurricular activities and "didn't go to any basketball games." His grades suffered from the time he had to devote to work. "I didn't make the honor roll my sophomore year as I did my freshman year, but I did good. . . . I never let the job go. During the season I would cut back one or two days a week, but by the time I was a senior in high school, that job at Dominick's was paying me like nine bucks an hour, and that for me, that was a lot of money back then." By the time Prince graduated, he had been promoted to the produce department and was a full-time employee working forty hours a week. He decided against college.

By December he'd changed his mind. "I can't do this no more, I can't," he told himself. "There's no way I can do this for the rest of my life." Prince enrolled in classes at a community college for one semester before transferring to a university. Grant money paid only some of the bills. He transferred to the Edwardsville store and continued working for the supermarket chain throughout college. He knew he had made the right decision when he returned to Evanston during a school holiday and saw the consequences of academic disengagement on his friends. "Wow, had it changed," especially "drug wise," he told me. The people who had been smoking weed when he left were involved in much more serious drugs when he returned. "I mean, that was like a real eye opener," he said, grateful that he had escaped this fate. Prince's story illustrates the extent to which black students were not being steered toward college. The most studious of our group, initially he opted out of college to work in a supermarket.

Low expectations were partly responsible. Prince wasn't encouraged to continue his education by school counselors or his family. Even though he knew "you could walk in there at any time," he "didn't pay much attention" to the counseling center. The only time he sought advice from a counselor was when he inquired about the VE program or "some kind of program where the kids could leave school and earn money and still earn class credit." His guidance counselor told him flat out, "You can't be a part of that program." When he pressed, she said it again: "That's not for you." Prince didn't understand that it was a program for "people that had no opportunity to go to college; it was more like career oriented to get them prepared for the workforce." While he was not steered toward VE, he was not tracked for college either. He didn't understand the importance of college admissions exams and didn't prepare before he took the ACT. "For me it wasn't something that was like, you gotta go do good on this test if you wanta go to a good college; it was like if you wanta go to college you have to take this test. I didn't put any time into studying or thinking about it; the day of the test I just went there and took it." Prince didn't have a frame of reference when it came to college. Most of his relatives had never finished high school. His mother demanded that he graduate from high school but didn't push him beyond that.

Jesse did not consider college beyond the possibility of being recruited by a sports program. When that offer did not come, he found work at Household Finance Corporation (HFC), a mortgage service company in Schaumburg, Illinois. His fond recollections of playing intramural sports against teams from other large corporations in the area, including Allstate Insurance and Sara Lee Foods, resonated with his dreams to be a professional athlete. They also revealed class disparities between workers and owners. He remembers that executives would "fly in on their helicopters and they'd land on the field." Instead of seeing this as evidence of a wage gap, Jesse bragged about it. HFC was a "good company"; it rewarded its employees after the game with "big banquets." Jesse also minimized inequalities by being an eager learner. He was proud that during the seven years that he worked for the company, he was trained to do a variety of tasks. "I learned how to do For Air, a fast messenger service," he told me. He also delivered parcels to "every big building in Chicago, handling business for Household Finance." In the mailroom he learned to ship packages through the United Parcel Service, sending out five to six hundred packages a day. Finally, he learned to repair tape; "they taught me how to splice and fix it back together." Jesse believed his time at HFC was well spent; he was "just trying to get more job skills to help me when I fill out my resume." He continued to believe that "life held something better."

I never considered the labor behind neatly arranged products on grocery-store shelves until Jesse told me about it. In his late twenties, Jesse was hired by A. J. Canfield to deliver and stock the company's products. The job afforded Jesse some of the autonomy he craved:

> I wanted to be my own boss, and working on the pop truck, I was my own boss. I didn't have to answer to nobody; all I had to do was handle four chain stores before lunchtime. You got to do all your main grocery stores, you got to do them before 12:00. Like a Dominick's store: you got to go in there, take a shelf order, whatever they're out of, go back out to your truck, write it down what you need, then whatever they got in their back room that hasn't been worked out on the floor, make sure the stuff that you wrote down, if it's in their back room, you got to take it from back there and then put it out on the shelf. You got to face all the stuff up if you have to build a display of pops on sale, and you got to drop five hundred cases of pop and build a display, and you got to know how to do it without the pop falling everywhere. I made good money. I stayed there for about three or four years.

Marketing strategies were important in an increasingly consumer-conscious culture.

More than the others, Jesse's employment history exemplifies the temporary work that was available to poor blacks without college degrees. He has had "maybe three or four jobs" while living in Tacoma, Washington. His story also illustrates the low-paying, dirty, and unpleasant tasks that members of minority groups routinely do and whites often refuse to perform. After working as a mover for Mayflower Transit Company, he was hired by Northwest Cascade, which sets up and maintains "honey buckets," or portable toilets, for summer camps, construction sites, and highway stops:

> They started me at $12.50; after three months you go to union wage, $13.50, then if you still there after a year you go to the union scale at $17.50 an hour. I was making $17.50 an hour, best benefits in the state of Washington. I worked there for almost two years, and then they laid me off. I mean if I wanted to, I'm sure I could probably go back out there, but who wants to do that? That's no career move. I used to take a bath and couldn't even get the smell off of me, and it ain't like it's just you dancing in the stuff, it's just you around it and it's feces, and they have 'em all in Seattle and homeless people sleep inside of them things, so you might go pick up a hundred of 'em and they bring 'em back to the yard, because people steady order them, and all they can do is bring 'em back, and they don't have time

to pump 'em out, so the stuff gets thrown all over the thing. By the time it gets to the yard and it's your day to be up on the wash rack washing 'em, and you got to stick your hand in there, you in a rubber suit, but you got to stick your hand down in there and grab. People might leave underwear, syringes from heroin addicts, it's all kind of stuff be down in there, but I did it because I'm trying to do right and take care of my family, and like I said, I didn't have much education. I didn't have much of a choice.

More recently, Jesse worked as a mover, a skill he had learned from his uncles as a child. When business slowed down, he was laid off again. "I'm not even working, and the money I'm getting from unemployment isn't that much; I'm only drawing about 150 bucks a week."

One afternoon we were driving in his car after picking up a state-issued voucher so that he could pay his electricity bill—his service was about to be disconnected. During our conversation I mentioned that I was working on my PhD at Yale University. His response, *"Yale!* That's Ivy League!," and its juxtaposition to our errand reiterated the race and class division between us—not because of anything either one of us did. Jesse worked hard. He had a difficult time finding work because of educational inequalities and the socioeconomic status of his parents.

I worked less hard. I had experimented with drugs and didn't excel in school. The stakes were never so high that I had to really care about much. I took acting lessons but wasn't determined enough. After years of waitressing I simply decided to go back to school. I started by taking classes at a community college in San Diego. Eventually I transferred to the University of California, Los Angeles. I was unprepared for a rigorous academic program but did well. I had grown up around highly educated adults. I didn't know grammatical rules per se, but I could tell when something sounded right. I read my papers out loud after I wrote them. I graduated with honors.

Jesse's parents never finished high school. He was forty-six and marginally illiterate. He asked, "Do you know how it is to go for a job and you can't really fill out a application and can't spell some of the words?" Then he explained his strategy for overcoming his handicap: "I would have to get a application from the job, take it home, get help filling it out, then bring it back to the place. Some places won't let you take the application, you have to fill it out right there, so I'd have to fill out an application and bring it with me and then copy off of that." Jesse knew that his future was precarious: "I'm still trying to survive, still trying to make it off of what I know and what I can do physically. Once the physical part goes and I can't do anything physical no more, I don't know where I'm going to be, because my body's not going to be able to do this back-breaking work too much longer. So I need to try and find something I can do that's not so strenuous. It's like times right now I wake up in the morning, I be hurting all over."

Unwelcome and untrained for the mainstream economy, Chip was forced to look for an alternative. He joined the Black Mob, a gang of twenty teenagers that soon exploded to more than 250. In the heart of Evanston's west side, near Foster School at Simpson and Payne, they would "gamble and serve" or shoot dice and sell drugs. Power and territory were not incentives. Instead it was about living life. Like everyone else, the boys wanted to have "our cars clean, look good, talk crazy to women, and go to the club on the weekend." Chip explained, "All we were trying to do is live." Dealing weed escalated to selling guns, freebasing cocaine, jail time, and addiction to heroin and crack. In the beginning Chip played by the rules and controlled his urges. "When you serve, and even if you ain't in a gang, you don't want to use, because you know you going to mess up." It's a conflict of interest: "saying you going to sell when you your best customer, that's not good."

Chip's life went downhill when he started "spilling," giving his customer half and doing the rest himself. He'd travel on the train to Chicago's west side to buy drugs and return to Evanston to sell them. One day he was busted on the "L" platform. The police took him to jail but failed to find all of the drugs on his person. A couple of "foils" used to package heroin sustained Chip, by now a full-fledged addict. Other addicts weren't so lucky. Chip could hear them screaming "Turnkey, turnkey," hoping the guard would bring relief. After three days his wife arrived, and they took the bus home together. Back in his neighborhood, Chip saw "niggers on both corners" and "jumped out of the bus." His addiction was so severe that at night he slept with sweat socks on his hands to keep from scratching and opening the sores that covered his body. After five years, Chip told me, "I was tired of being tired," and he quit cold turkey.

With no concrete goals, my white friends and I drifted after high school. Financial and emotional support from families provided a bottom we could not fall below. Living at home with no substantial responsibilities, Carla worked part time in a restaurant and by her own account did "nothing." A small inheritance—"I got like sixteen thousand dollars"—from her father let her quit work altogether. He had struggled with alcoholism and died from cirrhosis in 1979, soon after Carla's eighteenth birthday. She used the money to spend a month in

New York with Jennifer and get "my first apartment alone." She remembers that she "got high" a lot. Her brother would tease her. He would hold his hand up to shield his eyes and look out the window, imitating her job search. Carla did not incur debt. Her inheritance paid for her indulgences. She took classes at the American Academy of Art. "I liked to draw," she told me. Her mother supported her "creative endeavors." Carla completed two years but "didn't finish" the program. She continued to drift: "I was aimless, I had nothing going on, I was pretty depressed."

Jennifer practiced her art and worked part time. She thought about going to college but had "barely got through high school." She lived at home with her parents. At night she took classes at the Art Institute of Chicago. "I didn't go there having any clue as to what I wanted to do with the experience, but art has always been an outlet." In 1983 she moved to New York City, where she lived with a family friend, worked as a waitress, and went out every night "till like the sun came up." She made and sold scarves and jewelry. She had connections. Eventually she started working as a fashion stylist. The industry propelled her further away from the integrated world she had known as a child. Racial segregation in the workplace is common in fashion and advertising. Jennifer's coworkers were mostly white. Interactions with minority groups were limited to casting days when clients were looking for models to represent specific ethnic or racial groups. Artistic directors come to these sessions with explicit instructions to "mix up the spreads" with Asian, black, white, and "mixed-race" peoples. They craft advertisements that show a balanced multiracial cast of characters interacting and consuming their products, suggesting that discriminatory racial barriers have been dismantled. The commercial spreads no longer reflected Jennifer's real life.

What began as a hobby for Ronny evolved into a music career. Like those of Carla and Jennifer, his talents were supported by socioeconomic advantage. His parents had available resources to indulge their son's musical interests and hobbies early. When he was in seventh grade, his father found an ad for a used drum set for sale in the *Review*. Because he didn't need an after-school job, Ronny had hours on end to practice. He'd sit in his room with his stereo "right there behind my head," listening and playing along to Jimi Hendrix, Diana Ross, and Marvin Gaye's *Let's Get It On* album. Ronny and Perkey made weekly excursions to Evanston's west side to hear funk music: "We'd go watch this guy's band rehearse in his basement and maybe sit in a little bit—

I'd play a couple songs and Perkey would sing. I was the only white guy." Every Tuesday they went to a church on the west side to listen to a father and son play. "It was just the two of them drums and organ."

"There was never any talk of going away to college" in Ronny's family. After high school he played drums for a jazz band in New Orleans. His whiteness gave the group legitimacy in a desegregating South. He got the job because the band "needed a white guy to get the gig." The boys lived at the Holiday Inn for the entire summer, playing six nights a week in the hotel lounge. When management offered to extend the engagement, Ronny declined: "I'm going back, I'm going to school." Back home he took recording, jazz band, marimba, and sight-reading classes. He did that for a year, and then "that was that, I didn't go back." Ronny didn't feel the same urgency to settle or find a job that his black friends did. He lived life day to day while they "got city jobs." He gave private music lessons and says, "There's something about the structure of the teaching that is really healthy for me." When he was just a musician, "it was that same sort of drifting feeling I had growing up, like 'whatever, I got a gig tonight' and 'basically I don't have anything to do all day.'" When whites complained that their childhoods lacked both structure and strict boundaries, they were referring to parents who did not prioritize education or emphasize self-discipline and delayed gratification. Some felt that they did not reach their full potential in life because of their parents' lackadaisical attitudes.

Carla echoed Ronny's sentiments when she told me, "It meant everything to me to all of sudden have a structure." She exercised her privilege when she *decided* to go to college. Loyola University Chicago wouldn't accept her "without SAT or ACT scores, and my grades weren't high." She felt entitled to try again. Mundelein College told her, "We'll give you a shot for a semester," and put her on probationary status. Carla excelled. She was on the dean's list every year and studied abroad in Italy. She took her time and switched majors several times before deciding on math. To fulfill an elective requirement, she took a Spanish class, and that was when she "fell in love" with Latin American history. She changed majors one last time and graduated after six years. The next fall she enrolled in a master's program and after that received her doctorate. Her dissertation explored themes of race, class, and power. Her interests developed over many years but stemmed from Evanston's integration plan and the courageous individuals who demanded racial equality for all schoolchildren.

My white friends knew deep down that they were expected to succeed. They couldn't identify the source of their intuition. For Regina, dropping out of high school was not an option—"no way." She knew that "at a minimum" she had to graduate from high school, "no matter how fucked up everything was around me." The educational backgrounds of her family may have been influential. "I just knew that my grandparents would never forgive me. I'd done enough," she said, referring to her interracial relationship with Earl. Graduating from high school, "that was a given." College was not mandatory. Neither of her grandparents had gone to college, and they "were fine." In fact her grandfather, an immigrant, became very wealthy without a high school diploma. He made his money through real estate. Regina regrets that neither school authorities nor her parents stressed the importance of college. "I really resent that, and I really resent my family not being more proactive. . . . It's a big sore spot for me. . . . Nobody took an interest in me going to college." Somehow she knew that she had to take ACTs and SATs, but "I didn't know what that meant, and I had no real grasp." After high school she took classes at DePaul University. "I always intended on finishing, it's just that life kind of got in the way." Unconsciously noting the lack of intergenerational social mobility, she said, "I suppose I could have gone on public aid and finished school, but I wasn't brought up to be in the system; there's just certain things that aren't . . . options because it's not in my world. It's like children of doctors become doctors and children of lawyers become lawyers and . . ."

Interpersonal relationships are strained by class differences. Regina felt the tension when Earl did not graduate from high school and she did. Young and in love, they moved into a studio apartment together. Regina paid her bills by working as a waitress and as a clerk at a gas station. Earl worked in the informal economy selling drugs. "He just was on a downward path. He just went from bad to worse. He went from good to bad to worse, instead of good, great, greater . . ." Regina made efforts to improve her life. "I was not young and stupid anymore." They fought a lot. Three months later, it was over. "I'm not gonna live in the ghetto," she decided. "I don't remember the breakup itself; it was pretty violent, and I just left, and I left everything, what little I had, in my studio apartment—my few possessions, my TV, and my stereo, which I had gotten for my birthday, clothes, everything—and I moved into my mother's house for a little while. I was growing and he wasn't, and I was moving on and he wasn't." Seven years earlier Earl had followed her home on his bike, worried because she was crying. It took only that long for the city to turn an innocent boy with so much promise into a desperate criminal. Wrongfully accused once, he was imprisoned twice. He thought about Regina from his cell. He wrote her letters and tried calling her too. She avoided him and lied to his family so that he couldn't find her. "He thought I was in California, and anybody in my family would tell him nothing."

With no high school diploma and a felony charge, finding work was all but impossible. Earl did odd jobs, working as a day laborer. He painted houses. By this time he was a grown man and didn't want to stay with his family. He started following "the trail," a route that ran along Lake Michigan south from Milwaukee to Chicago. The Potawatomis had traveled this same path, following the seasons, hunting and gathering, before their land was stolen from them. Today men and women struggling with drug addiction, homelessness, and unemployment take this same journey, looking for a place to sleep. While day shelters offer various services, most transport clients to "the pads," churches or community centers set up with mattresses at night. Regulations require individuals to move on to the next town and a new shelter every few days, but "you can just stay on the trail" indefinitely.

Struggling with addiction, Chip and his wife also followed it. They could have stayed with family too, but not together, and they didn't want to leave each other's side. "I could have went to family—I didn't want to," Chip told me. Imagine what it must have been like when Chip saw his old friend from Evanston. He told me, "I'd seen Earl. Earl was on the trail." Eventually Earl found work cooking in the kitchen at a men's shelter in Chicago. A staff member who later attended his funeral said Earl was a loved guy. Remembering Earl's fate, Chip told me, "I think a nine-millimeter to the leg would explain to Earl their situation, too, . . . especially when I came from the service, you know, and I know a well-played shot didn't have to be a kill shot for a man with a fork."

On nights when the shelters were full, Chip and his wife rode the "L." "We get our sleep at night on the train, south out to O'Hare Airport and back." When I met with him in Beloit, he was making ends meet collecting supplemental security income (SSI) because of his disability and selling some of his prescription painkillers. His condition had deteriorated to the point where he could no longer work. I asked him if he had any regrets, and he responded, "I always thought with some more education, I could have stepped through quite a few more doors, you know."

Quick cash and a flexible work schedule made waitressing an appealing job for white girls without college plans. Regina and I worked at Yesterdays across from Northwestern's campus. Undocumented workers filled positions behind the scenes in the kitchen. Regina's first husband was a cook. He didn't use his real name; he went by Juan Martinez, the name printed on his green card. Restaurant work is readily available, and the skills are easily transferable. When the couple left Evanston and moved to Naples, Florida, they didn't have a problem finding work. After reading an advertisement in a newspaper, they applied at the Glades, a new country club, and were hired on the spot. When the marriage didn't work out, Regina returned to Evanston. Again, she found work readily,. "I worked for my mother for about seven years, and I was making good money, and I really didn't need to go back to school."

Carla worked her way through college and graduate school as a waitress at Un Grand Café, an upscale French bistro in Chicago. She met her first husband, a busboy, while she was an undergraduate. They did their best to resist ethnic and social class differences. She felt "out of place in academic settings" and was more comfortable in a "less educated environment," and "he was bright but he was not educated." Narrowing the gap, he earned his GED. The marriage did not last. Carla divorced him around the time she was taking her comprehensive examinations and "starting the heavy dissertation phase." Initially, she had not wanted to go to college, having "kind of screwed up" in high school. She thinks she was "one of those people that wasn't supposed to make it." She explains her academic success by the fact that both of her parents were intellectuals: "although I like to talk shit, I have grammar capital, as postmodernists would say." Carla's vocabulary and ability to express herself were shaped at an early age at the dinner table. Growing up, she never worried about money. Later she worked hard but also felt comfort knowing that if she needed something her family was there to provide it. Like other white group members, she never got into too much trouble; "there's some part of me that would stop myself before getting heavy into drugs," and "my family wouldn't have let me stray too far."

The decision to go to college was made for Barbara by her parents. It also ended her romance with Mario, who didn't go. She earned a master's degree in mental health. She worked as a grief counselor at a hospice before she became a paralegal in a personal injury family law firm. "After ten years of working in the field of death and dying," she says, "I needed a little change, and my divorce attorney, who is now my boss, asked me if I wanted to try working with him." While most paralegals go to school to train, she learned through experience because the boss "basically liked me." The job entailed "everything that the attorney would do except go to court and argue the case." Prompted by a client who was reconsidering his divorce and needed someone to talk to, she asked her boss about starting a new business alongside his. He welcomed the idea and let her use his office space. As a licensed grief therapist and a senior paralegal, she targeted clients who were divorcing, because that "taps into feelings of grief and loss."

Candy majored in French. She took advantage of the resources that her private college offered and spent a semester abroad. She participated in campus life, becoming president of the French club. She did graduate work at Middlebury College, including a year in Paris studying French literature. When she decided to stay in France, she used powerful social networks and the "strength of weak ties" to secure jobs and residency. Mark Granovetter's pathbreaking work measures how a person's distant relatives and acquaintances pass along information about job opportunities.[50] An individual with high socioeconomic status (SES) usually has access to a vast array of contacts from similar backgrounds. With no "working papers," Candy contacted the president of the American Chamber of Commerce in Paris, who was also an alumnus from Middlebury, where she had earned her master's. Candy worked as a real-estate developer before getting her next job. She found work through a friend of her father, the director of the Christian Children's Fund organization. Candy was hired to oversee the development of a French subsidiary.

Another opportunity came from a friend who worked at the American embassy in Paris. At the time of our interview, Candy was directing a five-million-dollar restoration project for the consulate building, located on the Plaza Le Concorde. Her husband was doing similar work as the director of development and operations for the Chateau de Chantilly, where the family was residing. Her first love, Jesse, could not rely on the same kind of powerful social networks to secure work.

Social networking operated differently for low-income blacks. Bernie applied seven times before he was called in for an interview at Commonwealth Edison, an electric utility company. Every time "I'd go back out there, they had lost my application." Eventually he used his brother-in-law's name to get his foot in the door. Unlike the connections of white members of the group, his connection did not give him an edge; rather it righted a wrong. Bernie was relieved that he wouldn't need his backup plan. "Well, I ain't going to the army," he thought to himself. Proud of his perseverance, he told his new boss.

His supervisor confided, "Well, I'm going to tell you the truth—I'm not supposed to tell you this. They usually steer clear of people that live in Evanston because most of 'em, we give 'em the physical and the drug test, and they come back with drugs in their system." Applications would "disappear," because "80 percent of the people they tried to hire that lived in Evanston wouldn't pass the physical because of drugs."

Beset with negative stereotypes, employers sometimes discriminate against whole census tracts or zip codes usually where poor minorities live.[51] Bernie tried to ignore the racist implications of this policy. "I really didn't get into it, 'cause I just wanted a job." He could not help but think about all of the times that he applied and how each time his application had been "lost."

Bernie experienced discrimination again while working as a meter reader in Mount Prospect. When residents saw him approaching their neighbors' homes, they became suspicious. He explained, "This was back in the eighties; you didn't see too many black faces out there when you got to Schaumburg, Hoffman Estates, Barrington, Arlington Heights, Mount Prospect, all that—that was the end of the black people. They'd let the dog out on me, stuff like that." The police would pull up and then turn away: "They'd see me reading meters; they knew what it was going to be 'cause they were used to the calls. They would either see the car or they'd see me, I had on a uniform say Com Ed with cards in my hand." Eventually Bernie was promoted. As an overhead troubleshooter, he assessed problems on the overhead grid, the wiring that runs aboveground on electrical poles. "If there's wire down, I have to isolate it to make it safe for the crew. . . . So it's my job to find out where it's bad at, to isolate it, and then pick up and turn on as much as I can. And then tell the crew what they need and where they have to go." Bernie worked a rotating shift to supply Evanston residents with electricity twenty-four hours a day.

After college, Prince worked as a manager for Osco Drug Store, a job that he was obviously overqualified for. He was ambitious and hoped to move up the corporate ladder quickly. Asked about his career goals during the job interview, he had no qualms about stating his aspirations: "I want to work in the finance department and do some recruiting." A year and a half later, Prince was asked to train a new employee. Following precedent, Prince asked the white male, "Where do you want to go with Osco?" Like Prince, the new hire replied, "I want to go into the finance department."

For six months Prince trained him in store operations. "He learned a lot from me." The two became fast friends, which made it all the worse when the new employee pulled Prince aside to tell him that he was being transferred to the finance department. Prince remembered hearing the news, "I was just floored. And they knew that position is what I wanted, and I sat and trained him, and then he gets the job." Prince left Osco because "you only have to do me one time." He went to work for a mortgage company in Westchester, Illinois. Eventually, he and a partner started their own company. Building on his expertise, Prince bought out his partner and downsized to one office in Evanston.

Group members were part of a self-perpetuating cycle of recruitment, one that seemed impossible to break. During my interviews, I discovered that white parents were either professionals or artists, while their black counterparts were domestic helpers or factory workers. Today that pattern continues: white members of our group have stable and professional careers, while blacks hold temporary, undesirable, and poorly paid jobs. Even whites who did not apply themselves in school, or make their education a priority, did not suffer because of bad choices. Like their parents, white friends had the freedom to explore artistic and creative avenues before settling on careers that would be both gratifying and financially rewarding and were not necessarily reliant on college credentials. Meanwhile blacks, like their parents before them, performed jobs that epitomized the alienation of the worker: unsatisfying labor that required little skill and paid a low wage. Unlike the case with whites, there were grave costs for academic disengagement. In Jesse's case, the available work was backbreaking, filthy, and degrading.

Everyone in the photo flirted with delinquency. We liked to get high and hang out during high school. The one exception was Prince, a black male who excelled in school, was the first in his family to attend college, and went on to become a successful businessman. But Prince had to surmount major obstacles in order to do so, including low expectations from academic advisers and racial discrimination in the workplace, before his hard work paid off. Class reproduction, or the ways in which social class is reproduced across generations, ensures not only that the poor remain disadvantaged but also that privilege remains in the hands of those who are well-off to begin with.

Together Again, One Last Time

It is frightening; it is ludicrous. It is typical; it is freakish. It is Americana suited for a tremendous sociological study. WILLIAM GUY

Frances Willard and Osceola Spencer described Evanston in remarkably similar terms. Both women used religious metaphors to praise its beauty. They were impressed by the opportunities available to disenfranchised members of the community. Years later, Robert Douglas Mead also marveled at the big houses and tree-lined streets but saw cracks in the facade when black alumni boycotted their high school reunion. My photograph points to an even deeper fissure between what's said about Evanston and what really happens there. The city rests on and reproduces racial inequality and injustice, but most people don't want you to know that.

Race and class diversity shaped the early suburb. Founding fathers espoused principles of Methodism, including abolitionism and prohibition, while subtly excluding blacks from the political and social spheres. Whites monopolized the lakefront for luxury homes and recreational activities. They pushed blacks to vacant land hidden from view, near industry and a sanitary canal. Separation was reinforced through street circulation, racial covenants, and zoning policies ensuring that there was little social interaction between racial groups. A white privileged class enjoyed economic advantage working as professionals in Chicago's Loop during the day, retreating to comfortable homes for family life at night. A black working class serviced wealthy lifestyles that placed white women at the center of the domestic sphere. A nonpartisan city government consisted of a mayor and eighteen aldermen, but Evanston was a solidly Republican town until Lyndon B. Johnson carried it in 1964.

Segregated diversity was celebrated. There were two Evanstons, one white and one black. Every major city in America leads the same double life. There were separate hospitals. There were two YMCAs. Religious institutions were also segregated. There were many churches, but no synagogues until 1964, when Beth Emet was built and welcomed Martin Luther King Jr. to sleep in the basement. The elementary schools were also racially divided. Whites were not openly hostile but viewed blacks in patronizing terms and would not have considered them social equals. Advancement did not come because of the intense involvement of whites. Blacks demanded their fair share, threatening the city with a lawsuit if it didn't comply with *Brown*. Black children and parents carried the burden of seeking school integration, while white liberal groups controlled school boards and school systems. A conflict brewed between traditionalists and an expanding base of political liberals over control of social and educational initiatives and organizations. Hardly any white women worked outside the home. Black women formed a countable minority. During the 1960s blacks and whites banded together to desegregate schools and neighborhoods. Their resolve expanded the civil rights movement outside the South and northern urban centers.

There were twenty elementary and four middle schools. Oscar Chute was the highly respected superintendent overseeing seven school board members elected for three-year terms by a caucus system designed to assure noncontested elections. Residential patterns dictated school assignment, sending blacks to one elementary school on the city's west side and whites to the rest. They shared the high school, but blacks were made to feel unwelcome and in some cases didn't even make the pages of their yearbooks.

Gregory Coffin arrived to do what the law demanded and make Evanston the first northern city to "voluntarily" desegregate. Coffin constructed an integrated rather than merely desegregated school system. Through redistricting and a massive busing program, he achieved a salt-and-pepper mix in the student population. To entice white families to bus children to the previously all-black Foster, it was made a laboratory school supported by the education department at Northwestern University. As a result, black children from the Foster area were transported out to formerly all-white institutions. There was not an even distribution of teachers and administrators until Joe Hill was promoted and designed a minority recruitment program. The district applied for federal grants to support summer institutes. Teachers were trained to work in a multiethnic setting. Books and materials were examined for racial balance and absence of minority contributions to history and society. The curriculum was revamped.

Not everyone looked favorably on the vigorous thrust toward total integration. Phrases like "lowered standards" and "reverse discrimination" were bandied out. Coffin's abrasive personality didn't sit well with some members of the school board. He was accused of being arrogant and moving too fast. Divisions grew and battle lines were drawn. School board members were as divided as the town they represented, voting 4–3 against Coffin. Citizens for 65 formed to retain the superintendent. An "Oust Coffin" group tried to send him packing. Both groups organized to get out the vote and elect new board members who would favor their point of view. Community meetings overflowed. In the end, the innovative superintendent lost his bid.

School desegregation was less contentious than open housing. Evanston refused to pass or enforce a fair housing law. Powerful real-estate groups kept an open housing ordinance at bay for more than four years. When a law was passed by the city council, the mayor refused to sign it. Although the ordinance went into effect without his signature, the mayor's actions sent a message that was loud and clear: the government would not willingly intervene to overturn racial inequality. Loopholes and a wage gap preserved an east-west divide. Housing discrimination had set in motion a vast black-white economic gap that grew with each succeeding generation. The distribution of wealth was more unequal than income. There were many people who had nothing, and probably an equal number who had everything.

Although discrimination was now illegal, oppression took new forms. Nonracial dynamics were part of the story. Zoning laws and property rights discourse overshadowed declining social mobility. Busing and school lunch policies kept children apart after school and during the noontime meal. Evanston was dry in every sense of the word. The school board voted against federal money for a milk subsidy because Evanston didn't need charity. Home-cooked meals became the hallmark of good motherhood. In high school, youth were separated using hall assignments and an elaborate tracking system. Ability grouping and teacher expectations set the life course for students. Economics justified segregated residential areas and ended friendships. Charities supplemented low-wage work. Within-school segregation replaced separate educational institutions, and exorbitant taxes preserved lakefront property for the rich. In the 1970s, deindustrialization and the drug war did the work of de facto segregation.[1] Increasing credentialism, or employer emphasis on diplomas and licensing rather than an apprentice system, coincided with police crackdowns.

Great strides were made, but the community never fully committed itself. Still, Evanstonians were able to maintain a public image that did not include active bigotry, because while civil rights activists may have challenged inequality during the 1960s, elite lifestyles were never *really* threatened. Andrew Wiese writes that blacks and whites found comfort in their separation. A substantial black population let Evanstonians believe they were integrating without really doing so. Segregation regulated relationships and interactions. It was a reflection of dominance and subordination, if only because it was a one-way process. Instead of lessening, it increased as blacks threatened the status quo through migration, education, and employment. Geographic barriers such as busy streets, railroad tracks, and a sanitary canal separated residential neighborhoods. Physical separation helped justify the social distance that whites tried to maintain. Income, occupation, and power also separated the two groups. Abundance allowed social problems to go undetected. There was a degree of intimacy that was often mistaken for equality. Blacks and whites interacted in domestic service relationships. Longtime residents were often school friends.[2]

Good intentions didn't make much of a difference. Well-meaning whites sometimes think they know what's best for blacks. Plantation owners are said to have genuinely cared about their slaves. Segregationists believed that separate was equal. Evanston did not support Coffin's dynamic local school leadership. Liberals failed to bring change. Roy King explained that indifference was worse than hostility. Martin Luther King Jr. warned that blindness was more important than open hostility for maintaining the status quo. Disadvantage was explained in various ways. Conservatives blamed lifestyle. Liberals focused on poverty. Everyone ignored racism. Evanston chose feel-good symbolism over substantive gain.

While integration brought blacks into white spaces and expanded the black middle class, its benefits were not far reaching. Where whites saw progress and improvement, blacks saw dreams dwindle. Foster School closed in 1970, and Community Hospital shut down in 1975. Both buildings were saved and repurposed. They are reminders of black courage and perseverance. In 1986 the city named a park for William

Twiggs. We know that the ceremony was lovely because of his grand-daughter. The *Review* did not send a reporter to cover it. The *Examiner* was long gone. Integration meant the death of black-owned businesses and the demolition of historically black institutions. In 1980 the Emerson YMCA was cleared for a research park that as of 2013 remained a grassy lot. In 1989 the city demolished the last Henry Butler building, even though it was a designated landmark, and despite pleas to save it. Bennett Johnson recognized the symbolic value. The historic building would have served Evanston youth as a symbol of black entrepreneurial success. Instead city fathers were willing to obliterate Butler's mark on society.

Segregation was enforced even as stories of desegregation were generated, circulated, and celebrated through the media. In 2002 *People* magazine interviewed actor John Cusack, an Evanston native. When asked about his high school experiences, Cusack issued an all-too-familiar reply. Evanston had "pretty decent public schools. Our school had a really great demographic mix: black, white, Hispanic, rich kids, poor kids."[3] Chip and Cusack's sister Joan were classmates. Schooled in the same building, they didn't necessarily receive the same education. Both students are pictured with their homeroom class in the Nichols School yearbook. Joan is seated in the front row, and Chip is standing behind her in the back. After graduating from eighth grade, they both went to Evanston Township High School. Joan received her diploma, and Chip was expelled. She attended the University of Wisconsin–Madison, and he went into the army. Joan was nominated for an Oscar. Chip followed the Potawatomi trail in search of food and shelter.

Growing up in a progressive and affluent suburb certainly has its advantages, but not everyone reaps the benefits of their privileged surroundings. This book examines the differences that race, class, and gender can make, by focusing on the life stories of thirteen individuals, all of whom call Evanston their hometown. It is about the accumulation of discrimination (or privilege) in housing, education, and work that leads to different outcomes. Our life stories demonstrate the persistence of racial and class privilege and disadvantage beyond 1960s civil rights activism. It was the things our parents had, not our hard work, that determined our life chances and opportunities. We inherited the social position of our families. One sphere of social life influenced the next, a cycle that was perpetual and difficult to break; without education, work options were limited, and without a substantial income, living in a decent neighborhood and owning a home were all but impossible.

Compared to their parents, who had come of age before the civil rights movement and were hardworking domestic and factory workers, my black friends had fewer opportunities and options. School rejected them before they did the same thing back. Unwelcome in the formal economy, they found alternatives. Given social disadvantages, hard work didn't pay off. Things took a turn for the worse. Once-promising lives were cut short by early death. There was variety within racialized patterns. Some overcame challenges brought on by racial oppression and poverty. Mothers who were determined to break the racial caste system intervened when they saw their sons slipping away, and some were successful. Black teachers, guidance counselors, and staff formed an important support group.

The uncomfortable truth is that whites by and large fared better. In terms of education, wealth, employment, and health, we live under better circumstances. When we flailed in school, our parents, who had experience with educational institutions, used their knowledge, clout, and checkbooks to guarantee our graduation. Our labor was not necessary for the home to function. We never went without. We came and went as we pleased, and later in life, when we decided it was time to get serious, it wasn't too late. At every stage there were safety nets to catch us if we fell. We found jobs and promotions through powerful social networks and the strength of weak ties. We had grammar capital, learning by example from our well-educated parents. Our hard work paid off because of our social advantage. The older we got, the more the group in the photograph, or anything like it, became impossible. Today our lives are much more segregated than they were.

I used to think that I grew up in a racially integrated city, but today I know how wrong I was. Racism isn't something that happens somewhere else; it happens at home. Having black and white people together in the same city, schools, jobs, and photographs does not constitute racial integration. We didn't associate racism with our experiences. Even when confronted with racist patterns both in school and later, we had a hard time seeing them, insisting on interpreting our experiences in terms of the American dream of the rugged individual rising and falling on merit alone.[4] Did Evanston's experiment with integration work? Using humanity as a framework rather than racial categories, Chip's answer gave me pause: "We wouldn't call it that; we would call it friendship."

There is no doubt that we were friends and sometimes more. If we had prejudices, they centered on a preference for the Jackson Five or tube socks, not skin color. It had been nearly thirty years since I had seen Chip. In Evanston I had never been to his house or met his family. In Beloit his aunt insisted that I stay in her guest room. The night I arrived, Chip's wife cooked me dinner—turkey, macaroni and cheese, and greens. The meal took her two days to prepare. If Chip and I never shared a school lunch, that night made up for it. Later, when I was back in New Haven, he phoned. The photo, my visit, and reconnecting with old friends from Evanston,whom I had put him in touch with inspired him to call. I was the one in the group who was "blessed," he said, because I had brought everyone together again one last time. There was something irrevocable about the time when we were teenagers and were allowed to be together, if only for a short time; it shaped our lives forever.

In the end this book wasn't about the individuals in the photograph, not ultimately. Instead it was about what's deeply connected but is off the page, out of sight, past the borders. It's about what has come down from this photograph from the moment of history that is its context. While there is much to tell about the thirteen people suspended in my snapshot, my real interest is the social and historic conditions. Hidden in the colored rectangle are some modest surprises and small redemptions and blades of latter-day racial hope, however slender and promissory. The most important faces in this story are the ones you can't see. The book isn't so much about what is going on when the photo was taken as about what led to the moment and what happened afterward.[5] For me the photo was a chance to examine my beginnings, to think about how I got where I am. To learn about the impact of social structure on people's lives. To understand how racial privilege and disadvantage are reproduced and how little merit has to do with the opportunities and chances people have over the course of a lifetime. Mr. Guy was right; Evanston made for a "tremendous sociological study."

Notes

1. I have benefited from aspects of whiteness, a position of privilege typically associated with a set of social, economic, and historical advantages.
2. Sherry B. Ortner, *New Jersey Dreaming: Capital, Culture, and the Class of '58* (Durham, NC: Duke University Press, 1997). Our group is an example of a "post-community," that is a population that is spatially scattered, not all together in a local place, but one which is historically interrelated.
3. Gaston Bachelard, *The Poetics of Space* (Boston: Beacon, 1964), 9. Memories are motionless, and the more securely they are fixed in space, the sounder they are.
4. Sarah Maza, "Stories in History: Cultural Narratives in Recent Works in European History," *American Historical Review.* 1996, 1,515.
5. See Douglas Hartmann, *Race, Culture, and the Revolt of the Black Athlete: The 1968 Olympic Protests and Their Aftermath* (Chicago: University of Chicago Press, 2003). In 1968, track stars Tommie Smith and John Carlos made the Black Power salute during the medal ceremony at the Summer Olympics in Mexico City.
6. Paul Connerton, *How Societies Remember* (Cambridge: Cambridge University Press, 1989), 104. Memories are not formed, conveyed, or sustained on purely cognitive levels. Actors actually embody traditions through habitual performances because the body is ". . . socially constituted in the sense that it is culturally shaped in its actual practices and behavior."
7. Ed Guerrero in Isaac Julien, dir., *BaadAsssss Cinema: A Bold Look at 70's Blaxploitation Films*, DVD (Minerva Pictures, 2002).

8. George Nelson, *Elevating the Game: Black Men and Basketball* (Lincoln: University of Nebraska Press, 1992), 165.

9. Gerome Ragni and James Rado, "Black Boys," *Hair* (United Artist Music Group, 1967).

10. I borrow from Robert Zussman's work on his mother's photo album, which he claims contains an "idealized representation" of his family. "Picturing the Self: My Mother's Family Photo Albums," *Contexts*, 2006.

11. Connerton, *How Societies Remember*, 2. Connerton argues that just as present factors tend to distort our recollections of the past, so, too, past experiences influence present experiences.

12. Howard Winant, *The World Is a Ghetto: Race and Democracy since World War II* (New York: BasicBooks, 2001), 21. "Race" is not biological or inherent. Rather, it is a classificatory system that has been culturally and discursively constructed, beginning with processes of modernization that cannot be reduced to any one of a number of causal factors. An amalgam of sociohistorical transformations are responsible, including new forms of empire and nation, systems of capital and labor, and articulations of culture and identity, all of which called for racialized subjects and laborers.

13. Dalton Conley, *Honky* (Berkeley: University of California Press, 2000). These findings echo those of Conley, who wrote about his experiences growing up in a housing project on Manhattan's Lower East Side in his sociological memoir. Conley's parents may have been cash poor, but they were solidly middle class, and their environment seemingly had little effect on their children's opportunities. Expectations, social connections, and resources may have played greater roles than actual financial worth.

14. Sandra Harding, *Whose Science? Whose Knowledge? Thinking from Women's Lives* (Ithaca, NY: Cornell University Press, 1991).

15. Ibid., 143. If the larger culture is stratified by race and gender and lacks powerful critiques of this stratification, it is not plausible to imagine that racist and sexist interests and values would be identified within a community of scientists composed entirely of people who benefit—intentionally or not—from institutional racism and sexism.

16. Ibid., 150. A more critical understanding of social structure can actually be obtained from the perspectives of common people who are not invested in denial or ignorance. They can reveal social contradictions and can make "strange what had appeared familiar."

17. Lillian Smith, *Killers of the Dream* (New York: W. W. Norton, 1961). Smith has written about this inconsistency; she claims that education in racism begins with the black domestic.

18. See Ken Plummer, *Telling Sexual Stories: Power, Change and Social Worlds* (New York: Routledge, 1995).

19. Ron Crawford, dir., *Register Me from Evanston*, VHS (Evanston, IL: Fat Films, 1982).

20. Mary Pattillo-McCoy, *Black Picket Fences: Privilege and Peril among the Black Middle Class* (Chicago: University of Chicago Press, 1999).

21. Douglas S. Massey and Nancy A. Denton, *American Apartheid: Segregation and the Making of the Underclass* (Cambridge, MA: Harvard University Press, 1996), 70.

22. Andrew Wiese, *Places of Their Own: African American Suburbanization in the Twentieth Century* (Chicago: University of Chicago Press, 2004), 5.

23. Kenneth T. Jackson, *Crabgrass Frontier: The Suburbanization of the United States* (New York: Oxford University Press, 1985), 6.

24. Robert Fishman, *Bourgeois Utopias* (New York: Basic Books, 1987), 4.

25. Richard Harris, "Working-Class Homeownership in the American Metropolis," *Journal of Urban History* 17 (November, 1990): 46–69. Harris's work expands the class composition of suburbs to include blue-collar workers and their families, who in 1940 proved as likely to be homeowners as were members of the white-collar middle class.

26. Richard Harris and Robert Lewis, "The Geography of North American Cities and Suburbs, 1900–1950: A New Synthesis," in *The Suburb Reader*, ed. Becky Nicolaides and Andrew Wiese (New York: Routledge, 2006), 129.

27. Sixty percent of black suburban growth took place around the four largest metropolitan areas: New York, Detroit, Philadelphia, and Chicago. See Andrew Wiese, "Black Housing, White Finance: African American Housing and Home Ownership in Evanston, Illinois, before 1940," *Journal of Social History*, 1999, and Wiese, *Places of Their Own*, 2004.

28. Wiese, *Places of Their Own*, 4–6.

29. Thomas Sugrue, *Sweet Land of Liberty: The Forgotten Struggle for Civil Rights in the North* (New York: Random House, 2009), 447.

30. Stan West et al., *Suburban Promised Land: The Emerging Black Community in Oak Park, Illinois, 1880–1980* (Oak Park, IL: Soweto, 2009).

31. Carole Goodwin, *The Oak Park Strategy: Community Control of Racial Change* (Chicago: University of Chicago Press, 1979), 41.

32. Amanda Seligman, *Block by Block: Neighborhoods and Public Policy on Chicago's Westside* (Chicago: University of Chicago Press, 2005), 184–85, and Goodwin, *Oak Park Strategy*, 160–63.

33. Wiese, *Places of Their Own*.

34. Norbert Allen Simon, "The Politicization of Educational Issues" (PhD diss., Northwestern University, 1974).

35. Aldon D. Morris, *Origins of the Civil Rights Movements* (New York: Free Press, 1984)

36. Doug McAdam, *Freedom Summer* (New York: Oxford University Press, 1988).

37. Matthew D. Lassiter, "De Jure / De Facto Segregation: The Long Shadow of a National Myth," in *The Myth of Southern Exceptionalism*, ed. Matthew D. Lassiter and Joseph Crespino (Oxford: Oxford University Press, 2010), 32.

The earliest mention of de facto segregation appears to be a 1955 statement by the Urban League of Greater New York, which demanded "an emergency program to desegregate New York City's public schools" and accused education officials of culpability in the "presently de facto segregated Negro and Puerto Rican schools."

38. Lassiter, "De Jure / De Facto Segregation," 28.
39. See Eduardo Bonilla-Silva, *Racism without Racists: Color-Blind Racism and the Persistence of Racial Inequality in America* (Lanham, MD: Rowman and Littlefield, 2003).
40. See Lassiter, "De Jure / De Facto Segregation." Because the government could not be held accountable, it had no obligation to fix the racial inequalities it was creating. As a result, the North was insulated from civil rights litigation for two decades after *Brown*.
41. Stephen Meyer, *As Long as They Don't Move Next Door: Segregation and Racial Conflict in American Neighborhoods* (Lanham, MD: Rowman and Littlefield, 2000), 272. The Commission was established in 1957.
42. United States Commission on Civil Rights, Housing Hearings, 1959.
43. Ruth Frankenberg, *The Social Construction of Whiteness: White Women, Race Matters* (Minneapolis: University of Minnesota Press, 1993), 62.
44. For residential inequalities see Massey and Denton, *American Apartheid*; for educational opportunities see Gary Orfield and Susan Eaton, *Dismantling Segregation: The Quiet Reversal of "Brown v. Board of Education"* (New York: New Press, 1996); for discrimination in employment, see William Julius Wilson, *When Work Disappears: The World of the New Urban Poor* (New York: Alfred A. Knopf, 1996); and Joe R. Feagin and Melvin P. Sykes, *The Black Middle-Class Experience* (Boston: Beacon, 1994).

CHAPTER ONE

1. Francis Willard, *A Classic Town: The Story of Evanston, "by an Old Timer"* (Chicago: Women's Temperance Publishing Association, 1892), 13.
2. Gerald D. Suttles, "The Cumulative Texture of Local Urban Culture," *American Journal of Sociology*, 1984. 285. "Cities get to know what they are and what is distinctive about them from the unified observation of others."
3. Ibid., 284.
4. Andrew Jackson was elected president in 1828 on a platform that promised removal of all eastern Indians to western lands.
5. William Cronon, *Nature's Metropolis: Chicago and the Great West* (New York: W. W. Norton, 1991), 25.
6. Margery Blair Perkins, *Evanstonia: An Informal History of Evanston and Its Architecture* (Chicago: Chicago Review Press, 1984), 20.
7. Perkins, *Evanstonia*, 32.

8. Kevin Barry Leonard, "Paternalism and the Rise of a Black Community in Evanston, Illinois: 1870–1930" (MA thesis, Northwestern University, 1982).
9. Cronon, *Nature's Metropolis*, 263.
10. Ibid., 153.
11. Ibid.
12. Ira Katznelson, *City Trenches: Urban Politics and the Patterning of Class in the United States* (Chicago: University of Chicago Press, 1981), 67.
13. Ibid., 51.
14. Ibid., 52, 58.
15. Robert Fishman, *Bourgeois Utopias* (New York: Basic Books, 1987).
16. Karen Sawislak, *Smoldering City: Chicago and and the Great Fire, 1871–1874* (Chicago: University of Chicago Press, 1995), 34. For example, attorney John LeMoyne, his family, and their friends retreated to his summer cottage in Lakeview, staying on even after the chaos subsided.
17. Ibid., 29.
18. Ibid., 36.
19. Cronon, *Nature's Metropolis*, 347.
20. Perkins, *Evanstonia*, 52.
21. Cronon, *Nature's Metropolis*, 347.
22. Ibid., 350.
23. Ibid., 348.
24. Ibid., 350.
25. Ibid., 348.
26. Fishman, *Bourgeoise Utopias*, 135.
27. Cronon, *Nature's Metropolis*, 347.
28. Michael Ebner, *Creating Chicago's North Shore* (Chicago: University of Chicago Press, 1988).
29. Willard, *Classic Town*, 165.
30. Perkins, *Evanstonia*, 65.
31. Newton Bateman and Paul Selby, eds., *Historical Encyclopedia of Illinois* (Chicago: Munsell, 1906), 143.
32. Willard, *Classic Town*, 58.
33. Ibid., 57–58.
34. Ibid., 219.
35. Perkins, *Evanstonia*, 32. Evanston's dry spell continued until 1972, when the city finally allowed the sale of beer in restaurants. It was 1984 before the first retail liquor store opened.
36. Willard, *Classic Town*, 166.
37. Perkins, *Evanstonia*, 35.
38. Shawna Cooper-Gibson, "Sourcing the Persistence: A Portrait of Helen Cromer Cooper" (EdD diss., Boston University, 2011).
39. Willard, *Classic Town*, 170.

40. Ibid., 171.
41. Ibid., 173.
42. Ibid., 174.
43. Kathleen M. Blee, *Women of the Klan: Racism and Gender in the 1920s* (Berkeley: University of California Press, 1991)
44. Willard, *Classic Town*, 223.
45. Evelyn Brooks Higginbotham, *Righteous Discontent: The Women's Movement in the Black Baptist Church; 1880–1920* (Cambridge, MA: Harvard University Press, 1993).
46. Patricia A. Schechter, "Temperance Work in the Nineteenth Century," in *Black Women in America: An Historical Encyclopedia*, ed. Darlene Clark Hine (Brooklyn: Carlson, 1993), 2:1154–56.
47. Ida B. Wells, *Southern Horrors and Other Writings: The Anti-lynching Campaign of Ida B. Wells, 1892–1900* (Boston: Bedford Books, 1997), 144. Ida B. Wells minced no words with Willard while on tour in England in 1893 and 1894. She accused the WCTU president of not doing enough to put an end to lynching. Wells concluded that Willard was "no better or worse than the great bulk of White Americans on the Negro question." Willard's statement is from *Classic Town*, 173.
48. For a discussion of this legend, see Clyde D. Foster, *Evanston's Yesterdays* (Evanston, IL: Evanston Historical Society, 1956), and Ron Crawford, dir., *Register Me from Evanston*, VHS (Fat Film, 1982).
49. James P. Brawley, *Two Centuries of Methodist Concern: Bondage, Freedom and Education of Black People* (New York: Vantage s, 1974), 535–36.
50. Willard, *Classic Town*, 386.
51. Ibid., 264.
52. *Abraham Lincoln's Visit to Evanston in 1860* (Evanston, IL: City National Bank, 1914). Sometime after Lincoln's visit, the Julius White house was moved to 1227 Elmwood.
53. Willard, *Classic Town*, 176.
54. Ibid., 183.
55. "Henry Butler," in *Historical Encyclopedia of Illinois* [ed. Newton Bateman and Paul Selby] *and History of Evanston* [ed. Harvey B. Hurd and Robert D. Sheppard] (Chicago: Munsell, 1906), 2:635.
56. Morris E. Robinson Jr., *A Place We Can Call Our Home: The Emerging Black Community Circa 1850–1930* (Evanston: Shorefront, 1996), 14.
57. Willard, *Classic Town*, 142.
58. Andrew Wiese, *Places of Their Own: African American Suburbanization in the Twentieth Century* (Chicago: University of Chicago Press, 2004).
59. Willard, *Classic Town*, 208.
60. Ibid., 414.
61. Perkins, *Evanstonia*, 134.
62. Andrew Jackson Downing, *The Architecture of Country Houses: Including Designs for Cottages, Farm-Houses, and Villas* (New York: D. Appleton, 1866), 5–6.

63. *Plan of Evanston* (Evanston, IL: Bowman, 1917), 7.
64. Ibid., 8.
65. Ibid., 6.
66. Ibid., 12.
67. Ibid., 12.
68. Ibid., 9.
69. Ibid., 51.
70. Fishman, *Bourgeoise Utopias*, 148.
71. *Plan of Evanston*, 69.
72. Willard, *Classic Town*, 13.
73. *Plan of Evanston*, 64–65.
74. Ibid., 64–66.
75. Ibid., 59.
76. Zoning Ordinance, Evanston, Illinois, January 18, 1921.
77. "A Suburbanite Defends Racial Exclusion in Court, 1933," in *The Suburb Reader*, ed. Becky Nicolaides and Andrew Wiese (New York: Routledge, 2006), 235–37.
78. *Chicago Defender*, May 15, 1948.
79. See Stephen Meyer, *As Long as They Don't Move In Next Door: Segregation and Racial Conflict in American Neighborhoods* (Lanham, MD: Rowman and Littlefield, 1999), 93–94, and "Real Estate: 'Exclusive . . . Restricted,'" *US News and World Report*, May 14, 1948, reprinted in *Suburb Reader*, ed. Nicolaides and Wiese, 325–26.
80. See Wiese, *Places of Their Own*.
81. Executive Order 8802, signed in 1941 by President Franklin D. Roosevelt, prohibited racial discrimination in industries involved in the war effort.
82. See Joe William Trotter Jr., *The Great Migration in Historical Perspective: New Dimensions of Race, Class, and Gender* (Bloomington: Indiana University Press, 1991).
83. By 1910 five thousand blacks lived in suburbs of Chicago.
84. Wiese, *Places of Their Own*, 2.
85. Ibid.
86. Ibid.
87. Robinson, *Place We Can Call Our Home*, 13. Maria Murray was the first black resident in Evanston. She arrived in 1855 to work for the Allen Vane family.
88. Ibid., 23.
89. Andrew Wiese, "Black Housing, White Finance: African American Housing and Home Ownership in Evanston, Illinois, Before 1940," *Journal of Social History*, 1999, 433–34.
90. Wiese, *Places of Their Own*, 61–63.
91. Robert Douglas Mead, *Reunion: Twenty-Five Years Out of School* (New York: Saturday Review, 1973), 153.
92. Richard Wright, *Native Son* (rpt., New York: HarperCollins, 1993), 284.

93. William M. Tuttle Jr., *Race Riot: Chicago in the Red Summer of 1919* (Urbana: University of Illinois Press, 1970), 14.

94. Wiese, *Places of Their Own*, 59.

95. Wayne Watson, "Mrs. John J. Spencer," Evanston History Center, 1974.

96. Wiese, *Places of Their Own*, 59.

97. Ibid., 55.

98. Ibid.

99. Ibid. Andrew Wiese documents the sexual division of labor and the distinctive nature of black employment in Evanston, claiming that it is an important addition to our understanding of the intersections of race, class, gender, and suburbanization. US census figures from 1920 show that Evanston's black population numbered 2,522 and that women constituted 55 percent of that total.

100. Ibid.

101. Ibid., 56.

102. Ibid., 41–42.

103. Ibid.

104. Wiese, "Black Housing, White Finance."

105. Nicolaides and Wiese, eds., *Suburb Reader*. Nicolaides's work on prewar Los Angeles also revises suburban historiography.

106. Census data reveal that between 1920 and 1940, 25 percent of black Evanstonians used their houses as a source of rental income.

107. Wiese, "Black Housing, White Finance," 436.

108. Anne Meis Knupfer's work on black club women demonstrates that they reached "across" rather than "down" to their less fortunate sisters, because although there may have been class differences, both groups suffered equally from sexism and racism.

109. Cora Watson was a member of Ebenezer AME and vacationed in Idlewild, Michigan, a resort town for blacks.

110. Angela Jackson, "Caldonia Martin," Evanston History Center, 1974.

111. Anne Meis Knupfer, "Toward a Tenderer Humanity and a Nobler Womanhood: African American Women's Clubs in Chicago, 1890–1920," *Journal of Women's History* 3 (1995): 57–76.

112. "Department Store Branches in Suburbs Succeed, Multiply," *Business Week*, October 1, 1930, reprinted in *Suburb Reader*, ed. Nicolaides and Wiese, 117.

113. Anne Meis Knupfer, *Toward a Tenderer Humanity and a Nobler Womanhood: African American Women's Clubs in Turn-of-the-Century Chicago* (New York: New York University Press, 1996), 60.

114. Morris E. Robinson Jr., *Gatherings: The History and Activities of the Emerson Street Branch YMCA* (Evanston, IL: Shorefront, 2004).

115. Bennett Johnson, foreword to Robinson, *Gatherings*.

116. Robinson, *Place We Can Call Our Home*, 3.

117. Robinson, *Gatherings*.

118. Ibid.

119. Ibid.

120. *Examiner* 1, no. 4 (February 21–March 7, 1969).

121. Susan Hope Engel, dir., *Unforgettable: Memories of the Emerson Street Branch YMCA*, DVD (McGaw YMCA, 2010).

122. Robinson, *Gatherings.*

123. Median incomes increased 55 percent for the decade, climbing from 54 to 61 percent of the white median and reaching 72 percent in two-parent households.

124. Wiese, *Places of Their Own*, 2004. The proportion of African Americans working in white-collar occupations rose from approximately 8 percent in 1940 to more than 13 percent in 1960. By the 1950s, there were a growing number of black teachers, nurses, insurance agents, small business owners, civil servants, mail carriers, and stenographers.

125. Lois M. Quinn and John Pawasarat, "Racial Integration in Urban America: A Block Level Analysis of African American and White Housing Patterns" (Milwaukee: University of Wisconsin–Milwaukee, 2003), 4. This study claims that America's 8.2 million blocks provide a more accurate measure of interaction between blacks and whites. Examining smaller units permitted the researchers to see that social interaction between "races" seldom happens.

126. Wiese, *Places of Their Own*, 2004. Between 1910 and 1940 there was not a single area of expansion outside of west Evanston, in spite of a black population growth of almost five thousand. By 1930 Evanston's black population reached 4,938, and District 7 of the Fifth Ward was home to 79.8 percent of these residents. By 1940, 84 percent of black households in Evanston lived within these limits, and the core of the neighborhood was 95 percent black; it was this area of Evanston, referred to through at least the 1940s as "Colored Town," that set the city apart from the rest of the North Shore. In 1940, 6,026 blacks lived in Evanston. Between 1940 and 1950 the city's black community grew again by 50 percent. Returning soldiers would continue to ensure its growth.

127. Engel, *Unforgettable.*

CHAPTER TWO

1. Don Kazak, "Power Structure Challanged," *Daily Northwestern*, April 1, 1970.

2. In 1896, the Supreme Court ruling in *Plessy v. Ferguson* upheld the constitutionality of racial segregation in the public sphere under the doctrine of separate but equal, and gave states the legal right to, among other things, divide black and white children in the public school system. In 1954, *Brown v. Board of Education* held that separate but equal was inherently *unequal.*

3. Princeton (1948), Berkeley (1966), Champaign and Urbana, Illinois (1966), and Evanston (1967).
4. Jack Dougherty, *More Than One Struggle: The Evolution of Black School Reform in Milwaukee* (Chapel Hill: University of North Carolina Press, 2004), 38, 168–69. Dougherty documents similar practices in Milwaukee.
5. Charles T. Clotfelter, *After "Brown": The Rise and Retreat of School Desegregation* (Princeton, NJ: Princeton University Press, 2004). Clotfelter devotes only two pages to lunch programs.
6. Educational institutions were built to serve a geographical area within walking distances for a majority of children.
7. Foster and Dewey Schools had black enrollments of 100 percent and 67 percent respectively.
8. Frank Whiting, letter to Oscar Chute, October 30, 1965.
9. Editorial, *Evanston Review*, November 17, 1966.
10. *Evanston Review*, November 17, 1966.
11. Martin Luther King Jr., *Why We Can't Wait* (New York: Harper and Row, 1964).
12. *Evanston Review*, January 7, 1965.
13. *Evanston Review*, May 28, 1964.
14. The three academic years preceding integration were 1963–64, 1964–65, and 1965–66.
15. Dougherty, *More Than One Struggle*, 94.
16. *Evanston Review*, September 9, 1965.
17. *Evanston Review*, September 19, 1966.
18. *Evanston Review*, December 16, 1965.
19. *Evanston Review*, May 12, 1966.
20. *Evanston Review*, August 4, 1966.
21. *Evanston Review*, July 28, 1966.
22. Larry Brooks, dir., *The Integration of Foster School*, DVD (Evanston, IL: District 65, 1966).
23. Brooks, *Integration of Foster School*.
24. Ronald P. Formisano, *Boston against Busing: Race, Class and Ethnicity in the 1960s and 1970s* (Chapel Hill: University of North Carolina Press, 1991), 23.
25. *Evanston Review*, March 3, 1966.
26. *Evanston Review*, April 14, 1966.
27. Martin Luther King Jr. papers, King Center, Atlanta.
28. *Evanston Review*, March 24, 1966.
29. *Evanston Review*, August 11, 1966.
30. *Evanston Review*, December 8, 1966.
31. *Evanston Review*, February 9, 1967.
32. *Evanston Review*, August 24, 1967.
33. *Evanston Review*, March 10, 1966.
34. *Evanston Review*, April 28, 1966.
35. *Evanston Review*, September 22, 1966.

36. *Evanston Review,* October 20, 1966.
37. *Evanston Review,* May 1, 1969.
38. *Evanston Review,* November 17, 1966.
39. *Evanston Review,* November 10, 1966.
40. *Evanston Review,* November 17, 1966.
41. *Evanston Review,* November 3, 1966.
42. *Evanston Review,* October 27, 1966.
43. *Evanston Review,* November 17, 1966.
44. *Evanston Review,* December 16, 1966.
45. The Head Start program was offered in cooperation with District 65 and Neighbors at Work, a local Office of Economic Opportunity.
46. Susan Levine, *School Lunch Politics: The Surprising History of America's Favorite Welfare Program* (Princeton, NJ: Princeton University Press, 2010), 33.
47. Ibid., 76.
48. Sheila A. Taenzler, "The National School Lunch Program," *University of Pennsylvania Law Review* 119 (December 1970): 375.
49. *Evanston Review,* November 3, 1966.
50. *Evanston Review,* February 16, 1967.
51. *Evanston Review,* June 22, 1967.
52. *Evanston Review,* January 26, 1967.
53. Editorial, *Evanston Review,* February 2, 1967.
54. Editorial, *Evanston Review,* June 29, 1967.
55. *Evanston Review,* January, 26, 1967.
56. *Evanston Review,* January 26, 1967.
57. *Evanston Review,* July 27, 1967.
58. *Evanston Review,* July 27, 1967.
59. *Evanston Review,* January 26, 1967.
60. *Evanston Review,* July 27, 1967.
61. *Evanston Review,* August 10, 1967.
62. *Evanston Review,* September 14, 1967.
63. Ibid.
64. *Evanston Review,* September 28, 1967.
65. *Evanston Review,* October 5, 1967.
66. *Evanston Review,* September 14, 1967.
67. *Evanston Review,* September 28, 1967.
68. *Evanston Review,* September 21, 1967.
69. Ibid.
70. *Evanston Review,* September 28, 1967.
71. *Evanston Review,* September 21, 1967.
72. *Evanston Review,* September 28, 1967.
73. *Evanston Review,* October 12, 1967.
74. Ibid.
75. *Evanston Review,* September 28, 1967.
76. Ibid.

77. *Evanston Review*, October 5, 1967.
78. *Evanston Review*, October 19, 1967.
79. John J. Hillebrand, "Integration Side-Effect: New Lunch Plan May Be Needed," *Nation's Schools*, July 1968.
80. *Evanston Review*, October 26, 1967.
81. *Evanston Review*, December 7, 1967.
82. *Evanston Review*, October 19, 1967.
83. *Evanston Review*, October 26, 1967.
84. Levine, *School Lunch Politics*, 32.
85. *Evanston Review*, May 1, 1969.
86. *Evanston Review*, January 26, 1967.
87. Levine, *School Lunch Politics*, 82.
88. *Evanston Review*, April 14, 1969.
89. William Peters, dir., *The Eye of the Storm*, VHS (orig. ABC News, 1970). The film documents the efforts of Jane Elliott, an Iowa schoolteacher, to teach her students about discrimination by dividing them in to two groups, the brown eyes and the blue eyes.
90. *Evanston Review*, February 6, 1969.
91. *Evanston Review*, March 10, 1969.
92. *Evanston Review*, April 25, 1968.
93. *Evanston Review*, June 20, 1968.
94. *Evanston Review*, December 1, 1969.
95. *Evanston Review*, September 9, 1968.
96. *North Shore Examiner*, 1, no. 7 (August 2–23, 1969), and *School Outlook*, September 5, 1969.

CHAPTER THREE

1. *School Outlook*, 1969.
2. *Who's Who in America 1968* (Berkeley Heights, NJ: A. N. Marquis, 1968).
3. *Evanston Review*, August 12, 1968.
4. Public Forum, *Evanston Review*, August 19, 1968.
5. *Evanston Review*, January 18, 1968.
6. Charles W. Eddis, "Of Turtles and Establishment: The Great Evanston School Board Controversy," sermon delivered at the Unitarian Church of Evanston on February 15, 1970.
7. *Evanston Review*, October 31, 1968.
8. *Evanston Review*, March 3, 1969.
9. The Kerner Report was a 1968 federal report that investigated urban riots in the United States and found that violence reflected the profound frustration of blacks. *Evanston Review*, March 3, 1969.
10. Gregory C. Coffin, "The Black Administrator and the Nation's Schools," paper presented at the 102nd Annual Convention of School Administrators, Atlantic City, NJ, February 17, 1970.

11. *Evanston Review*, February 24, 1969.
12. *Evanston Review*, March 5, 1969.
13. *Evanston Review*, March 10, 1969.
14. *Evanston Review*, June 16, 1969.
15. Ronald P. Formisano, *Boston against Busing: Race, Class and Ethnicity in the 1960s and 1970s* (Chapel Hill: University of North Carolina Press, 1991), 23.
16. *Chicago Today*, July 20, 1969.
17. *Evanston Review*, June 30, 1969.
18. *Evanston Review*, June 28, 1969.
19. Ibid.
20. Public Forum, *Evanston Review*, n.d.
21. *Evanston Review*, July 17, 1969.
22. School board meeting held on July 14, 1969.
23. Gregory C. Coffin, "How Evanston, Illinois Integrated *All* of its Schools," speech delivered in Washington, DC, November 1967.
24. *Evanston Review*, July 17, 1969.
25. *Evanston Review*, July 14, 1969.
26. Gregory C. Coffin, "Wolves in Sheepskin: Working to Solve Racial Imbalance in Suburban School Districts," speech given at Purdue University, Fort Wayne, Indiana, January 23, 1970.
27. Bennett J. Johnson, "The Coffin Affair," statement given to the Board of Education, District 65, July 28, 1969.
28. *North Shore Examiner* 1, no. 7 (August 2–23, 1969).
29. Ibid.
30. Public Forum, *Evanston Review*, July 24, 1969.
31. Public Forum, *Evanston Review*, n.d.
32. *Evanston Review*, August 4, 1969.
33. *North Shore Examiner* 1, no 9 (October 3–22, 1969).
34. See Jayiia Hsia, "Integration in Evanston, 1967–1971: A Longitudinal Evaluation" (Evanston, IL: Northwestern University, 1971).
35. *North Shore Examiner*, 1, no. 9 (October 3–22, 1969).
36. Board of Education of School District 65, "The Report of the Board of Education on the Superintendency of Dr. Gregory C. Coffin," Evanston, 1969, 47.
37. *Evanston Review*, August 28, 1969.
38. *Chicago Today*, August 27, 1969.
39. *North Shore Examiner* 1, no. 10 (October 25–November 15, 1969).
40. Ibid.
41. *Evanston Review*, August 25, 1969.
42. *Evanston Review*, October 30, 1969.
43. United Black Employees of School District 65, "An Analysis of the Report of the Board of Education on the Superintendency of Dr. Gregory C. Coffin," April 4, 1970.

44. *Chicago Sun Times*, March 25, 1970.
45. *North Shore Examiner* 1, no. 10 (October 25–November 15, 1969).
46. *Evanston Review*, October 27, 1969.
47. Black Caucus, press statement, n.d.
48. Public Forum, *Evanston Review*, October 27, 1969.
49. Public Forum, *Evanston Review*, November 3, 1969.
50. Perspective, *North Shore Examiner* 1, no. 11 (November 16–December 6, 1969).
51. *School Outlook*, September 5, 1969.
52. *Evanston Review*, September 22, 1969.
53. *Chicago Today*, February 15, 1970.
54. *Evanston Review*, July 14, 1969.
55. Gregory C. Coffin, Response, February 1970.
56. *North Shore Examiner* 2, no. 3 (March 23–April 9, 1970).
57. Donald Lawson, April 10, 1970, speech given at Ebenezer AME Church.
58. *North Shore Examiner* 1, no. 10 (October 25–November 15, 1969).
59. *School Management*, December 1965.
60. For more on NAACP actions in northern and western states, see Robert L. Carter, *A Matter of Law: A Memoir of Struggle in the Cause of "Equal Rights"* (New York: New Press, 2005).
61. *North Shore Examiner* 2, no. 3 (March 23–April 9, 1970).
62. *School Management*, March 1970.
63. Ibid.
64. Robert Douglas Mead, *Reunion: Twenty-Five Years out of School* (New York: Saturday Review, 1973), 229.
65. *Evanston Review*, April 13, 1970.
66. Ibid.
67. Mead, *Reunion*, 225.
68. *North Shore Examiner* 2, no. 5 (April 25–May 15, 1970).
69. *Evanston Review*, April 13, 1970.
70. Ad Hoc Committee of Concerned Black Parents and Citizens of District 65, statement, April 16, 1970.
71. Neighbors at Work, statement, April 16, 1970.
72. *North Shore Examiner* 2, no 4 (April 7–25, 1970).
73. *North Shore Examiner* 2, no. 5 (April 25–May 15, 1970).

CHAPTER FOUR

1. "Jr. High Changes Proposed," *Evanston Review*, May 11, 1967.
2. *Evanston Review*, May 11, 1967.
3. "Boundary Changes Studies," *Evanston Review*, May 18, 1967.
4. Margherita Andreotti et al., "Preliminary Survey of Historic Art in the Evanston Schools," report by the Public Art Committee of the City of Evanston, 2007.

5. Jontyle Theresa Robinson and Wendy Greenhouse, *The Art of Archibald J. Motley, Jr.* (Chicago: Chicago Historical Society, 1991). Also see Amy M. Mooney, *Archibald J. Motley, Jr.* (Petaluma, CA: Pomegranate, 2004).

6. Norbert Allen Simon, "The Politicization of Educational Issues" (PhD diss., Northwestern University, 1974), 236.

7. Ibid., 239.

8. Ibid., 323.

9. Ann Pollak, statement to members of subcommittee on community involvement, District 65 Board of Education Rights and Responsibilities Committee, September 6, 1969.

10. Alice Kreiman, statement to Committee on Rights and Responsibilities, August 6, 1969.

11. Kevin Lynch, *The Image of the City* (Cambridge, MA: MIT Press, 1960), 92. Lynch calls this attachment "organization legibility."

12. Frederick C. Klein, "A Quiet Change: How Integration Came to One Neighborhood without Any Planning," *Wall Street Journal*, July 9, 1974.

13. Lynch, *Image of the City*.

14. Ibid., 87.

15. Ibid., 88–89. Also see Lynch for a description of the four stages of precision.

16. Dalton Conley, *Being Black, Living in the Red: Race, Wealth, and Social Policy in America* (Berkeley: University of California Press, 1999), 5, 25.

17. Evanston Planning Department, 1974.

18. Michel de Certeau, *The Practice of Everyday Life* (Berkeley: University of California Press, 1984), 29.

19. Jane Jacobs, *The Death and Life of Great American Cities* (New York: Random House, 1961), 71.

20. Gwen Macsi, "The Mayor of Nichols," radio segment, *All Things Considered*, National Public Radio, 2005.

21. Jan Hoffman, "Why Can't She Walk to School?" *New York Times*, September 13, 2009.

22. Youth served as apprentices to skilled craftsmen, working in factories or on the family farm.

23. Annette Lareau, *Unequal Childhoods: Class, Race, and Family Life* (Berkeley: University of California Press, 2003), 245–48.

24. Bruce J. Schulman, *The Seventies* (Cambridge, MA: Da Capo, 2001), 246. In his comprehensive study of 1970s culture, Schulman claims that the privatization of everyday life was an ongoing trend during this period.

25. Jacobs, *Great American Cities*, 86.

26. Ibid.

27. *Evanston Review*, August 1, 1968.

28. Ibid.

29. *Evanston Review*, September 25, 1969.

30. *Evanston Review*, March 2, 1967.

31. Editorial, *Evanston Review*, January 13, 1969.
32. *Evanston Review*, September 25, 1969.

CHAPTER FIVE

1. Martin Luther King Jr., "Three Dimensions of a Complete Life," sermon delivered at First Methodist Church, Evanston, May 1963.
2. Editorial, *Evanston Review*, October 19, 1967.
3. 1970 US Census.
4. *Evanston Review*, September 9, 1965.
5. *Evanston Review*, June 5, 1969.
6. *Evanston Review*, August 10, 1965.
7. *Evanston Review*, September 16, 1965.
8. Ibid.
9. *Evanston Review*, October 14, 1965.
10. *Evanston Review*, May 6, 1965.
11. Ibid.
12. Douglas S. Massey and Nancy A. Denton, *American Apartheid: Segregation and the Making of the Underclass* (Cambridge, MA: Harvard University Press, 1996), 191.
13. Amanda Seligman, *Block by Block: Neighborhoods and Public Policy on Chicago's West Side* (Chicago: University of Chicago Press, 2005), 65.
14. *Evanston Review*, May 28, 1964.
15. Editorial, *Evanston Review*, May 21, 1964.
16. Ibid.
17. *Evanston Review*, July 9, 1964.
18. *Evanston Review*, May 28, 1964.
19. *Evanston Review*, May 27, 1965.
20. Ibid.
21. Editorial, *Evanston Review*, May 28, 1964.
22. *Evanston Review*, January 28, 1965.
23. Ibid.
24. *Evanston Review*, May 27, 1965.
25. *Evanston Review*, January 21, 1965.
26. *Evanston Review*, January 28, 1965.
27. *Evanston Review*, May 27, 1965.
28. *Evanston Review*, June 11, 1964.
29. Ibid.
30. *Evanston Review*, May 6, 1965.
31. NSSP brochure, 1965.
32. NSSP prospectus, 1965.
33. *Evanston Review*, April 1, 1965.
34. The North Shore Summer Project volunteers started work on June 25 and ended on August 21.

35. NSSP headquarters was located at 730 Elm Street in Winnetka, Illinois.
36. *Evanston Review*, May 27, 1965.
37. *Evanston Review*, July 29, 1965.
38. *Evanston Review*, November 8, 1962.
39. *Evanston Review*, July 29, 1965.
40. Ibid.
41. *Evanston Review*, July 15, 1965.
42. Ibid.
43. Ibid.
44. *Evanston Review*, August 26, 1965.
45. *Evanston Review*, September 2, 1965.
46. Ibid.
47. NSSP press release, August 13, 1965.
48. *Evanston Review*, September 2, 1965, italics mine.
49. *North Shore Examiner* 2, no. 9 (July 16–31, 1970).
50. *Evanston Review*, May 26, 1966.
51. *Evanston Review*, January 21, 1965.
52. Massey and Denton, *American Apartheid*, 195.
53. Public Forum, *Evanston Review*, April 11, 1968.
54. "Suburbanites March in King Tribute," *Chicago Tribune*, April 8, 1968.
55. David Pyle, "Let Us Dare," sermon delivered on January 24, 2010.
56. Reverand Jacob Blake, "NOW: A Brief History."
57. Public Forum, *Evanston Review*, April 25, 1968.
58. *Evanston Review*, April 25, 1968.
59. Ibid.
60. This was a common ploy. Milwaukee did the same. See Patrick D. Jones, *The Selma of the North: Civil Rights Insurgency in Milwaukee* (Cambridge, MA: Harvard University Press, 2009), 177.
61. See Seligman, *Block by Block*, 180. In 1963 Governor Otto Kerner had issued an executive order prohibiting brokers from accepting or acting on discriminatory listings. The Chicago Board of Realtors had filed a lawsuit that blocked this order. The order was finally upheld in by the Illinois Supreme Court in 1967. It was made irrelevant by the 1968 federal Fair Housing Act.
62. *Evanston Review*, May 2, 1968.
63. *Evanston Review*, July 11, 1968.
64. Editorial, *Evanston Review*, July 29, 1968.
65. In 1968 Oak Park passed a stronger open housing ordinance that included unusual injunctive powers. See Carole Goodwin, *The Oak Park Strategy: Community Control of Racial Change* (Chicago: University of Chicago Press, 1979), 149–50.
66. *North Shore Examiner* 1, no. 1 (December 1968).
67. *Evanston Review*, June 5, 1969.
68. Ibid.

69. Ibid.
70. *North Shore Examiner* 2, no. 10 (August 14–31, 1970).
71. *North Shore Examiner* 1, no. 4 (February 21–March 7, 1968).
72. *Evanston Review*, November 13, 1969.
73. "N.U. Called Slumlord," *North Shore Examiner* 2, no. 14 (February 1970).
74. *North Shore Examiner* 2, no. 11 (September 1970).
75. "Evanston Housing: Some Facts, Some Problems," interim report submitted by Mayor Ingram's committee on postwar planning, 1943.
76. *Evanston Review*, November 13, 1969.
77. Public Forum, *Evanston Review*, November 20, 1969.
78. *North Shore Examiner* 2, no. 10 (August 14–31, 1970).
79. *Evanston Review*, December 1, 1969.

CHAPTER SIX

1. *Evanston Review*, December 4, 1975.
2. *Chicago Tribune*, March 21, 2000.
3. An early leader in American education, Horace Mann believed that free public schools would end poverty as the populace became more educated.
4. Robert Douglas Mead, *Reunion: Twenty-Five Years out of School* (New York: Saturday Review, 1973), 170.
5. Ibid., 181.
6. Ibid., 184–85.
7. Ibid., 148–49, 185.
8. Ibid., 159.
9. Ben Burns, "Robeson Writes History at Erlanger with Masterful Acting in 'Othello,'" *Chicago Defender*, 1945, 17.
10. Mead, *Reunion*, 3.
11. Ibid., 149.
12. Paul Willis, *Learning to Labor: How Working Class Kids Get Working Class Jobs* (New York: Columbia University Press, 1977).
13. *North Shore Examiner* 2, no. 15 (November 20–December 5, 1970).
14. *Evanston Review*, November 16, 1967.
15. *Ladies' Home Journal*, May 1968.
16. *North Shore Examiner* 1, no 1 (December 21–28, 1968).
17. *Evanston Review*, February 8, 1968.
18. US Bureau of Labor data.
19. *Jet*, November 13, 1989.
20. "1968 + 40: The Black Student Movement at Northwestern and Its Legacy," conference held at Northwestern University, Evanston, IL, October 31 and November 1, 2008.
21. *Evanston Review*, October 21, 1968.
22. *Evanston Review*, November 21, 1968.

23. *Evanston Review,* December 2, 1968.
24. *Evanston Review,* December 16, 1968.
25. *North Shore Examiner* 1, no. 4 (February 21–March 7, 1969).
26. *Evanston Review,* January 20, 1969.
27. *Evanston Review,* March 3, 1969.
28. *Evanston Review,* May 22, 1969.
29. *North Shore Examiner* 1, no. 5 (March 21–April 4, 1969).
30. *Evanston Review,* May 22, 1969.
31. Ibid.
32. *Evanston Review,* March 28, 1968.
33. Ibid.
34. *Evanston Review,* May 22, 1969.
35. Bacon: Mary; Beardsley: Carla and Chip; Boltwood: Bernie, Perkey, and Candy; Michael: Jennifer, Ronny, and Prince.
36. Jeannie Oakes, *Keeping Track: How Schools Structure Inequality* (New Haven, CT: Yale University Press, 2005), 64–67.
37. See Samuel Bowles and Herbert Gintis, *Schooling in Capitalist America: Educational Reform and the Contradictions of Economic Life* (New York: Basic Books, 1976).
38. Oakes, *Keeping Track,* 133–34.
39. Ibid., 4.
40. Ibid., 167.
41. Ibid., 153.
42. Ibid., 168.
43. See Bowles and Gintis, *Schooling in Capitalist America,* 1976.
44. Oakes, *Keeping Track,* 131.
45. See Paul Willis, *Learning to Labor: How Working Class Kids Get Working Class Jobs* (New York: Columbia University Press, 1977).
46. Oakes, *Keeping Track,* 9, 143.
47. Ibid., 111.
48. Ibid., 131.
49. See ibid.

CHAPTER SEVEN

1. *Evanston Review,* January 8, 1964.
2. James Grossman, "Great Migration," in *The Encyclopedia of Chicago,* ed. James R. Grossman, Ann Durkin Keating, and Janice L. Reiff (Chicago: University of Chicago Press, 2005), http://www.encyclopedia.chicago history.org/pages/545.html. Chicago attracted slightly more than 500,000 of the approximately seven million blacks who left the South between 1916 and 1970. The migration outlasted the expansion of Chicago's job market. By the 1960s Chicago's meat-packing factories had closed, and its steel mills were beginning to decline.

3. Black life in northern cities received increasing scholarly attention in the 1960s and 1970s, focusing on the ghetto to document the social isolation of blacks.

4. Sociologist William Julius Wilson singles out work, not residential segregation, as the root cause of social disorganization and its attendant problems. His argument, developed over the course of several texts, culminated in *When Work Disappears: The World of the New Urban Poor*, an examination of chronic unemployment and its devastating effects on social and cultural life. See William J. Wilson, *The Declining Significance of Race: Blacks and Changing American Institutions* (Chicago: University of Chicago Press, 1978); *The Truly Disadvantaged: The Inner City, the Underclass, and Public Policy* (Chicago: University of Chicago Press, 1987); *When Work Disappears: The World of the New Urban Poor* (New York: Alfred A. Knopf, 1996). Exacerbated by the "out-migration" of middle-class blacks to suburban areas, the associated loss of cultural values and financial support were "fundamentally a consequence of the disappearance of work" (Wilson, *When Work Disappears*, xiii). His assumptions regarding the causal effects of joblessness, however, do not address inequalities pervasive in the social spheres of housing and education. Nor does he account for suburban areas where blacks were poor despite the wealth of their surroundings. Furthermore, Wilson offers little historical analysis of US labor relations, a process that uniformly made room for blacks only at the floor of the economy.

5. *Evanston Review*, August 12, 1965.

6. *Evanston Review*, December 14, 1967.

7. Public Forum, *Evanston Review*, December 14, 1967.

8. Eventually economics won out. In 1971 the Holiday Inn approached Jack Siegel, the city's attorney. The company wanted to expand and build a hotel in Evanston, but wanted to serve alcohol. Siegel sent a proposal to the city council, and in the end tax revenue won out over a flailing WCTU. On January 5, 1972, the city council voted Evanston wet and approved a limited number of licenses to restaurants and bars. The gesture attracted a new hotel and drew customers back to the city's restaurants.

9. *Evanston Review*, December 25, 1968.

10. See Antonio Gramsci, *Selections from the Prison Notebooks*, ed. Quintin Hoare and Geoffrey Nowell-Smith (New York: International Publishers, 1971).

11. *Evanston Review*, September 9, 1965.

12. *Evanston Review*, September 9, 1965.

13. *Evanston Review*, March 4, 1965.

14. Ibid.

15. *North Shore Examiner* 1, no 4 (February 21–March 7, 1968).

16. *North Shore Examiner* 1, no. 12 (December 6–23, 1969).

17. *North Shore Examiner* 1, no. 4 (February 21–March 7, 1968).

18. *North Shore Examiner* 2, no. 3, (March 23–April 9, 1970).
19. *North Shore Examiner* 1, no. 11 (November 16–December 6, 1969).
20. *North Shore Examiner* 2, no 6 (May 15–31, 1970).
21. Ira Katznelson, *City Trenches: Urban Politics and the Patterning of Class in the United States* (Chicago: University of Chicago Press, 1981), 112.
22. Ibid., 179–80.
23. *Evanston Review*, May 27, 1965.
24. *Evanston Review*, February 20, 1969.
25. *Evanston Review*, July 25, 1968.
26. *Evanston Review*, August 15, 1968.
27. *Evanston Review*, July 22, 1968.
28. *Evanston Review* May 8, 1969.
29. *Evanston Review*, November 19, 1964.
30. Katznelson, *City Trenches*, 118.
31. Ibid., 120–21.
32. In 1926, Carter G. Woodson chose the second week of February for Negro History Week to commemorate the birthdays of Frederick Douglass and Abraham Lincoln. In 1976, as the nation reached its bicentennial, the week was expanded into an entire month.
33. *Evanston Review*, February 10, 1969.
34. Ibid.
35. William E. Cross Jr., "Encountering Nigrescence," in *Handbook in Multicultural Counseling*, ed. Joseph G. Ponterotto et al., 2nd ed. (Thousand Oaks, CA: Sage), 30–44.
36. *Evanston Review*, May 12, 1969.
37. Frances Fox Piven and Richard A. Cloward, *Regulating the Poor: The Functions of Public Welfare* (New York: Pantheon Books, 1993), xiii.
38. Katznelson, *City Trenches*, 110.
39. *Evanston Review*, August 5, 1965.
40. *Evanston Review*, June 8, 1967.
41. *Evanston Review*, August 29, 1968.
42. *Evanston Review*, August 3, 1967.
43. *Evanston Review*, May 11, 1967.
44. *Evanston Review*, June 8, 1967.
45. *Evanston Review*, August 28, 1968.
46. *Evanston Review*, July 7, 1966.
47. *Evanston Review*, June 24, 1968.
48. Approximately one-third of juvenile offenders were black.
49. *Evanston Review*, September 9, 1965.
50. Mark S. Granovetter, "The Strength of Weak Ties," *American Journal of Sociology*, 78, no. 6 (1973): 1360–80.
51. Joleen Kirschenman and Katherine Neckerman conducted a study in Chicago to discover the extent to which employers discriminate against young black people. Kirschenman and Neckerman, "We'd Love to Hire

Them But . . . ," in *The Urban Underclass*, ed. Christopher Jencks and Paul E. Peterson, 203–32 (Washington, DC: Brookings Institution, 1991).

CONCLUSION

1. See William J. Wilson, *The Declining Significance of Race: Blacks and Changing American Institutions* (Chicago: University of Chicago Press, 1978); *The Truly Disadvantaged: The Inner City, the Underclass, and Public Policy* (Chicago: University of Chicago Press, 1987); *When Work Disappears: The World of the New Urban Poor* (New York: Alfred A. Knopf, 1996).
2. Andrew Wiese, *Places of Their Own: African American Suburbanization in the Twentieth Century* (Chicago: University of Chicago Press, 2004).
3. John Cusack, interview, *People*, July 15, 2002, 22.
4. For a similar account, see Jay Macleod, *Ain't No Makin' It: Aspirations and Attainment in a Low-Income Neighborhood* (Boulder: Westview, 1995).
5. I borrow these phrases from Paul Hendrickson, *Sons of Mississippi: A Story of Race and Its Legacy* (New York: Alfred A. Knopf, 2003)

Index

Italicized page numbers refer to figures.

ism in, 25, 39, 236–37; as Best Shaded
City in the West, 43–44; blacks on city
council of, 52; children's freedom to
roam in, 150–51; as City of Homes, 42;
demographics of, 17, 19; as domestic
service hub for North Shore, 47; doors
not locked in, 151; as dry town, 33–34,
35, 227–28, 267n35, 282n8; employment discrimination against residents
of, 253; end of prohibition in, 282n8;
founding of, 27, 28–29; geography of,
17–18, 142–43; gradual integration in,
143; growing up black versus white
in, 1; hanging out on Church Street
in, 219; as Haven of the Negro, 48; as
headquarter city, 41; as Heavenston,
27, 35–36, 45; hiring of blacks in,
225; homes in, 41–44; home tours
in, 150; integrationist self-image of,
19, 21, 258; invention of ice cream
sundae in, 35–36; Martin Luther King
Jr. in, 176–77; Martin Luther King
Jr.'s mention of, 164; lack of social
services in, 167; legal prohibitions in,
36; liberals attracted to diversity of,
57, 59–61, 67, 143, 156; libraries in,
40; Lincoln Republicans in, 36–37;
maps of, 58, 81, 144–48, 150–51, 151;
migration to, 18–19, 22–23, 28–32, 37,
44, 59–67; monumental buildings in,
40; multiple manifestations of racism
in, 257–58; naming of, 33; versus Oak
Park, Illinois, 16–17; partisanship in
city government of, 256; places of
worship in, 256; poverty in, 227–30;
prosperous self-image of, 228; as proud
of liberality, 16; public image of, 27; as
quasi-integrated, 21; racism as organizing principle in, 2–3, 255–56; rapid
growth of, after Chicago Fire, 31, 32; as
Ridgeville, 28, 29; Sabbatarian laws in,
227–28; segregated diversity in, 256;
as site for sociological study, 255, 261;
social imagination of, 5; as village and
township, 29; westward direction of
traffic and sewage and, 42–43; white
versus black youth hanging out in, 219.
See also black community of Evanston;
Great Migration
Evanston Black Caucus: aid to tenants
from, 191; King LAB school renaming

and, 123–25; protest against new parks
and, 192; support for Coffin from, 112,
114, 115, 118, 119; threat by, to burn
down LAB School, 117
Evanston Child Care Center Association,
237–38
Evanston Council of Churches, 175–76,
183
Evanston History Center, 14–15, 38
Evanston Human Relations Commission,
112
Evanstonian (school newspaper), 200
Evanston–North Shore Board of Realtors,
128, 170–71, 176, 178–81, 186–87
Evanston Planning Commission, 190,
191–92
Evanston Public Library, 14
Evanston Real Estate Brokers' Council,
171–72
Evanston Review (newspaper): advertising
space in, during Coffin controversy,
122, 125; bicycle registration and,
239; Black Power thinking in, 235–36;
boasting about size of black population in, 165; Carla and Earl pictured
in, 194–96, 195; class divide in, 226,
228–29; Coffin and, 107, 112, 118–19,
132–33; endorsements of, in school
board election, 130; fair housing movement and, 171; integration's success
evaluated by, 194–96; King LAB school
renaming and, 123, 124–25; letters
against school desegregation in, 82;
on mural at West Side Service Center,
235; Neighbors at Work in, 231; open
housing ordinance and, 185, 187; open
lunch plan and, 90; publication history
and content of, 13–14; on racial tension
at ETHS, 209; restrictive covenants
and, 46; school lunch policies and,
92–93, 96, 101; William Twiggs Park
and, 258–59
Evanston Sanitarium, 39–40
Evanston Township High School (ETHS):
black boycott of 1946 reunion of,
197–98, 255; black college-bound
students at, 199, 242–43; black enrollment and dropout rate in, 199, 206;
black personnel and, 206–7, 215; black
student activism at, 24, 201–2, 204,
205–10, 208; black students forced out

house and, 160; map-drawing exercise and, 147, *148*; memories of teachers and, 161–62; on night school, 216; parents of, 62, 66, 141–42, 149, 154; on Project Prejudice racism simulations, 100; on racism in Evanston schools, 224; Ray's death and, 3
Project Prejudice, 99–100
Proviso East High School, 201–2, 205
Purdue University, 115–16

Question Box Club, 53

Raby, Al, 136
race and racism: author's black friends' perceptions of, 223–24; bicycle riding and theft and, 238–39; black absence from school curriculum and, 115–16; black neighborhoods excluded by home tours and, 150; black pride and, 194, 198; black resilience and agency and, 22; black underclass and preservation of privilege and, 22; Chicago as research site and, 15; colorblind racism and, 20–21; color line and, 142, 150–51; commodification of black bodies and, 7; conflict between white and black girls and, 154–55; construction of race and, 264n12; declining significance of, 282n4; discipline disparities in middle schools and, 142; domestic workers and, 10–13, 264n17; end of interracial friendships and, 8; in fashion and advertising, 247; generational differences in experience of, 143; geographical units of study and, 271n125; ghetto and, 282n3; harassment of black high academic performers and, 222–23; home visiting and, 153–54; integration and racial identity and, 201; interracial dating and, 152–53; interracial marriage and, 176; multiple manifestations of, in Evanston, 257–58; networking contacts and, 252; nostalgia versus reality and, 7–9; opposition to Coffin and, 122; as organizing principle in Evanston, 2–3, 255–56; overcoming educational deficiencies and, 25; owning versus renting home and, 149; poverty as black problem and, 228–29; public narratives versus institutional realities,

5, 9, 12, 13, 14–15; race as criteria for school assignment and, 82; racialization of urban space and, 50; racism simulations and, 99–100, 274n89; recommendation for restrictions on black population growth and, 191–92; school lunch policies and, 96–97; in scientific community, 264n16; separate black history courses and, 202; suburban employment opportunities and, 16; in teacher training, 78–79, 101–2; temperance movement and, 35; as urban organizing principle, 2–3; wealth of whites versus blacks and, 149; white versus black disengaged students and, 212, 213–17, 224, 227, 245–47, 254. *See also* black community of Evanston; housing discrimination; integration and segregation; school desegregation; white privilege
Rahr, Sumner G., 128
Raskin, Mrs. Nathaniel, 173
Ray, *xii–xiii*; addictions and, 218–19; baseball and, 156; bicycle theft and, 239; clothing styles and, 6; death of, 3, 219; ditching school, 219; as dropout, 223; employment for, 65–66; group picture and, 6, 7; Jennifer and Ronny's house and, 157; as Jennifer's brother, 4; Job Corps and, 218; memories of teachers and, 162; parents of, 65–66
Raymond, Miner, 36–37
Raymond Park, *183*, 184
recreation. *See* parks and recreation
Regina, *xii–xiii*; day job and, 215; Earl and, xiii, 1, 152, 156, 160, 196, 220, 223, 241, 249–50; first marriage of, 250–51; on graduating from high school, 248–49; home life of, 60; interview of, 4; as Jennifer's sister, 4; Lighted Schoolhouse and, 160; memories of teachers and, 161; night school and, 215; parents of, 60, 64, 142; post–high school work experience of, 249, 250–51; postsecondary education and, 223, 249–50
Register Me from Evanston (film), 15
Reid, Jimmy, 235
Reporter and Directory (periodical), 38
reproduction and resistance, 21–22